Praise for *Understanding the Palestinian–Israeli Conflict*

"This balanced and highly useful 'primer' presents in question-and-answer form extensive explanations of recent events in the Israeli-Palestinian struggle ... An essential volume by an experienced scholar and analyst ...."
—*Library Journal*

"In her compact, concise, and highly useful guide, Bennis ... explains various aspects of the longstanding conflict between the Palestinians and Israel ... This is an excellent addition to any Middle East collection."
—*Multicultural Review*

"Phyllis Bennis has produced a simple and educational work about a highly complicated conflict ... [T]he author is deeply knowledgeable of the conflict and its history ... [T]his is a competent, direct, and accessible introduction to the issue."
—*Journal of Palestine Studies*

"Bennis (Institute for Policy Studies) utilizes a question and answer format in order to provide a well-informed and, considering its brevity, surprisingly detailed primer on Israeli-Palestinian history and politics for an American audience seeking to understand US policy in the region ... All but the most expert will likely learn something and the neophyte will greatly benefit in understanding by reading this book."
—*Book News*

UNDERSTANDING PALESTINE AND ISRAEL

BY PHYLLIS BENNIS

FOREWORD BY OMAR BADDAR

OLIVE
BRANCH
PRESS

An imprint of Interlink Publishing Group, Inc.
Northampton, Massachusetts

First published in 2025 by
OLIVE BRANCH PRESS
An imprint of Interlink Publishing Group, Inc.
46 Crosby Street, Northampton, Massachusetts 01060
www.interlinkbooks.com

Based on *Understanding the Palestinian–Israeli Conflict: A Primer*, 7th updated edition, 2019

Library of Congress Cataloging-in-Publication Data available
ISBN 978-1-62371-647-9

To download our catalogs, please visit our website at www.interlinkbooks.com
Printed and bound in the United States of America

10 9 8 7 6 5 4 3 2 1

For Gaza

ACKNOWLEDGEMENTS

Hope has been in short supply this year. Shadows were everywhere, and darkness seemed to overtake the light too often as a horrific war in Gaza quickly escalated, and the word "genocide" was suddenly being used as a normal way to describe what we were seeing daily on our phones, computers, televisions, and front pages of newspapers. And we were paying for it. Our government, with our tax dollars, was writing the checks, shipping the bombs, the warplanes, the tank ammunition.

It was hard. But there *was* light. There was outrage, sooner than before, and it turned into protests. Palestinian leaders, Rabbis for Ceasefire, Black for Palestine, Jewish Voice for Peace, the Uncommitted movement, the students—the students! Hundreds of thousands in the streets, occupations of Grand Central Station and congressional offices, student encampments spread across the country. A broad new movement demanding Ceasefire Now. The public letters of outrage and repudiation, the resignations by government workers unwilling to be part of enabling Israel's war. The light began to sneak through, and a little bit of hope began to stir.

For me, it was the South African initiative at the International Court of Justice—holding Israel accountable for its crimes. Brilliant teams of lawyers, of diplomats, of activists, a global community waking up at 4 in the morning to watch the legal team across the pond begin their presentation in The Hague, texts racing around the world from Palestine to Johannesburg to New York as we cheered. One South African friend of mine wrote, "I have never been so proud to be a South African—and I've never been so proud to be a human being."

It was hope, finally. The Palestinian Anti-Apartheid Movement and the BDS movement leadership, the South African BDS Coalition, the incredible team at South Africa's foreign ministry, the activists and others who work at and on the United Nations—all played crucial roles in making that initiative possible. And I am so grateful for having been able to work closely with those and other friends and colleagues to strengthen and publicize that campaign—it's what gave me hope through the darkness.

I remain thankful to the Palestinian rights movement here in the US, whose members kept the pressure on Congress and the White House and made sure that everyone in this country knew that even with a desperately important election looming, it still wasn't acceptable to have to choose between supporters of fascism and supporters of genocide. Working with them made strategizing in a time of crisis more doable than I would have expected. Leaders and others in and around Jewish Voice for Peace—Stefanie Fox, Eran Efrati, Rebecca Vilkomerson, Rabbi Alissa Wise among them—remain among the most strategic thinkers I know. Richard Falk, Craig Mokhiber, David Wildman, Francesca Albanese, Michel Moushabeck, Tamara Alrifai, Khaled Mansour, Andy Shallal, Nadia Hijab, Mona Younis, Margaret Zaknoen, Omar Baddar, Zeina Ashrawi Hutchison, Ahmad Abuzneid, and so many others in and around the UN and the Palestine movement brought years of experience, incredible knowledge, passion, and a commitment to collaboration. The leaders of the Uncommitted and other parts of the newer, broader component of the ceasefire movement brought a fresh energy and innovative ideas.

My longstanding gang at the Institute for Policy Studies, including our amazing leadership team of Tope Folarin, Kathleen Gaspard, John Cavanagh, and LaShawn Walker, along with my colleagues Sarah Anderson, Lindsay Koshgarian, Sarah Gertler, and many more, provided crucial support for work on this book even in the midst of other demands. My extraordinary IPS project co-director, Khury Petersen-Smith, remains an amazing collaborator, partner, and co-conspirator as we work to help educate, build, and consolidate movements through these difficult times. Edgardo Lander remains a deep mainstay of friendship and solidarity. Michel Moushabeck and his wonderful team at Interlink, always understanding the urgency of movement moments and the need for education, pushed and prodded to get this book underway, and somehow managed to move at the speed of light to get it out faster than I could have imagined.

And my scattered family—created and otherwise—remain crucial in my life. I couldn't do it without them. My far-flung sisterhood of movement partners and family share all of what it takes for us to continue working and living through the darkness: Judy Bennis, Linda Gordon, Monica White, Nancy Parson, Laura Flanders, Jeanne Butterfield, Ellen Kaiser, Jenny Daniell, Leslie Cagan. And in DC, my fourth-floor pod of John Harrison, Joey Thompson, Ram Hansen provide the love of home.

Early this morning, the ICC issued war crimes warrants for Israeli leaders. Last night, nineteen senators voted to oppose sending more weapons to Israel. Things are changing. The light is starting to show.

Phyllis Bennis
November 21, 2024

CONTENTS

CONTENTS

PART III: THE ASSESSMENTS—Where Are We Now?

PART IV: OCTOBER 7 AND ITS AFTERMATH

CONTENTS

FOREWORD

By Omar Baddar

This is a dark time in the world. Israel's decades-long war on Palestinian existence has now escalated into a full-fledged genocide in Gaza, and spilt beyond the borders of Palestine and Israel into a conflagration that has the potential to escalate even further into a regional catastrophe.

Here in the United States, outgoing president Joe Biden, renowned for his supposed empathy, has overseen unconditional U.S. support for Israel's live-streamed genocide in Gaza with unimaginable callousness and indifference to the lives of Palestinians. He is being replaced by President Donald Trump, who has promised to give Israel an even freer hand to "finish the job," and who has nominated anti-Palestinian fanatics for leading positions in his administration. It is difficult to find the words to describe how perilous things look at this moment, and yet so little is understood about how we got here and how to stop the slide towards greater violence.

Every debate over the Palestinian–Israeli conflict devolves into an endless backward chronology: *Israel did this because Palestinians did that before, but Palestinians only did that because Israel did this first*, and so on and so forth. One can carry this logic all the way back to the origin of this conflict, when the Zionist movement planned the systematic ethnic cleansing of Palestinians and the destruction of their towns and villages in order to create the Jewish state of Israel. But even more pressing than the history of this conflict is the dynamic that exists between Palestinians and Israelis today: The status quo is that one people rules over another. Every day, regardless of whether an act of violence takes place or doesn't, Palestinians live under Israeli control without freedom or basic rights, and their existence is shrinking by the day. To miss this fundamental dynamic—as much of our misinformed public does in the US—is to miss everything.

We in the United States live in a paradoxical corporate media environment: Despite the fact that what's happening in Palestine and Israel gets endless coverage in our papers and on our screens, the average American has no adequate understanding of the basics of what is happening there. The problem lies in the quality of this media coverage, which too often is biased and devoid of context, leaving the audience either with no sense of what's unfolding beyond aimless violence or, worse, an inverted impression in which Israel is somehow the victim of Palestinian aggression. Our media is obsessed with the invaders' and occupiers' right to "self-defense" against the people they're oppressing, but never a word is said about the right of an occupied people to defend themselves against their oppressors. This bias distorts perceptions of the reality on the ground beyond recognition.

Yet Americans can't afford the luxury of being misinformed because the US is more involved in this so-called conflict than any other in the world. No country receives more military funding nor more diplomatic cover from the United States than Israel. This has been most devastating for Palestinians who are enduring the brunt of US-backed Israeli atrocities, but it has also not been good for Israelis, nor for US interests in the region or across the globe.

Understanding what's happening in Palestine and Israel, and the US role in it, is an imperative for Americans, and Phyllis Bennis is an exceptional analyst who not only has a deep understanding of this issue, but is uniquely skilled at identifying the most important core issues and explaining them in a very accessible way for an audience that wants to understand what is unfolding. This book is precisely what this moment calls for in order for our country to understand how destructive our role has been in this conflict—and to mobilize that understanding towards advocacy for justice before it's too late.

November 2024

Omar Baddar is a DC-based Palestinian-American political analyst and a member of the National Policy Council of the Arab American Institute. He has appeared on CNN, MSNBC, BBC, Al-Jazeera, and Democracy Now, and his writings have appeared in Salon, Newsweek, HuffPost, the Daily Beast, Jadaliyya, and other outlets.

INTRODUCTION

When Israel went to war against the people of Gaza on October 8, 2023, following the Hamas-led attack on southern Israel the day before, something unprecedented happened in the United States. For the first time in the long history of Israeli wars against Palestinians, people across the country were suddenly seeing, hearing, talking about—and soon being outraged by—the brutality of the assault, the pain that Palestinian children and elders and everyone else in Gaza were experiencing. The call for a ceasefire started almost immediately, and within days we could see the beginnings of what would soon become a huge, broad movement demanding "Ceasefire Now!"

The need was urgent—and the huge mobilizations of protest, of petitions, of pressuring Congress and the White House, of working for city council and state assembly resolutions, for campus encampments and campaigns for divesting from corporations profiting from Israeli occupation—all reflected the passion, the commitment, and the need for more.

Never before had so many people across the US responded so powerfully to an attack on Palestinians, with the demand for a ceasefire and the determination to do something to make it happen. And right from the beginning, for many that meant insisting on an end not only to Israeli violations but to the US military and economic support that made those violations possible.

People were certainly shocked by the violence of the attack on Israel on October 7, and the demand to release the hostages remained important. Yet the images of massive Israeli bombing—using US-made and to a large degree US-funded warplanes, bombs, drones, helicopters, and other weaponry, attacking the entire population and wreaking absolute devastation across Gaza right in front of us, on our phones, computer screens, televisions, newspapers, podcasts 24/7—were too powerful to ignore. The movement was growing very quickly—faster than ever before. And many of the hundreds of thousands—eventually millions—of people outraged and responding to the war hadn't been exposed to much of the history, the politics, the culture, or the US and international roles in this longstanding but suddenly urgent crisis. People began to look for information.

At the same time, though, campaigns rooted in longstanding myths, deliberate historical falsehoods, biased media, careless or intentional distortion, and carefully crafted disinformation all took hold, making accurate information difficult or impossible to find. Legacy organizations in the US that had for decades worked to build official and broad popular support for Israel escalated their efforts. They ramped up their efforts to paint those demanding a ceasefire as "antisemitic," and claimed that all those calling for Israel to be held accountable for its war crimes and violations of human rights were supporting Hamas. From the beginning of the war, they pressured members of Congress and especially the White House to reject calls for a ceasefire despite the war's atrocities. Soon they were lobbying Congress to punish South Africa for bringing Israel's violations of the Genocide Convention to the International Court of Justice. And they did all of that hoping that most people in the US—including the millions calling for a ceasefire and demanding an end to the US military support that was enabling Israel's war—would not know enough to challenge their claims.

But they were wrong. Because the movement for ceasefire had sprung up so fast and so strong, those campaigns of falsehoods did not go unchallenged. Students creating ceasefire encampments on their campuses included teach-ins in their programs to share their knowledge. Israel's exclusion of foreign reporters from Gaza meant that even mainstream media turned to Palestinian journalists already on the ground, who continued their work documenting the war even as their colleagues were killed in unthinkable numbers. Independent media outlets upped their game. Unions, faith-based, and other types of organizations, worked to provide fact sheets for members wanting to learn and to protest. Focusing on racial and climate justice, anti-militarism, immigrant and economic rights, and women's and LGBTQ rights, social movements built partnerships with Palestinians and others to lead webinars and discussions. It was all aimed at providing the background information, the talking points, and some of the history for new supporters of ceasefire who had never thought much about the issue before, for activists who had questions they had never investigated before, and for longtime supporters of Palestinian rights and a just peace in the Middle East who simply had never had the time to learn all they wanted to. This book is part of that effort, to foster discussion and share information where it has too often been unavailable.

That public outrage and the demand for a ceasefire didn't fade away. They continued to grow as the war entered its second year, escalating as Israel's war—which the International Court of Justice ruled was plausibly a genocide—escalated. And while the demand for ceasefire remained the central message, the ceasefire movement altered the very definition of its watchword. The cries of "Ceasefire Now!" continued, but in the war's second year, they signified more than just the demand for a permanent stop to the bombing. "Ceasefire" now also included humanitarian aid for a devastated people now facing death from famine as well as bombing. It meant the resumption of funding to the key UN agency working in Gaza to provide support for Palestinians, and crucially, "ceasefire" soon was understood to also mean an end to weapons transfers to Israel. "Ceasefire Now" was transformed into a three-part demand.

And this demand was being raised by millions of people. Four months into the war, 67 percent of all Americans, of all political affiliations, supported the call for a permanent ceasefire. By June 2024, a CBS poll showed 61 percent of all Americans, and 77 percent of Democrats and young people of all stripes, believed the US should not send weapons to Israel.

That massive public demand to protect Palestinian lives had never happened in this country. The violence, the deaths, and the forcible displacement of this magnitude had not happened since the war of 1948. Certainly the International Court of Justice's acknowledgement calling the war plausibly genocidal reflected the shocking level of violence. But this violence has been part of Israel's occupation of Palestinian land since the beginning. Some of the questions in this book address that reality.

My first trip to occupied Palestine, in early 1988, was with my old friend Neal Cassidy, a photographer at the small newspaper we both worked for. We carried many questions, and were learning as we traveled. We arrived during the first intifada, or uprising, which had started in December 1987 but was already well underway and reflected an extraordinary society-wide mobilization of people. The images of "children of the stones" tossing rocks at giant Israeli tanks quickly became iconic, along with the women and men, the elders, everyone challenging the occupation and a longstanding colonialism. Although it had begun as a spontaneous response to the death of four Palestinian workers hit by an Israeli truck in Gaza, the uprising had quickly transformed into something else. It linked the grassroots-based mobilization that had erupted in the occupied territories with the exiled Palestinian leadership's diplomatic efforts underway internationally. What emerged over the next six years or so was strategically clear, tactically creative, and inclusive across generations, political affiliation, gender, class, location, and work. Support for the intifada's actions—its civil disobedience, strikes, tax resistance, protests, boycotts of Israeli goods and creation of an alternative cooperative economy, underground schools and clinics—was virtually unanimous.

The intifada was overwhelmingly nonviolent—but the Israeli response was certainly not. Military and settler violence skyrocketed across the occupied territories, with armed soldiers blocking roads and establishing new checkpoints, round-the-clock shoot-to-kill curfews, towns and villages being shut down, illegal Jewish settlements built and expanding, while thousands of Palestinian homes were demolished. Schools, universities, clinics were forcibly shuttered. Settlers threatened and attacked school children and uprooted ancient olive trees. New laws were imposed, making possession of the Palestinian flag, even clothing in the colors of the flag, a crime. The Israeli human rights organization B'Tselem reported that during the years of the first uprising, Israeli troops killed 1,070 Palestinians, 237 of them children. Jewish settlers killed 54 more.

As we worked on a book on the uprising, we always stopped first at the local hospital in every Palestinian city or town as soon as we arrived. That was the place to get the news of the day, because much of the news involved Israeli violence. At the time, Prime Minister Yitzhak Rabin, later heralded as a peacemaker for his role in the long-failed Oslo process, had responded to the nonviolent uprising with an official doctrine of "might, force, and beatings." In case anyone didn't understand what that meant, he ordered his military forces dealing with Palestinian protesters to "break their bones," including those of children. The soldiers did so, first with rocks—it sometimes took thirty minutes of beating before a young bone shattered—later with bullets. Israeli soldiers shot Neal in Nablus in October 1988, and after surgery to remove the bullet, he recovered in a hospital ward filled with teenagers and young men who had suffered broken legs and arms as the result of being beaten or shot.

Thirty years later, breaking bones was still a policy. In response to Gaza's explicitly nonviolent "Great March of Return" mobilizations that began in May 2018, organized by a noted Palestinian poet, Israel announced plans to send sharpshooters to attack the unarmed protesters who were still besieged in the walled-off Gaza Strip. They did—and the marksmen consistently took aim at the legs of teenagers and other young people. A year later, in May 2019, United Nations humanitarian coordinator Jamie McGoldrick reported that 7,000 unarmed Palestinians had been shot by Israeli snipers during that first year of the protests, and that 1,700 of them, almost all young, still faced the likelihood of amputation in the future, mostly of their legs, because Gaza doctors didn't have access to the advanced techniques needed to preserve their limbs.

And it continued. In just the first three months of Israel's assault against Gaza that began in October 2023, UNICEF reported that along with thousands of children killed, about 1,000 children had lost one or both legs. It was the equivalent of ten children losing a limb every day from Israeli bombing, the group said. British-Palestinian surgeon Ghassan Abu Sittah described performing six amputations on children in one day during his work in a Gaza hospital during the first months of the war, part of what he called "the biggest cohort of pediatric amputees in history." Because the Israeli siege blocked access to vital medicines, many of the amputations were carried out on children without anesthesia.

One of the things that people in the US were beginning to grasp, especially those who had become part of the ceasefire movement, was that understanding history always depends on when you start the clock. As many people have begun to realize, the terrible events in Gaza did not begin with the events of October 7. Rather, they were rooted in the long legacy of colonialism, ethnic cleansing, occupation, and apartheid that have characterized Israel's relationship with the Palestinians from the beginning. As a young pro-Israel activist, I absorbed much of the same false and incomplete information that we see today. When I first began learning about Palestine—its land and its history, its people and its poets—I had to challenge all those ideas and all the information I thought I knew. The clock was already ticking. It took me a long time to catch up.

This book is for looking back to what has happened since then. Most of all it's for people who recognize why we still urgently need a permanent three-dimensional ceasefire now, right now—and for those who also want to understand what led to the current crisis and what is happening now, and who want to at least begin to think about what, beyond a ceasefire, may lie ahead. The clock is still ticking.

Phyllis Bennis
Washington, DC
November 2024

GLOSSARY OF TERMS, ABBREVIATIONS & KEY FIGURES

Abraham Accords: US-orchestrated diplomatic deals for Arab regimes to normalize relations with Israel in return for upgraded military and economic ties with US.

AIPAC (American-Israel Public Affairs Committee): One of main components of the pro-Israel lobby.

Apartheid: A system of "inhumane acts committed for the purpose of establishing and maintaining domination by one racial group of persons over any other racial group." It forms the basis for the UN's 1973 convention against Apartheid.

Apartheid (or Separation) Wall: Erected in 2002 supposedly to separate the West Bank from Israel, but built mostly inside Palestinian land. The wall divided Palestinians from their own land, ensured Jewish settlements and Palestinian water sources remained on Israeli side, and separated East Jerusalem from the rest of the West Bank. It was ruled illegal by ICJ in 2004.

Yasir Arafat: Chairman of the Palestine Liberation Organization (PLO), president of Palestinian Authority.

BDS: The movement for Boycott, Divestment & Sanctions.

Camp David Summit: A failed effort by President Clinton in 2000 to reach a "peace deal" between Israel and Palestinians. The last effort based on Oslo "peace process."

Gaza Strip: Palestinian territory bordering Israel, Egypt, and the Mediterranean, militarily occupied, with settlements built by Israel after the Six-Day War. In 2005, settlers were withdrawn and troops redeployed to surround Gaza in a permanent siege. Gaza's 2.3 million residents have faced frequent military assault from Israel since 2008.

Geneva Conventions: Part of the laws of war identifying obligations of an occupying power over an occupied civilian population.

Genocide: Using inhumane acts with specific intent to destroy all or part of a racial, religious, ethnic, or other group.

Genocide Convention: Refers to the Convention on the Prevention and Punishment of the Crime of Genocide. It defines the crime of genocide and identifies illegality for perpetrators and obligations of state parties to prevent and halt genocide.

Golan Heights: Israel-occupied Syrian territory with Jews-only settlements built after the Six-Day War and annexed in 1981. The annexation was not recognized by any other country until Trump recognized it in 2018.

Green Line: The armistice line ending war in 1949, which divided Israel from the West Bank, East Jerusalem, and Gaza.

Hamas: Palestinian Islamist organization founded in 1987 that won Palestinian elections in 2006; administered occupied Gaza from 2007; and led the 2023 attack on Israel.

ICC (International Criminal Court): Holds individuals criminally accountable for war crimes, crimes against humanity, and apartheid.

ICJ (International Court of Justice): Rules on cases between countries; in 2023, South Africa brought charges against Israel for violating the Genocide Convention.

IDF: Israel Defense Forces.

Intifada: First Palestinian uprising (1987–1993); second uprising 2000–2005.

Israel: State created by the Zionist movement on historic land of Palestine; declared independence in 1948 and never declared borders.

Knesset: Parliament of the State of Israel.

Law of Return: Israeli law guaranteeing the right of every Jewish person from anywhere in the world to emigrate to Israel and immediately be granted full citizenship and nationality rights.

Nakba: Meaning "catastrophe" in Arabic, the Nakba is the term Palestinians use to refer to the forced dispossession and expulsion of 750,000 Palestinians from their homes and land in the 1947–49 war.

Benjamin Netanyahu: Israeli prime minister from 1996–1999, 2009–2021, and 2022–.

Occupied Territories: Territory in which a foreign power maintains effective control of land and population. The Occupied Palestinian Territory (OPT) is the UN's term for the Israeli-occupied West Bank, East Jerusalem, and Gaza Strip.

Oslo Accords: The 1993 agreement for mutual recognition and security arrangements between the PLO and Israel, which failed to lead to the creation of a Palestinian state.

PA (Palestinian Authority): Created by the Oslo Accords.

Palestine: Recognized as distinct region within the Arab world, ruled as part of Ottoman Empire until World War I, then by British. The UN took over and partitioned the land and recognized the Jewish-controlled state of Israel after 750,000 Palestinians were dispossessed from their land, but it never created a Palestinian state.

Palestine Mandate: Form by which the League of Nations granted Britain control of Palestine after the defeat of the Ottoman Empire.

Right of return: A guarantee in international law that every person displaced by war has the right to return to their home. UN resolution 194 provides even stronger specific guarantees to Palestinians, yet Israel has denied the exercise of that right for Palestinians since creation of the state.

Settler colonialism: Claiming territory for foreign control by permanent settlers replacing or suppressing the indigenous population, not only for extracting resources.

Ariel Sharon: Israeli general, defense minister, and prime minister.

Six-Day War: The 1967 war in which Israel attacked and defeated Egypt, Syria, and Jordan and occupied the Palestinian West Bank, East Jerusalem, and Gaza, along with the Sinai Peninsula in Egypt and Golan Heights in Syria.

United Nations: Global organization created in 1945. The "Palestine Question" was one of first crises it faced.

UNRWA (UN Relief and Works Agency): UN organization with a mandate from 1949 to the present to provide humanitarian support to Palestinian refugees until there is a just solution to the refugee situation.

West Bank: Palestinian territory that includes East Jerusalem and borders Jordan and Israel, occupied by Israel after 1967 War. In 2024, about 3 million Palestinians lived in the West Bank and East Jerusalem, along with 750,000 illegal settlers.

Zionism: Political movement for the creation of and continued support for a Jewish-dominated state in historic Palestine.

PART I:
THE BACKGROUND—
People, Places, and Ideas

Why is the Middle East so important to the US and internationally?

From earliest history, the Middle East and the area known as Palestine were global crossroads of trade, science, scholarship, and religion. In more recent times, the discovery of oil in the region and the need of powerful empires for reliable local allies led to the creation of western protectorates throughout the Middle East. After World War I, newly demarcated Arab nation-states emerged and began fighting for independence. Following the devastation of World War II, the European powers long dominant in the Middle East struggled to rebuild, and lost both their official colonial mandates and much of their influence. France remained influential in Syria and Lebanon, but with the UN's 1947 Partition Agreement, Britain pulled out of Palestine. Soon afterward, the US moved into the breach.

From 1967 through the beginnings of the twenty-first century, US policy in the region has been based on protecting the triad of oil, Israel, and stability. "Stability" had always been understood to include access to markets, raw materials, and labor forces for US business interests, as well as the stability imposed by the expansion of US military capacity throughout the region, including the creation of an elaborate network of US military bases. Beginning after the 1967 Six-Day War, the US relied on Israel as a Cold War cat's paw—a military extension of its own strategic reach—both within the Middle East region and internationally, in places as far-flung as Angola, Guatemala, Mozambique, and Nicaragua. At the same time, widespread domestic support for Israel—initially concentrated in the mainstream Jewish community and later among the increasingly powerful right-wing Christian evangelical fundamentalists in the US—took root in popular culture and politics, giving Israel's supporters great influence over Washington policymakers.

Till the end of the Cold War, Israel remained a close and reliable ally, in the region as well as internationally. With the end of the Cold War and the rise of the so-called global war on terror, the strategic value of a military alliance with Israel was less important and the role of the pro-Israel lobbies became ever more influential in maintaining the close US-Israeli tie. Well into the twenty-first century, as US strategic interests focused more on escalating competition with China and Russia while still being shaped by Washington's efforts to dominate countries and regions across the Middle East, Israel's strategic value appeared to be diminishing. US lobbies remained strong, however, and ties with Israel, shaped by unparalleled levels of US military, economic, and diplomatic support, never weakened.

Who are the Palestinians? Where did they come from?

Palestinian Arabs are descendants of the indigenous people of Palestine, who lived under the vast Arab/Islamic empire that from the seventh century dominated Palestine, during the rise of the Arabic language and Arab/Islamic culture. While Palestine was primarily agricultural, Palestinian cities, especially Jerusalem, were hubs of Arab civilization, where scholars, poets, and scientists congregated and where, enriched by a constant influx of traders, they forged the city's identity as an important regional center.

Islam's and Christianity's religious and moral teachings remained the dominant social forces, but small indigenous Jewish communities remained as integral parts of the Palestinian community. They were the remnants of Palestine's ancient Jewish kingdom, which was conquered by Rome in 70 CE, its people largely scattered. Along with larger groups of Christians, those Palestinian Jews maintained their faith and communal identities within broader the Palestinian society throughout the rise of Islam.

Throughout the years of the Arab and then Ottoman empires across what is now the Arab world, there were no nation-states; instead the political demography was shaped by cities and regions. As in most parts of the Arab world, modern nationalist consciousness for Palestinians grew in the context of demographic changes and shifts in colonial control. During the 400 years of Ottoman Turkish control, Palestine was a distinct and identifiable region within the larger empire, but linked closely with the region then known as Greater Syria.

With World War I and the defeat of the Ottoman Empire, Palestine was taken over by the British Empire. But even before that, beginning in the 1880s, the increasing influx of European Jewish settlers brought about a new national identity—a distinctly Palestinian consciousness—among the Muslims and Christians who were the overwhelming majority of Palestinian society. Those indigenous Palestinians resisted the colonial ambitions of European Jewish settlers, especially when the numbers expanded with the rise of political Zionism, resisted British colonial rule until 1947, and resisted the Israeli occupation and colonial settlement since 1948 and 1967.

Why are there Palestinians in Israel at all and what is the Nakba?

When Israel was created as a state in 1948, 750,000 indigenous Palestinians, whose families had lived in Palestine for hundreds of years, were forcibly expelled by, or fled in terror of, the powerful Zionist militias that would soon become the army of the State of Israel. The Israelis call it their War of Independence—Palestinians call it the Nakba, or catastrophe. The 2.1 million or so Palestinians living today inside the 1949 borders of Israel, who constitute about 21 percent of the Israeli population, are those that remained and their descendants. Israel's admission to the UN in 1949 was conditioned on its stated willingness to abide by General Assembly Resolution 194 calling for the right of Palestine refugees to return to their homes and receive compensation for their losses. But despite international law and specific UN resolutions, none of those forced into exile have ever been allowed to return.

From Israel's creation in 1948 until 1966, the indigenous Palestinian population inside the country lived under military rule. Since that time, Palestinians inside Israel have been considered citizens, can vote, organize political parties, and run for office; several Palestinians serve in the Israeli Knesset, or parliament. But not all rights inside Israel are granted on the basis of citizenship. Israeli nationality is defined by religion, not citizenship. And those rights and obligations defined as "nationality rights" legally favor Jews over non-Jews (who are overwhelmingly Palestinian) in social services, the right to own land, access to bank loans and education, military service, and more. In 2018 Israel passed a "Basic Law" (equivalent to a constitutional amendment in the US) stating explicitly that "the right to exercise national self-determination in the State of Israel is unique to the Jewish people"—so self-determination is denied to Israel's millions of Palestinian citizens.

About three times as many Palestinians live under Israeli military occupation in the West Bank, Gaza, and East Jerusalem than remain inside Israel's 1949 borders. Millions more remain refugees.

Have Palestinians always relied on armed force in their fight for freedom?

Palestinian resistance to the expropriation of their land, their forced displacement and dispossession, home demolitions, and the stranglehold of military occupation, has been overwhelmingly nonviolent. And from the 1936 general strike declared in Palestine years before the creation of the state of Israel to the overwhelmingly nonviolent first Intifada or uprising in 1987, from Gaza's 2018 Great March of Return organized by a well-known Palestinian poet to the explicitly nonviolent global Boycott, Divestment, and Sanctions movement, nonviolent Palestinian resistance has been met with violence from pre-state militias and later from the Israeli state itself. Episodes of armed resistance have been far less frequent than nonviolent struggles.

There are many definitions of "terrorism." The US State Department defines terrorism as "pre-meditated, politically motivated violence perpetrated against noncombatant targets by sub-national groups or clandestine agents, usually intended to influence an audience." That definition is specifically crafted to ensure that state terrorism is excluded (by specifying "sub-national" perpetrators), and by identifying "noncombatant" targets (which means an attack on soldiers who happen to be off duty would count as "terrorism," unlike identifying "civilian" targets).

Under that definition, the rare Palestinian attacks on civilians inside Israel would be considered terrorism; of course, so would the far more frequent and far more lethal attacks on Palestinian civilians, and their homes, marketplaces, mosques, churches, schools, or hospitals, by Israeli settlers in the occupied West Bank, occupied East Jerusalem, or the occupied Gaza Strip. Palestinian attacks on Israeli soldiers, military checkpoints, or other military targets, which are legal under international law for people living under military occupation, would not fall under the definition of "terrorism," although Israeli and US politicians and pundits routinely describe them as such.

The vast majority of Palestinians have never participated in any armed attack against anyone. In the spring of 2002, a large group of well-known Palestinian intellectuals signed a public statement condemning suicide bombings against civilians. But virtually all Palestinians understand the desperation and hopelessness that fueled the rage and resistance to occupation by those forced to live for decades under military occupation and siege.

What do the Palestinians want?

Like any population, Palestinians have different opinions, different dreams, whether they live as second-class citizens inside Israel, under military occupation, or as stateless refugees or exiles in a far-flung global diaspora. The oldest cohort of Palestinian exiles, those in their eighties or 90s, still remember being expelled from their homes inside what is now Israel but what was then Palestine, in 1947–48. Some of them, even as they grow old, still hold the keys to their homes that their parents kept as they fled, thinking they would be back in days or weeks. Many more remember the terror of being expelled from their homes in the West Bank and Gaza and East Jerusalem in 1967, finding minimal shelter in refugee camps that became home for nearly sixty years. Like most people everywhere, most Palestinians want dignity, human and national rights, freedom and equality—and that's true whether they hope for a state of their own or life in some kind of a multinational democratic state.

In 1988, in an enormous, historic compromise, the Palestine National Council, or parliament-in-exile, voted to accept a two-state solution that would return to Palestinians only the 22 percent of their land that had been occupied in 1967. They accepted that the other 78 percent would remain Israel. Many Palestinians and some factions rejected, and still reject that historic compromise, because it gave away so much. Even among the majority of Palestinians who endorsed the goal of an independent state—a fully realized and truly independent, sovereign, and viable state, encompassing all of the West Bank and Gaza, with East Jerusalem as its capital—many now believe that a so-called two-state solution is no longer an option: after decades of land theft and settler-colonial expansion, there is simply no land left.

The struggle for Palestinian rights has become the dominant narrative among many Palestinians both inside Palestine and in the far-flung diaspora, rather than the earlier focus on recognition of a state. Virtually all Palestinians also insist on the internationally guaranteed right for refugees to return to the homes from which they were expelled. The right of return is central to international law, and Palestinians are also specifically guaranteed that right by UN Resolution 194, which states unequivocally that "refugees wishing to return to their homes and live at peace with their neighbors should be permitted to do so at the earliest practicable date, and that compensation should be paid for the property of those choosing not to return."

Who are the Israelis? Where did they come from?

Israel defines itself as a state of and for the Jewish people, and about 79 percent of the population are Jews. It is, however, a country of immigrants, and unlike the indigenous Palestinian citizens of Israel who make up about 21 percent of the population, the vast majority of Jewish Israelis (or their forebears) have come to Israel from all over the world in the last 120 years, but mostly since 1948. The tiny indigenous and intensely orthodox Jewish communities in places like Safed and Tiberias largely remained separate from the growing mainstream Israeli population of Jewish immigrants in the late nineteenth and into the twentieth century.

The Israeli Jewish community is roughly divided into Ashkenazi, or European, Jews—of whom about one-fifth are Russians who arrived in the 1990s—along with Mizrachi and Sephardic Jews, as well as Ethiopian Jews. The Sephardim come from Spain, many having been expelled during the Inquisition of 1492. Mizrachi Jews constitute a wide-ranging category from across North Africa and West Asia. The Mizrachim are Arab—they or their forebears having emigrated to Israel from Morocco, Yemen, Syria, Iraq, Egypt, or other Arab countries— or from Iran, Turkey, Kurdistan, or elsewhere in the Middle East. The Ethiopians came to Israel primarily in 1984, during a terrible famine, and in 1991, as civil war erupted in Ethiopia. In that case, thousands of Ethiopian Jews were picked up and flown to Israel directly by the Israeli government. While many Israelis denied the Jewish credentials of the Ethiopians, the government eventually accepted them as Jews under the requirements of Israel's "law of return" guaranteeing any Jew anywhere in the world the right to settle in Israel.

Historically there has been significant tension within Israel between Jews of European descent and those whose ancestors come from the Arab world and Africa, since Israeli society is heavily racialized and, since the beginning of political Zionism and Jewish settlement in Palestine, has privileged European Jews in economic and social power.

It was European and Russian Jews, back in the late 1880s, who first began significant Jewish immigration to what was then Ottoman- and later British-ruled Palestine. They came fleeing persecution and violent pogroms, or communal attacks, in czarist Russia and Eastern Europe, and smaller numbers came in answer to mobilizations organized by a movement known as Zionism, which called for all Jews to leave their countries of origin to live in a Jewish state the Zionists wanted to create in Palestine. The use of Hebrew, recreated as a modern language beginning in the late 1800s, an orientation toward and identification with Europe and the US rather than the neighboring Middle Eastern countries, and nearly universal military service (excepting only Arabs and ultra-orthodox Jews) became the central anchors around which national Zionist, and later Israeli consciousness was built.

Israel defines itself as a state of the entire Jewish people, wherever they live, not simply a state for its own citizens. It encourages Jewish immigration through what is known as the Law of Return, under which any Jew born anywhere in the world, with or without pre-existing ties to Israel, has the official right to claim immediate citizenship upon arrival in Israel, and the right to all the privileges of being Jewish in a Jewish-dominated state—including state-financed language classes, housing, job placement, and medical and welfare benefits. Only Jews automatically have the right to immigrate to Israel; the indigenous Palestinians and their descendants, including those expelled from their homeland in 1947–1948 and 1967, are denied that right, despite the guarantees of UN Resolution 194 (institutionalizing the Palestinian right of return) and those of the Universal Declaration on Human Rights.

In 2018, Israel further institutionalized Jewish privilege with the passage of the Nation-State Law of Israel's Basic Law (equivalent to the US Constitution). It stated explicitly that only Jews have the right of self-determination in Israel, officially ensuring that that right would be denied to the millions of Palestinian citizens of Israel.

Who are the Israeli settlers? Why are the Israeli settlements located outside Israel's borders?

Immediately after the 1967 war, with 250,000 Palestinians having been forced from their homes and land, Israelis moved to establish Jewish colonies in the newly occupied territories.

The first, created in Hebron in the West Bank in 1968, was led by American-born extremist Rabbi Meir Kahane and sanctioned by a Labor Party government. Since then, Israeli governments have continued to justify construction, expansion and arming of the settlements both for security and ideological reasons. The Labor Party, committed to Israeli military control of all land west of the Jordan River, justified settlements in the name of security. The right-wing Likud Bloc supported settlements to assert its claim of Jewish sovereignty over the entire Biblical-era "Greater Israel," and when a Likud government won power in 1977, settlement construction expanded dramatically.

According to international law, the acquisition of territory by force is illegal. According to the Geneva Conventions, it is specifically illegal to transfer any civilians from the occupying country to the occupied territory. So the building of colonial settlements and the moving of Israelis to live in the Israeli-occupied territory is all completely illegal. That illegality was explicitly re-affirmed by the International Court of Justice in 2024, when the ICJ ruled that "Israel's continued presence in the OPT is unlawful," and that it has an obligation "to end its unlawful presence" and "to evacuate all settlers" from the OPT.

Despite that illegality, the settlement population has continued to grow, under both Labor and Likud governments. As settlement expansion increased, more secular Israelis moved to settlements. Government stipends kept mortgages low, amenities accessible, and commuting to jobs inside Israel easy because of a network of settler-only roads known as "bypass roads," designed to connect settlements to each other and to Israel without traversing or allowing entry or exit to Palestinian towns or villages.

Regardless of illegality, the settler population has vastly increased. As of 2024, more than 750,000 Jewish settlers lived in the occupied territories, about 234,000 of them in Arab East Jerusalem and the rest throughout the West Bank. Israel annexed East Jerusalem shortly after the 1967 war, but that annexation is not recognized by any government except for the United States.

Most US administrations have identified the settlements variously as "illegal," as "obstacles to peace," or as "unhelpful." But in 2018 the Trump administration changed course, saying explicitly that "the establishment of Israeli civilian settlements in the West Bank" was not illegal. It wasn't until more than three years into his term that the Biden administration partially distanced itself from that position, when Secretary of State Antony Blinken answered a reporter's question saying that West Bank settlement expansion, at least, is "inconsistent with international law." He did not comment on the legality of the existing settlements, however, nor did he even hint at imposing any consequences on Israel for its violation.

In the first seven months of 2024, during the first year of Israel's assault on Gaza, the Israeli organization Peace Now documented land confiscations by troops and settlers of over 9 square miles of the occupied West Bank—more than all the land confiscated over the last 20 years combined. In the same period the army and settlers displaced 1,285 Palestinians, and destroyed 641 structures, many of them people's homes.

What does "military occupation" mean?

Under international law, occupation is defined as effective control over territory and the people in it by an outside military force. In the Occupied

Palestinian Territory (OPT), military occupation means complete Israeli control over every facet of Palestinian civil and economic life. Since 1967, when Israel captured the West Bank, Gaza, and East Jerusalem, the goal has been to squeeze Palestinians into smaller and smaller pieces of territory, while claiming more and more land for settlement and use by Israeli Jews. The Oslo Accords of 1994–95 divided the West Bank into numerous non-contiguous pieces of land, with different levels of Israeli control in each of three categories—but none that actually allowed Palestinian governance or control over its territory or people. Since then, the division of land and the separation of people from their land, the walls built to surround the West Bank but actually extending deep into the Palestinian territory thus seizing even more land, the dramatic expansion of Israeli settlements and other land-use available only to Israeli Jews, and the reoccupation of Palestinian cities by Israeli military forces, all exacerbate the suppression of Palestinian life.

In the summer of 2005, Israel withdrew its soldiers and settlers from the territory of the Gaza Strip. But that did not end the occupation, because the Israeli military remained in "effective control" of Gaza, redeploying soldiers from inside the Strip to instead surrounding the territory, now also surrounded by a wall. Israel remained in complete control of Gaza's borders, the entry and exit of goods and people, Gaza's airspace, the sea off Gaza's coast, access to water, the electrical grid and more. Israel had destroyed the small Gaza airport in 2000, and after 2005 prohibited the rebuilding of the airport and prevented the construction of a seaport. Gaza remains very much part of the occupied territory.

What are the occupied territories?

In 1947, when the British ended the Palestine Mandate granted to them by the League of Nations, they turned control over to the new United Nations. The UN Partition Agreement of November 29, 1947, divided Palestine into sectors: 55 percent for a Jewish state (although the Jewish population was only 30 percent) and only 45 percent for a Palestinian Arab state (while Palestinians made up about 70 percent) with Jerusalem to be left under international control as a "corpus separatum" (separate body). War broke out immediately. After the 1947–1948 war, the new state of Israel was announced in May 1948.

Instead of the 55 percent granted by the UN, the new state was made up of 78 percent of the land of what had been British Mandate Palestine since 1922. Only 22 percent of the land was left, made up of the Gaza Strip (a small piece of land along the Mediterranean coast abutting the Egyptian border), the West Bank, along the Jordan River, and Arab East Jerusalem. From 1948 until the 1967 Six-Day War, the Gaza Strip was controlled by Egypt; the West Bank and East Jerusalem were governed by Jordan.

In the 1967 war, Israel took over the West Bank, Gaza, and East Jerusalem, the last 22 percent of historic Palestine. Those areas are now identified collectively by the United Nations as the Occupied Palestinian Territory (OPT).

In July 2024 the International Court of Justice ruled that Israel's "continued presence in the OPT is unlawful" and that it has an "obligation to end its unlawful presence in the OPT as soon as possible." It also ruled that all states are under an obligation "not to render aid or assistance to maintain that presence."

Whose capital is Jerusalem?

When the United Nations voted to partition Palestine in 1947, it identified land that was supposed to become an Israeli Jewish state, and land for a Palestinian Arab state. It also imposed a special status—*corpus separatum*, or "separate body"—for Jerusalem, ordering that Jerusalem remain under international, that is UN, jurisdiction, separately from the two new states that were to be created. The UN recognized the international significance of Jerusalem, whose holy sites are central to the tenets of the three Abrahamic monotheistic religions (Islam, Christianity, and Judaism), and viewed international jurisdiction as the best way to ensure both protection of the holy sites and free access to all.

When the 1947–48 war ended, Israel controlled 78 percent of the territory of Palestine, but only the western half of Jerusalem, comprising largely the "new city," and excluding both the Old City and the overwhelmingly Arab East Jerusalem. Israel promptly announced that Jerusalem would be its capital. East Jerusalem, like the rest of the Palestinian West Bank, came under Jordanian administration.

In 1967, when Israel occupied the last 22 percent of historic Palestine, including East Jerusalem, it immediately annexed East Jerusalem, declared the "unification" of the city, and began construction of huge settlement blocs in Arab East Jerusalem. By 2024, more than 220,000 Israeli Jewish settlers lived in East Jerusalem.

The US Congress has routinely voted to recognize Jerusalem as the official capital of Israel and to move the US embassy to Jerusalem, and US presidents have routinely campaigned for office on such commitments. But before 2017 no US president had taken that step, recognizing such a move as a threat to regional stability. Despite the routine congressional votes, operative US policy meant that the US embassy, like every other embassy in Israel, was located in Tel Aviv, not Jerusalem.

Until Donald Trump reversed longstanding US policy in 2017 to recognize Jerusalem as the capital of Israel and move the US embassy to Jerusalem in violation of international law and a host of specific UN resolutions, no country in the world officially recognized Jerusalem as the capital. After Trump's move, five countries moved their embassies—Paraguay, Honduras, Guatemala, Kosovo, and Papua New Guinea. Paraguay moved back to Tel Aviv within a few months; in 2022 reports surfaced in the Honduran parliament that the new government was considering moving out of Jerusalem, and in 2023 Honduras recalled its ambassador from Israel in protest of what it called genocide in Gaza. Kosovo and Guatemala remained with the US in Jerusalem, along with Papua New Guinea, whose new embassy was financed by Israel.

When Congress voted to require the relocation of the US embassy to Jerusalem, administrations including those of Bill Clinton, George W. Bush, and Barack Obama all made use of the legislation's six-month waiver clause given to the president in order to keep the status quo. However, when Joe Biden took office in 2021 following Trump, his administration rejected use of the waiver and announced his intention to maintain the Trump policy of recognizing Jerusalem as the capital and moving the embassy to Jerusalem. So the United States remained complicit in Israel's violations of international law and UN resolutions regarding Jerusalem, and Trump's extremist policies, unchanged, became Biden's policies.

Palestinians have long claimed Jerusalem as the capital of their would-be state. Throughout the Oslo years, their proposal was based on the idea of "one city, two capitals," in which the city would remain undivided, but there would be two national capitals within it—Israel's capital in West Jerusalem, Palestine's capital in East Jerusalem. The models of Italy and the Vatican—which each have capitals in Rome, as well as other historical examples—were often invoked.

During the negotiations that led to the Oslo Accords, particularly at the Camp David summit of August 2000, the Israelis rejected the Palestinian proposal. Their position was based on maintaining full Israeli sovereignty over all of Jerusalem. The Palestinians were offered a kind of municipal autonomy in some Arab neighborhoods of East Jerusalem (excluding the Jewish settlements in East Jerusalem), and the right to fly a Palestinian flag from the mosques of the Haram al-Sharif in Jerusalem's Old City. Israel would also extend the municipal border of Jerusalem to encompass three small Palestinian villages east of the city, and the Palestinians would be allowed to change the name of one of those towns, Abu Dis, to al-Quds (the Arabic name for Jerusalem). In theory, Abu Dis would become the capital of Palestine. The problem, of course, was that changing the name of a tiny, dusty village to al-Quds would not transform it into the city of Jerusalem—and calling it "the capital" wouldn't make it so.

International law governing the illegality of holding territory obtained through war, and a host of UN resolutions specifically calling for an end to Israel's occupation of East Jerusalem, prohibit Israeli annexation of occupied East Jerusalem and its claim to "unify" the entire city under their control. Israel's insistence on maintaining full sovereignty over the occupied Arab sector of the city violates those international decisions, particularly after the municipal borders of "Greater Jerusalem" were expanded from four square miles in 1967 to about forty-seven square miles at the expense of more than twenty Palestinian villages in the West Bank, which then came under Israeli control.

Who controls the West Bank, East Jerusalem, and the Gaza Strip?

Israel occupied those areas in the 1967 Six-Day War and imposed military control on all of them through the imposition of walls, checkpoints, soldiers, and weapons. The 1993 Oslo Accords created a Palestinian Authority (PA) whose limited power derived directly from and was controlled by Israel. Its official purpose was to provide administrative governance, but no real control of Gaza and small parts of the West Bank when Israeli troops withdrew. Unofficially it also functioned as the Palestinian liaison to the Israeli military occupying the territory.

The Oslo Accords divided the West Bank into "A, B, and C" areas. Areas A (the main cities), which originally amounted to only about 3 percent of the West Bank and by 1999 had risen to about 18 percent, were ostensibly placed under full Palestinian control of both civilian and security affairs. The B areas (over 400 Palestinian villages and rural areas) comprised 23 percent of the West Bank, where the PA was supposed to have civil control, but security remained entirely in Israeli hands. Area C, about 60 percent of the land (including Israeli settlements, military bases, designated green zones and other state-seized land that formerly was cultivated by Palestinian farmers), remained officially under complete Israeli control civilian and security control and largely inaccessible to Palestinians.

The areas where the PA was allowed to function at all were tiny disconnected islands surrounded by roads, settlements, military zones and other lands that remained under direct control of the Israeli military forces. In 2002, during the second Palestinian uprising, Israel moved to reoccupy all but one of the major cities that were supposed to be under Palestinian control and moved to tighten complete Israeli control of the roads, bridges, and agricultural land throughout the West Bank.

The 2002 reoccupation of the cities made clear that the Oslo version of Palestinian "control" was incomplete, temporary, and thoroughly reversible. In June 2002, the Israeli government began construction of a huge wall completely surrounding the West Bank—though the wall's route brought more than 15 percent of West Bank land onto the Israeli side. Israeli military occupation remained in place, controlling the land and the lives of Palestinians.

Israel remains in control of the economic life of Palestine through road and town closures and border controls in the West Bank as well as through the separation of towns and villages, farmers from their land, people from their schools and hospitals. It controls social life by separating families and denying residency permits both in Jerusalem and in the West Bank and Gaza; by denying access to Jerusalem's, Bethlehem's, and Hebron's Muslim and Christian shrines. In Gaza, even before the war that began in October 2023, control was maintained by a wall built to surround Gaza, and by imposition of a complete economic embargo on the Palestinians there, beginning in 2007. Over the years, the PA's capacity to serve as a governing body has waned; elections have not been held since 2006, and public support has diminished since.

Why does Israel still occupy those areas?

The first settlers after the 1967 war established settlements as part of asserting Israeli Jewish domination over all of Palestine, which they called "Eretz Israel," or the "Land of Israel." Later settlers, and the governments that supported them, claimed the settlements, especially those in the Jordan Valley, played a vital role in protecting Israel from possible attack from Arab states to the east.

In the 1990s, secular "yuppie settlers," uninterested in nationalist or religious rationales and concerned only with the amenities of settler life, became the majority; many indicated they would be willing to give up their homes if they were properly compensated. But increasingly, the number of ideologically driven settlers, both religious and nationalist extremists, increased, and became far more politically powerful even than their numbers, especially within the ranks of the right-wing Likud Bloc and a group of smaller parties much further to the right. Holding on to the settlements, even the most isolated, became an article of faith and a domestic political necessity for one Israeli government after another. Likud leader and then prime minister General Ariel Sharon, speaking before the 2005 Gaza "disengagement," described Netzarim, for example, a tiny isolated settlement in Gaza, as "the same as Tel Aviv" in importance.

Beyond the politics and their value in justifying the maintenance of large numbers of Israeli troops in the West Bank, the settlements played another important role in Israeli national life. They provided an excuse for the diversion of almost all of the West Bank water sources, its underground aquifers, to Israeli settlements and ultimately to Israel itself. Indigenous Palestinians, farmers on parched land, and villagers with insufficient water pressure even for a household tap pay the exorbitant price for that diversion of water, even as they watch the settlements' sparkling swimming pools and verdant, sprinkler-watered lawns.

In more recent years, especially as Benjamin Netanyahu was elected prime minister over and over beginning in the late 1990s and into the 2000s, public opinion across Israeli society began shifting sharply to the right. Popular support grew for the colonial project of settlement expansion and expulsion of Palestinians from the land, more ideologically driven extremists moved into settlement blocs, and settler representatives became a potent political force in the Knesset. The once-fashionable notion that settlers might voluntarily leave, get paid off, and move back to Israel, simply vanished. The settlers intended to stay—denying all legitimacy of indigenous Palestinian claims to the land.

If Jerusalem is the capital of Israel, why are there so many Palestinians in the eastern part of the city?

During the 1948 war, the Israeli military conquered only the western half of the city, most of which was still owned by Palestinian Arabs, and declared it the capital of Israel. Many Jerusalem Palestinians on the west side of the city were forced out of their homes and never allowed to return. East Jerusalem remained virtually entirely Palestinian, with the exception of a handful of religious Jews who remained in the Old City's ancient Jewish Quarter, even during the city's 1948–1967 years under Jordanian administration. In those years, Israeli Jews were prohibited from entering East Jerusalem, and Palestinians from inside Israel's border were kept out of West Jerusalem.

In 1967, when the Israeli army conquered East Jerusalem along with the West Bank, Gaza Strip, the Syrian Golan Heights, and Egypt's Sinai

Peninsula, one of Israel's first acts was to declare Jerusalem an eternally "united" city. In fact it was never unified; the old border, or Green Line, was legally erased, but remained vivid in the minds of Jerusalemites on both sides. During the first Palestinian intifada, or uprising, from 1987–1993, which pitted unarmed stone-throwing children and youths against the tanks of Israel's occupation forces, taxi drivers from West Jerusalem would routinely refuse to take passengers into the eastern part of the city, claiming they or their passengers would be at risk.

At the same time, starting immediately after the 1967 occupation, Israel began building huge settlements blocs within East Jerusalem, such as French Hill and Pisagot, which were quickly incorporated into Jewish Jerusalem and never acknowledged as settlements. As of 2024 there were more than 234,000 Israeli Jews living in East Jerusalem settlements, mostly primly defined as "neighborhoods." They made up about 39 percent of the population of what the United Nations still recognizes as Occupied East Jerusalem.

As the Jewish settler population grew, Palestinian Jerusalemites found their rights severely constrained. Permits for building new houses or additions to overcrowded homes were and remain virtually unobtainable for Palestinians. Marrying a partner from outside the city can put one's residency permit at risk. Palestinian Arabs in East Jerusalem are considered legal residents of the city—thus they have the right to vote for city council—but are denied full Israeli citizenship. And Israeli extremists continue provocative threats and actions, often in violation of Israel's own laws, aimed at erasing the Palestinian presence that had been central to Jerusalem's identity for centuries.

Well into the 2020s, the population of Jerusalem overall remained about 40% Palestinian, overwhelmingly in the eastern part of the city, and 60% Israeli Jews. Huge inequalities in government spending and lack of equal rights between Palestinian and Jewish Jerusalemites, as well as serious repression, land confiscation, and house demolitions facing Palestinians, all aim to drive Palestinians out of the city. But Palestinians in Jerusalem have largely refused to leave their homes.

Who are the Palestinian refugees?

There are two categories of Palestinian refugees. The first wave, about 750,000 at the time, were expelled by force or driven out by fear before, during, and after the 1947–48 war and attacks waged by pre-state Zionist militias. This massive dispossession was the *nakba*. Some were physically driven out, others fled in fear after hearing stories of massacres, such as that at the village of Deir Yassin outside of Jerusalem in April 1948, in which 254 Palestinian civilians were killed by soldiers from the various Zionist militias. Following the massacre, soldiers drove trucks through other Palestinian villages using loudspeakers to threaten "Deir Yassin, Deir Yassin!" in a kind of psychological warfare warning to any Palestinians who remained.

Many fled the campaign of ethnic cleansing, believing the onslaught by the militias would end within a few weeks and they would be able to return home. Many of them carried with them the keys to their houses, believing they would soon return, and thus the key has become a symbol of Palestinian refugee rights. Some, but far fewer now, are still alive of that aging first generation of refugees, living in refugee camps or in exile with their children and grandchildren, clinging to the keys and the hope that they will be allowed to go home before they die.

After seventy-five years, none have been allowed to return to their homes.

For many years, Israeli officials and many defenders of Israel claimed that the Palestinians who left did so only because they were ordered to by Arab leaders broadcasting on local radio, who allegedly promised them they would be able to return victorious. But throughout the 1990s, an increasingly large number of Israeli academics, the "new historians," carefully researched and completely debunked that myth. There were no such radio broadcasts.

Some of the civilians fled direct attacks by the Haganah, Palmach, and Irgun militias. Others fled in fear that they would be next. They believed they would eventually be able to come home because it is a longstanding tenet of international law that war-time refugees, regardless of the particular circumstances under which they flee, have the right to return to their homes.

When Palestinians were expelled from their homes in the 1948 war, many fled to neighboring Arab countries, others to the West Bank and Gaza Strip, the parts of Palestine not yet under the control of the new Israeli army. In all those places, corrupt and/or impoverished Arab governments had neither the will nor the resources to care for the sudden influx of refugees. The United Nations, recognizing its responsibility for the crisis through its role in dividing Palestine in the first place, took on the work of caring for the new exiles. It created the United Nations Relief and Works Agency (UNRWA), designed to provide basic housing, food, medical care, and education to the Palestinian refugees until they could return home; UNRWA was initially envisioned as a short-term project. But Israel refused to allow the refugees to return home. Instead, the months turned to years, and tent camps were transformed over time into squalid, crowded mini-towns, made up of concrete block houses with tin roofs held down by old tires and sometimes scraps of iron bars. For decades electricity remained sporadic, and streams of raw sewage were a common feature between tightly packed houses. But UNRWA schools educated Palestinian children to such an extent that until the 2023 Israeli war against Gaza destroyed almost all UNRWA schools and ended education for a whole generation of Gaza children, Palestinians maintained the highest percentage of literate and of college-educated people in the entire Arab world.

The second wave of Palestinian refugees was created during and following the Six-Day War of 1967, when Israel occupied the last 22% of Palestinian land—the West Bank, Gaza, and East Jerusalem. About 250,000 refugees were driven out of their homes, about half of whom were already refugees from 1948.

Some remained in what became known as the Occupied Palestinian Territory (OPT), where they found homes in already overcrowded refugee camps. Others, who had fled to Lebanon, Jordan, and Syria, crowded into similarly packed camps.

What are the rights of Palestinian refugees and why are they still living in refugee camps?

Some have claimed that Arab governments have used Palestinian refugees to score propaganda points, or to divert their own people's anger away from the regimes and toward Israel. Certainly the Arab regimes had little interest in serious political defense of Palestinian rights, let alone serious protection of Palestinian refugees. Only Jordan allowed Palestinians to become citizens. Everywhere else, Palestinians were kept segregated. In Lebanon, they were viewed as a potential disruption to the country's delicate confessional system balancing Christian and Muslim parties and interests, and well into the twenty-first century Palestinian refugees in Lebanon remain locked out of dozens of job categories. Egypt kept the Palestinians confined to the Gaza Strip.

But the refugee camps remained in place primarily because Israel blocked the refugees' right of return. The Palestinians themselves were determined that they wanted to go home—they did not want to be "integrated" into other Arab countries, despite the common language. Palestinians were—and remain—afraid that leaving the camps to integrate into some other part of the Arab world would result in the loss of their homes and their rights. The Arab world after 1948 was no longer an integrated "Arabia": nation-states had been created by lines drawn in the sand by colonial powers, as in so many other places in the world. National ties combined with specific ties to a village or town, creating for Palestinians a communal yearning to return home.

In 2000 there was discussion at the Camp David summit about allowing some of the 1967 refugees to return to their homes in a future Palestinian state, made up of parts of the West Bank and Gaza, but no consideration of the right of the 1948 refugees to return to their homes in what is now Israel. Ultimately none of the refugees were allowed to return at all. Israel remained in control of Occupied Palestine's borders, determining who would or would not be allowed to enter the territory. Since 1967, the majority of Palestinians have lived as exiles or refugees outside the original territory of the Palestine Mandate of 1922 (comprising Israel within the 1949 armistice lines, the occupied West Bank, Gaza Strip, and East Jerusalem).

A year before the United Nations created UNRWA in 1949, it passed Resolution 194 in December 1948, which went beyond customary international law protecting all refugees, to provide special protection for the Palestinians. The resolution reaffirmed that Palestinian "refugees wishing to return to their homes and live at peace with their neighbors should be permitted to do so at the earliest practicable date, and that compensation should be paid for the property of those choosing not to return." The UN even made Israel's own entry to the world body contingent on Israeli acceptance of Resolution 194.

But Israel refused to allow Palestinian refugees to exercise that right to return. There are now about 8.4 million 1948 refugees and their descendants around the world. All the refugees have the right to return to their homes. But despite international law and the specific requirements of Resolution 194, Israel has never allowed Palestinian refugees to return to their homes.

Israel claims that allowing the Palestinian refugees to return would change its demographic balance, more than doubling the current 21 percent Palestinian population inside pre-1967 Israel. That would indeed be the consequence. However, international law does not allow a country to violate UN resolutions and international law and principles in order to protect its ethnic or religious composition. The parallel would be if Rwanda's new Tutsi-dominated government, after the 1994 genocide, announced that they would not allow the overwhelmingly Hutu refugees who fled during the war to return home, because it would disrupt the new ethnic balance in their country. The United Nations and the world, appropriately, would have made very clear that such a prohibition was unacceptable and that the refugees had to be allowed to return home. (In fact the UN did provide protection to all Rwandan refugees who wanted to return.) Palestinian refugees, despite the passage of time, have the same rights as their Rwandan counterparts.

Most Palestinians recognize that while rights, including the right of return, are absolute, how to implement those rights can always be discussed. It is likely that once their right to return has been recognized, some Palestinian refugees may choose options other than permanent return to their mostly demolished villages in what is now Israel. But the key factor will be the ability of individual Palestinians to choose for themselves what to do. Some will choose to go home; some may wish to go only for short visits; some may wish to accept compensation and build new lives in a new Palestinian state; many may choose to accept compensation and citizenship in their place of refuge or in third countries. Some, especially among the most impoverished and disempowered Palestinian refugees living in Lebanon and especially those in Gaza who survive the genocide and razing of the Strip that began in October 2023, may indeed choose to return to their homes in Israel. All of them have the right to any of those choices. But discussion of how to implement this right of return cannot begin until Israel acknowledges its responsibility for the refugee crisis, and recognizes the internationally guaranteed right of return as an absolute right.

What is the Palestine Liberation Organization (PLO)?

In 1964, the PLO was created and largely controlled by leaders of the Arab states. At the same time, small groups of Palestinian activists were building nationalist organizations, some of which, the *fedayeen*, moved toward guerrilla tactics to challenge Israel. In 1968, Yasir Arafat became head of the PLO, uniting a number of factions that advocated a wide range of strategies and political principles. The organization was cobbled together, with a complicated web of eight separate political factions represented in the leadership; a broadly representative parliament-in-exile, the Palestine National Council; and a host of sector-based institutions including students' and women's unions, medical and relief agencies, and more. In many Palestinian-populated areas, particularly in Jordan and later in Lebanon, the PLO took on the responsibilities, and often the trappings, of a full government.

In the early years the PLO demanded a democratic secular state in all of Palestine—including what was then Israel as well as the 1967 occupied territories. There was no recognition of Israel having the right to exist as a separate Jewish-dominant state. But after the shock of the 1967 war and the resulting occupation began to wear off, Palestinians began to broaden their strategic approach. By the mid-1970s, the majority view in the PLO was moving toward acceptance of a two-state solution, an approach already accepted in the UN and elsewhere as reflecting an international consensus. In Israel, where refusal even to consider negotiations with the PLO was the norm, such a shift was viewed as potentially damaging, as it stripped away the key rationale for Israeli rejection of all Palestinian claims.

In 1974, the United Nations General Assembly recognized the PLO as the "sole legitimate representative of the Palestinian people." It established November 29 (the day the original partition resolution was signed in 1947) as an International Day of Solidarity with the Palestinian People and invited the PLO to participate as an observer within the General Assembly and other UN agencies.

In January 1976, a PLO-drafted resolution backed by a number of Arab countries as well as the Soviet Union was put before the UN Security Council. It called for a two-state solution, Israeli withdrawal to the 1967 borders, and other aspects of the international consensus. Israel refused to participate in the meeting, and the US cast its veto, killing the resolution.

In 1982, the PLO led the joint Lebanese-Palestinian resistance to the Israeli invasion of Lebanon and weeks-long bombardment of Beirut. Soon after, diplomatic efforts led to the organization's expulsion from Lebanon, with thousands of PLO activists and fighters boarding ships to a new, long exile in Tunis, even while hundreds of thousands of vulnerable Palestinian civilians remained in Lebanon.

Still, the two-state approach remained the majority view within the PLO for some years. In 1988, at the height of the first intifada, it became official when the Palestine National Council, the PLO's parliament in exile, convened in Algiers. In a unanimous vote, the PNC proclaimed the "establishment of the State of Palestine on our Palestinian territory with its capital Jerusalem." Within the political program was official recognition of Israel and of the two-state approach, despite the fact that Israel still considered the PLO an outlawed "terrorist" organization, and PLO officials were prohibited from even visiting Israel or the occupied territories.

The US opened mid-level diplomatic ties with the PLO a month later, but the organization remained excluded from the US-led international diplomatic efforts. With the Iraqi invasion of Kuwait in 1990, the PLO's decision to side with Iraq resulted in intense anger from the oil-rich Gulf countries that had long bankrolled the organization. Palestinians were summarily expelled from Saudi Arabia, Kuwait, and other Gulf states, and the PLO fell into severe poverty and political isolation in the region.

After the Gulf War, with the PLO at perhaps its weakest point, the US government, flush with its victory over Iraq, approached the PLO to negotiate Palestinian participation in the post-war peace talks in Madrid. The terms were insulting—no separate Palestinian delegation, participation only as a subset of the Jordanian team, no participation allowed for PLO members, no participation for Palestinian residents of Jerusalem, no role for the United Nations—so the PNC vote that finally approved participation in the Madrid process was bitterly contested. But eventually, the PLO, through its well-known but officially unacknowledged representatives in the occupied territories, accepted. The post-Madrid talks, ostensibly based on UN Resolutions 242 and 338 and the principle of "land for peace," moved from capital to capital, grinding on uneventfully for almost two years, when the surprise announcement hit the press that secret Israeli–PLO talks had been underway in Oslo, and that a Declaration of Principles was about to be signed.

The ceremony on the White House lawn on September 13, 1993, in which President Clinton presided over a handshake between a reluctant Yitzhak Rabin and an eager Yasir Arafat, provided a photo-op of global proportions. A Nobel Prize for Peace, split between Arafat, Rabin, and the Israeli Foreign Minister Shimon Peres, soon followed. The Oslo peace process was born.

Within two years and after extensive negotiations, Oslo's substantive agreements were signed; their crucial beginnings allowed the return of all the PLO exiles from Tunis to the West Bank and Gaza, where they would be allowed to create a new Palestinian Authority (PA) to administer small parts of the still-occupied territories under overall Israeli "security" control. As the PA took over, led by the same organizations (primarily Arafat's own Fatah party) and indeed mostly the same individuals that had led the PLO, the role of the PLO both inside occupied Palestine and in the international arena diminished, and the demand for recognition of the PLO as the sole legitimate representative of the Palestinian people faded away as well.

What is the Palestinian Authority (PA)?

The PA was created under the terms of the Oslo peace process. It is a quasi-governmental body, with derivative power limited to what is granted to it (or taken away from it) by Israel. It is not a fully independent government, even in the limited areas under its jurisdiction from which Israeli troops have temporarily withdrawn, but rather analogous to a municipal council, with carefully delimited authority. It has the authority, in most Palestinian towns and cities, to orchestrate day-to-day life for residents, but not to control the land. It is responsible for cleaning the streets, deploying local police, and keeping economic and social life functioning, but it is denied the authority to control its own borders. It does not have any authority over Israeli soldiers or settlers within or surrounding its land; it does not control a single contiguous territory but rather scores of tiny scattered and disconnected areas; and, according to the language of the Oslo agreements, any law passed by the PA's parliament is subject to approval or rejection by Israel.

Beginning in the spring of 2002, as the intifada escalated, Israel moved to reoccupy almost all of Palestine's major cities, from which its troops had been withdrawn under the terms of Oslo. While Palestinian resistance was fierce in one or two of the cities (Jenin and Nablus in particular), the speed of the Israeli military's return gave the lie to any notion that Palestinian control, already limited, was designed to be permanent.

Following the redeployment of Israeli soldiers and withdrawal of settlers from the territory of the Gaza Strip in 2005, the PA was assumed to have full control over Gaza. But Gaza remained occupied—because under international law "occupation" does not require the physical presence of troops on the ground, but is defined by an outside force having effective control over the occupied territory. Gaza remains completely under Israeli control—entry and exit, access to water, control of the economy, water, the electrical grid, and more. Even before the genocidal war that began in October 2023 led to the virtual destruction of the entire Gaza Strip. Continuing Israeli control of Gaza, and the lack of any viable connection between Gaza and the West Bank, made a mockery of PA authority.

After the January 2006 parliamentary elections, when the Islamist Hamas organization won majority control of the PA, the US and Israel orchestrated a global economic boycott of the PA that further limited its ability to govern. By the summer of 2006, with Israel routinely bombing and attacking Gaza's infrastructure and carrying out "targeted assassinations," the Israeli military had arrested more than forty members of the PA's legislature and about eight members of the cabinet; other PA officials went into hiding or on the run, undermining further any capacity to govern.

Over time, the challenges facing the PA—as well as issues of corruption—made clear its inability to successfully challenge the Israeli occupation. While it remains in place, its level of support from the occupied Palestinian population has been significantly reduced.

What is the wall that Israel built in the occupied West Bank?

According to Israeli officials, the huge wall built in the West Bank—known to Palestinians as the "apartheid wall"—is designed to protect Israel by keeping potential attackers out. Begun in 2002 with the support of both the Labor Party and the right-wing Likud, the Wall is composed largely of 24-foot high cement slabs, and includes electrified fences, trenches, gun emplacements, and security patrols, completely surrounding the West Bank.

But the Wall was not built to follow the Green Line, as the border between Israel and the West Bank is called; instead it curves significantly eastward in many areas to encompass huge swathes of Palestinian land—settlement blocs, large tracts of Palestinian farmland, and major Palestinian water sources—on the Israeli side. According to the UN, in the Jerusalem area alone, 55,000 Palestinians live in the area between the Green Line and the wall—an area that in some places became a closed military zone. Thousands of acres of Palestinian land on both sides of the wall have been seized by the Israeli military and cleared of houses and farmland. Palestinian farmers are supposed to be allowed to cross the wall to farm their land, but in many areas the wall extends for huge distances without access gates, and even where gates exist, Israeli soldiers are often either missing altogether or simply refuse to open the gates to allow Palestinian access to their own land. Israeli and Palestinian human rights organizations estimate that when completed, and matched by the planned parallel wall in the Jordan Valley, 90,000 Palestinians will have lost their land.

The wall completely surrounds the large Palestinian town of Qalqilya in the northern West Bank, separating the town from the West Bank. Besides isolating its population, the effect will also bring the valuable Western Aquifer System entirely under Israeli control, since its Palestinian portion lies beneath additional lands in Qalqilya.

The result was to ensure then-Prime Minister Ariel Sharon's stated goal of allowing a Palestinian non-sovereign and non-state "entity" of no more than about 40 percent of the West Bank, divided among several small noncontiguous chunks, plus most of Gaza.

As the Palestinian human rights group LAW pointed out, under the Fourth Geneva Convention, to which Israel is a signatory, the destruction or seizure of property in occupied territories is forbidden, as is collective punishment. Article 47 prohibits occupying powers from making changes to property in occupied territories. Seizure of land in occupied territories is prohibited under Article 52 of the Hague Regulations of 1907, which is a part of customary international law. And according to international humanitarian law governing occupation, occupiers cannot make any changes in the status of occupied territories. Israel's apartheid wall seizes land, destroys, and permanently changes the status of occupied territories.

The United Nations estimates that the wall transferred at least 15 percent of West Bank land into Israeli control and cut off tens of thousands of Palestinians from the West Bank, leaving them on the western, or Israeli, side of the wall. Significant West Bank aquifers that provide much of the water for Israel's high-tech agricultural production are also located on Palestinian land that ended up in Israeli hands. Within the wall-enclosed Palestinian areas, hundreds of Israeli military-run checkpoints remain in place, cutting off most towns and especially smaller villages from each other and from the larger cities that once provided commercial, educational, medical, and cultural facilities. Some towns, such as Qalqilya, were soon completely cut off, physically surrounded by the wall and dependent on the whim of Israeli soldiers, who control the only two gates into the town.

By 2005, Israeli officials had admitted that they intended the route of the wall to be the basis for the future, unilaterally imposed border of an expanded Israeli state.

What does the rest of the world think about the wall?

In December 2003, the UN General Assembly requested that the International Court of Justice in the Hague advise them on the legality of the wall. In its July 9, 2004, opinion, the ICJ ruled explicitly that the wall was illegal and that Israel must stop construction and dismantle any part of the wall inside the occupied territory, including Arab East Jerusalem. "Israel," the ICJ said, "is under an obligation to terminate its breaches of international law; it is under an obligation to cease forthwith the works of construction of the wall being built in the Occupied Palestinian Territory, including in and around East Jerusalem, to dismantle forthwith the structure therein situated, and to repeal or render ineffective forthwith all legislative and regulatory acts relating thereto." Significantly, the ICJ opinion was not limited to the wall alone. It also stressed the illegality of all the colonial settlements built throughout the Palestinian territory, and in doing so linked the illegality of the wall to that of the broader settlement project Israel had undertaken since its occupation of the West Bank, Gaza, and East Jerusalem in the 1967 war.

Israel rejected the ICJ's opinion before it was even issued. In January 2004, Prime Minister Ariel Sharon admitted that the wall was causing problems for ordinary Palestinians, and that the route of the wall, which cut off huge swathes of West Bank territory, could cause "legal difficulties in defending the state's position." But he went on to assert that "there will be no change as a result of Palestinian or UN demands, including those from the [International] court." Then-Justice Minister

Yosef Lapid called on his own government to move the wall, recognizing that "the present route will bring upon us isolation in the world." But Israel continued construction of the wall on Palestinian land.

The ICJ also stated directly that other countries have their own responsibility to pressure Israel to comply with the court's opinion. "All States," the court declared, "are under an obligation not to recognize the illegal situation resulting from the construction of the wall and not to render aid or assistance in maintaining the situation created by such construction." The US government quietly criticized the wall early in its process of construction, but soon dropped the critique and agreed, in direct violation of the court's ruling on the obligation of other states, to pay Israel almost $50 million—taken out of the $200 million the US provided in humanitarian support to Palestinian NGOs—to construct checkpoints and gates in the wall.

What is Hamas?

Hamas is a Palestinian Islamist and nationalist organization. It believes in a form of political Islam in which religion forms the basis for social and political governance and strategy for ending Israeli control. Its origins are in the Muslim Brotherhood, a pan-Arab Islamist organization based in Egypt. Hamas was created in Gaza in December 1987, immediately following the eruption of the first Palestinian intifada.

Even before Hamas came into existence, Israel covertly provided support to the Muslim Brotherhood; when Hamas was created, Israel allowed funds to flow to it both directly and through other governments. Hoping to create a counterweight to the nationalist secular PLO, Israel allowed Hamas to gain popularity with less of the repression and obstacles it imposed on the PLO, viewing Hamas as a potential competitor with the PLO for Palestinian loyalty, and believing the Islamist organization would be less of a serious challenge to Israel than the nationalist PLO. Although the PLO is itself a coalition of organizations, Hamas was never a member of the PLO.

Throughout its years, Hamas's activities have always been far broader than those of its well-known military wing. Especially in Gaza, always the poorest part of Palestine, Hamas created a widespread network of social welfare agencies, including schools, clinics, hospitals, and mosques. During the years of the first intifada (1987–1993), as well as the years of the Oslo process and the Palestinian Authority (from 1993 on), Hamas provided many of the basic services that Israel as the occupying power refused to provide, and that the PA, lacking real power and facing both poverty and problems of corruption, could not. As a result, Hamas's popularity grew.

Hamas's first suicide bombing was in 1993, and for many in Israel and internationally, that method of attack came to characterize the organization. Some of the attacks were against Israeli soldiers in the occupied territories—acts of military resistance recognized as legal under international law—but others targeted civilians inside Israel itself, in violation of international law. Hamas declared a unilateral cease-fire in March 2005, which it maintained until June 2006, when it announced its intention to break the cease-fire in response to a continuing and then escalating set of Israeli attacks. Of particular relevance in the Hamas decision was the Israeli attack just days before on a Gaza beach, which killed nine Palestinians, seven of them from one family, including five children. The end of the ceasefire led to Hamas's attack on an Israeli military patrol just over the Gaza border, culminating in the capture of one Israeli soldier.

Over the years, Israeli repression of Hamas increased. In 1994, Israel forcibly expelled 415 Palestinians, many of whom were connected to Hamas, to Lebanon despite the opposition of the government in Beirut. Israel has targeted many Hamas leaders for assassination, including Sheikh Ahmed Yassin, the paralyzed and wheelchair-bound founder and spiritual leader of Hamas, who was killed by an Israeli missile in Gaza in March 2004. His position was taken over by Abdel Aziz Rantisi, who was assassinated by Israel a month later. Rantisi, a Gaza physician, was among those kidnapped by Israel and expelled a decade earlier. Returned to Gaza in a prisoner exchange, Rantisi was killed by a "targeted" Israeli missile strike in Gaza.

In another ostensibly "targeted" assassination, this time of Hamas leader Salah Shihadeh, fourteen other people, nine of them children, were killed by the Israeli military air strike. State Department officials reportedly attempted to warn Secretary of State Colin Powell about Israel possibly violating the US Arms Export Control Act through its use of US-provided weapons in the assassination. But according to *US News and World Report*, then Undersecretary of State and later George W. Bush's Ambassador to the United Nations John Bolton prevented the warning from being passed on to Powell.

International observers, including US government officials and mainstream media, often misrepresented Hamas's political stance, which changed in response to political developments over the years. For years, Hamas had rejected a two-state solution, holding out for what it called an Islamic state in all of historic Palestine. But the Palestinian majority that elected Hamas to lead the Palestinian Authority in January 2006 included many who did not endorse that program. Reflecting that public view, in the midst of the summer 2006 Israeli attacks on Gaza, Hamas leader and then-Palestinian Prime Minister Ismail Haniyeh wrote in the *Washington Post* that the Gaza crisis was part of a "wider national conflict that can be resolved only by addressing the full dimensions of Palestinian national rights in an integrated manner. This means statehood for the West Bank and Gaza, a capital in Arab East Jerusalem, and resolving the 1948 Palestinian refugee issue fairly, on the basis of international legitimacy and established law."

That carefully articulated set of Palestinian goals—clearly "moderate" even by US and European standards—matched closely what Haniyeh called Palestinian "priorities." Those included "recognition of the core dispute over the land of historical Palestine and the rights of all its people; resolution of the refugee issue from 1948; reclaiming all lands occupied in 1967; and stopping Israeli attacks, assassinations and military expansion." It was significant that the Hamas leader, often accused of calling for "the destruction of Israel," actually distinguished between the need to "recognize" all the lost lands and rights of pre-1948 historical Palestine and the need for Palestinians to "reclaim" only those lands occupied in 1967.

Haniyeh's openness to negotiations was not reciprocated. Later in 2006, Israel imposed a crippling siege on the Gaza Strip, walling off the territory by a physical wall and the continued deployment of Israeli troops surrounding it. That siege continued—and was exacerbated by major Israeli assaults on Gaza in 2008–09 (Operation Cast Lead), 2012, 2014 (a fifty-five-day assault that killed at least 2,200 Palestinians), 2018, and 2021. In 2023, it was the desperation caused by almost two decades of siege and assault, with a whole generation having grown up never allowed to leave the crowded, impoverished Strip, that sparked the deadly Hamas-led attack of October 7, 2023, that broke out of the besieged territory and took hostages and killed both civilians and military troops in southern Israel (see pages 234–268). The Israeli response was to initiate an unprecedented genocidal assault on Gaza, resulting in more than 43,000 killed, disproportionately children and women, and the forced displacement of 90 percent of the population. In July 2024, Ismail Haniyeh, who for months had served as the leader of the Hamas negotiating team trying to reach a ceasefire, was assassinated in Tehran in an attack widely attributed to Israel.

What are Israel's "targeted assassinations"?

"Targeted assassination" is Israel's euphemism for its deliberate killing of Palestinian militants or leaders. In legal language, this is known as "extrajudicial killing," referring to a government's decision to kill someone without charges, without trial, and without any kind of judicial proceeding. Israel has carried out such killings of Palestinians since the 1970s, but the use of so-called targeted assassinations became far more commonplace with the beginning of the second intifada in 2000.

The term "targeted assassination" is designed to disguise two huge problems. First, the "targeting" is not so precise. According to the Israeli human rights organization B'Tselem, of 331 Palestinians killed in "targeted assassination" operations between September 2000 and June 2006, 127 were not targets at all; many of them were women and children. Second, calling these killings "targeted" does not make them legal; the Fourth Geneva Convention prohibits *all* killings by the occupying power of anyone in the occupied population. There are no exceptions.

Most of the assassinations are carried out long-distance—using missiles, rockets, or bombs that hit cars or houses or whole residential neighborhoods. In 2002, the killing of Hamas leader Sheikh Salah

Shihadeh at 3 AM in a crowded Gaza apartment building resulted not only his death but also the deaths of fourteen others, including nine children. Four years later, Israel's implementation of the assassination policy escalated again, following the Hamas victory in the Palestinian elections. In response, the Public Committee Against Torture in Israel noted that the problem of people being killed who were not the "official" target was made "abundantly clear during the 7 February 2006 air strike [in Gaza] that killed the two targeted people but also injured four children, one critically." A few months after that attack, on July 12, another Israeli air assault on a Gaza house missed the "targeted" Hamas leader but did kill two other adults and seven children.

During Israel's genocidal assault on Gaza that began in October 2023, hundreds of people, disproportionately women and children, were killed in attacks Israel justified on the grounds that they were "targeting" a particular Hamas leader. In July 2024, Israel bombed a displacement camp in southern Gaza, in an area that had been designated a "safe zone" for Palestinians fleeing Israel's attacks elsewhere in the Strip. At least ninety Palestinians were killed and over 300 wounded, many of them children. Israel justified the attack saying it was aimed at Mohammed Deif, a Hamas military leader. Prime Minister Netanyahu said he had approved the strike when he was assured no Israeli hostages were nearby; the presence of Palestinian civilians was either not considered at all or was deemed insufficient to matter. The first year of Israel's war was characterized by a sequence of Israeli assassinations of Hamas and (Lebanese) Hezbollah leaders and most of the time numerous other people, in Gaza, in Beirut, and even in Tehran. Those actions played an important role in making ceasefire negotiations impossible. (Haniyeh, for instance, was not only the Hamas leader but their key negotiator in the ceasefire talks).

The Fourth Geneva Convention, under Article 3 (1) (a) prohibits all "violence to life and person" and "murder of all kinds." Giving murder the clinical term "targeted assassination" does not make it legal. Israel has attempted to disguise the clear illegality of these killings by asserting that each is individually approved by the prime minister, but in fact, the authorization by any Israeli official, or even by Israel's highest courts, is thoroughly irrelevant as a defense to the Geneva Convention's absolute prohibition.

What is the international response to the Israeli–Palestinian conflict? Is there international agreement?

Beginning in the mid-1970s, when the Palestine Liberation Organization was deemed the sole legitimate representative of the Palestinian people and welcomed as an observer member of the United Nations, most of the world has been part of a clear international consensus on how to deal with the seemingly endless conflict.

Security Council Resolution 242, passed after the 1967 war, is widely recognized, officially, as the basis for a permanent settlement. The operative language of the resolution calls for two things: Israeli withdrawal from the land it had occupied in June 1967, and the right of every state in the region to " live in peace within secure and recognized boundaries." It also called for "a just settlement of the refugee problem" without stating that those refugees were Palestinian. Palestine, of course, was not a state, and so was not included in the rights of "every state in the region" to "secure and recognized boundaries."

In fact, neither Palestine nor Palestinians are even mentioned in the resolution, so the land for peace trade that the resolution is thought to require was really about Israel pulling out its troops from the land it had occupied—Palestinian, Syrian, and Egyptian—and peace from the surrounding Arab states. Palestinians were not granted statehood in 242.

Outside of the US, the resolution is understood in a much different way than simply calling for an exchange of land for peace. The international consensus puts much greater emphasis than the US does on the preamble of the resolution, which unequivocally asserts "the inadmissibility of the acquisition of territory by war." That is understood to mean that all the territory Israel captured by war must be returned—that to keep it is "inadmissible."

In terms of process, the international community has long recognized as inadequate the notion of bilateral talks under US sponsorship, in which Israel and Palestine, with such enormous disparities of power, face each other as if on a level playing field. That they are forced to negotiate before a mediator that is itself the strategic, financial, diplomatic, and military champion of the stronger of the two parties, makes the process even less legitimate. Instead, the UN has repeatedly called for convening an international peace conference, in which all the parties to the conflict, including Israel, the PLO, the Arab states, and others would negotiate in concert under the auspices of the UN Security Council. When the first international conference was convened in Madrid in 1991, following the US victory over Iraq in the Gulf War and just before the collapse of the Soviet Union, it was actually once again under the control of the United States. It was ostensibly based on the requirements of Resolution 242. Palestinian participation was allowed, but without even an independent delegation (the Palestinians were a subset of the Jordanian diplomatic team)—and the UN was prohibited from even participating in the conference.

Why is Israel so isolated in the United Nations?

In the United Nations, certain privileges and positions, including rotating membership in the Security Council, are determined within the regional groups of the General Assembly. The composition of the groups, determined at the height of the Cold War, was partly geographic and partly political (i.e., Eastern Europe and Western Europe constitute different regional groups). To protest its occupation and other policies toward Palestinians, Israel was excluded from participation in the Asian Group that includes the surrounding Arab countries.

In 2000, Secretary-General Kofi Annan orchestrated a campaign within the UN that managed to get Israel accepted into WEOG, the Western European and Others Group, first only in New York headquarters of the UN and later also in the Geneva headquarters. WEOG was and remained a geographic hodgepodge of both Cold War and colonial identities. When the regional groups were established in 1961, western European countries formed WEOG to separate themselves politically from the eastern European states with their ties to the Soviet-led socialist bloc. And despite its "Western European" title, WEOG also includes the "Others"—the United States and Canada, as well as Australia and New Zealand, none very close to Western Europe. Part of Wikipedia's definition describes WEOG members as "being part of the 'Western world' of affluent, developed liberal democracies, and are either part of

Western Europe or a majority European-descended [sic] state." Others might define WEOG, with the addition of Israel, as including most of the predominantly white wealthy countries as well as the most influential settler-colonial countries of the world.

Of course Israeli isolation at the UN goes beyond its official regional group positioning. Far more important is the widespread opposition throughout the UN system—including many US allies despite their reluctance to say so publicly—to Israel's occupation and apartheid. And while certainly not the only settler-colonial state in the UN—the US, Canada, Australia, and New Zealand remain powerful—Israel is the only settler-colonial state backed by a major western power where an active struggle between the indigenous and settler populations remains unresolved.

It should also be noted that Israel's consistent disregard for UN resolutions, its contempt for UN decisions, and disdain for UN personnel (including keeping relevant UN officials such as special rapporteurs accredited to the Human Rights Council, and in 2024 the secretary-general himself, persona non grata and kept out of Israel), and its persistent violations of human rights and international humanitarian law, all play a major role in Israel's isolation. It is the level of unconditional US backing, ultimately, that protects Israel from actually being held accountable for those violations in the United Nations, its various agencies, and the international courts and other legal structures of the multilateral system.

Why is the US the central player in the Middle East?

The main reason is power. By the time Israel was created, with the end of the British Mandate over Palestine, World War II was just over, and the European powers, victors and losers alike, lay decimated by war. Of all the major global powers, only the US survived the war intact, with economic and military power on the rise, and hungry for oil.

The US spent the Cold War years locked in contention with the Soviet Union, vying for influence in the strategic Middle East as much as anywhere else. With the end of the Cold War, the collapse of the

Soviet Union, and the US victory in the 1991 Gulf War, which profoundly altered the Middle East in favor of even greater US influence, Washington's superpower status significantly expanded. The decades of the US wars and occupations driven by the so-called global war on terror saw the massive expansion of US military bases, troop and naval deployments, and direct military engagement by US forces.

The combination of the US-Israeli "special relationship" and the vast superiority of Israel's power in the region further consolidated the US centrality. Iran, despite an economic crisis driven by US sanctions, emerged as the primary strategic challenger. But as long as Israel remains the strongest military force in the region, with the only nuclear arsenal in the Middle East and one of the most powerful conventional militaries anywhere, with unlimited backing by the US, Arab countries in the region have tended to limit their diplomatic imagination to what they think Israel—and the United States—will accept. So far, that has meant acquiescence to continued US control.

From the late 2010s on, much of US strategy focused on building an anti-Iran coalition, to be led in the region by Israel and Saudi Arabia, Washington's closest regional ally. The US remains the controlling authority in shaping the political map of the region.

What explains the US-Israeli "special relationship"?

When Israel was first created, its leaders chose to maintain the clearly Euro-American, rather than Middle Eastern, orientation that had characterized the Zionist movement even before the state was founded. With statehood, Israel maintained its military reliance primarily on France, Czechoslovakia, and other European powers, but it would soon turn for help and support to the leading Western power: the post–World War II United States.

Even before the State of Israel was declared, US support was strong, and the US was one of the first countries to recognize the new state in 1948. Relations remained close, but diplomatically and financially "normal" until the time of the 1967 war. When Israel demonstrated the extraordinary military prowess that enabled it to destroy three Arab armies and to occupy territories under the control of four separate countries, the Pentagon quickly recognized Israel's potential as a valuable Cold War ally, and the friendly alliance segued into the all-embracing "special relationship" and strategic alliance that continues today.

Economic assistance, military aid, and diplomatic protection all soared. Within US society, support for Israel grew exponentially. Existing pro-Israeli organizations (initially mostly based in the US Jewish community, but soon matched by the influential Christian Zionist movement primarily based in the Protestant evangelical churches) dramatically increased their influence in popular culture, in education, in the media, and among policymakers.

Is the US an "honest broker" in the conflict?

For many years the US called itself an "honest broker" in Palestine-Israel diplomacy, and that was correct, but only in a very particular context. The role of honest broker the US played through decades of failed diplomatic initiatives was never the role of a baseball umpire, independent and impartial. Rather, it is best compared to the role of a real estate broker who may deal honestly with both buyer and seller, but who is understood to represent the interests of only one side because her own economic (or in this case strategic) interests depend on it.

As longtime US negotiator Aaron David Miller described it, "American officials involved in Arab–Israeli peacemaking, myself included, have acted as Israel's attorney."

Perhaps even more dangerously, the US position has always refused to base its diplomacy on the principles of international law and UN resolutions. If it did, the necessity of Israel unilaterally ending its colonial occupation of the 1967 territories and unilaterally implementing the right of return of Palestinian refugees, both explicitly required by international law and UN resolutions, would be understood as the necessary starting point for any kind of negotiations over a future peace between Israelis and Palestinians.

In July 2024, the UN's International Court of Justice issued a powerful new assessment of Israel's occupation and apartheid practices. As

Craig Mokhiber, an international human rights lawyer and the former Director of the New York Office of the UN High Commissioner for Human Rights described it, the court "rejected arguments by the U.S. and other Western governments that sought to claim that the Court should defer to post-Oslo negotiations between the occupier and the occupied, and to the politics of the Security Council, rather than the application of international law."

Mokhiber went on, clarifying that "The Court, in rejecting these claims, declared that such negotiations and agreements do not and cannot trump the rights of the Palestinians and the obligations of Israel under international human rights and humanitarian law. The Court found first that, in any event, the parties have to exercise any powers and responsibilities under those agreements with due regard for the norms and principles of international law.

"Invoking article 47 of the Fourth Geneva Convention, the Court then put the matter to rest for good, reminding states that, as a matter of law, the protected population 'shall not be deprived' of the benefits of the Convention 'by any agreement concluded between the authorities of the occupied territories and the Occupying Power.' 'For this reason,' the Court continued, 'the Oslo Accords cannot be understood to detract from Israel's obligations under the pertinent rules of international law applicable in the Occupied Palestinian Territory.'

"In simple terms, the Court affirmed that Palestinians are human beings with human rights, that they need not negotiate for their human rights with their oppressor, and that Israel is not above the law."

How does the US support Israel?

US support for Israel emerges in several ways: economic, military, and diplomatic. While most Americans assume that US foreign aid goes to help the poorest people in the poorest countries, in fact it is Israel (wealthier than a number of European Union member countries) that since 1976 has received 25 percent or more of the entire US foreign aid budget and remains the highest recipient of US foreign aid in the world. (The sudden enormous escalation of military aid to Ukraine in 2023–24 surpassed aid to Israel, most likely temporarily.)

From the time of its founding until 1962, all of the US aid to Israel was economic aid. By 1971, military aid far outstripped the amounts of economic aid. And in 2008, at Israel's own request, the US ended its economic assistance and began sending only military aid—in the billions of dollars every year. In 2016 President Obama signed a ten-year agreement to provide Israel with $3.8 billion of US tax money every year—a huge increase from the earlier grant of $3 billion each year.

In 2022 Israel's military budget was about $23 billion—so Washington's $3.8 billion paid for almost 17 percent of Israel's entire military budget—something unheard of for any other country.

When Israel launched its war against Gaza following the attack on southern Israel in October 2023, military aid to Israel skyrocketed. Within just a few months, Congress had voted to send Israel $26 billion more of weapons, tank ammunition, bombs, drones and more—even including giant 500- and 2,000-pound bombs that can destroy an entire city block, killing virtually every person there. In May 2024, the Biden administration's National Security Memorandum 20, requiring an investigation of human rights issues in countries receiving US weapons, found that it was "reasonable to assess" that the Israeli military had used US weapons to violate the laws of war.

That same month, under enormous pressure, President Biden finally acknowledged that "civilians have been killed in Gaza as a consequence of those bombs," and said he would halt some weapons shipments to Israel if Netanyahu ordered an invasion of Rafah, a small city on Gaza's coast already overcrowded with refugees seeking shelter from the bombs. Days later, as Palestinians continued to be killed by Israeli air attacks in Rafah, Biden "paused" one shipment of the giant bombs, but a short time later he released the massive 500-pound bombs, holding back only the 2,000-pound behemoths. According to the *Washington Post*, even at the height of Israel's deadly war in Gaza, "the Biden administration views weapons transfers as off-limits when considering how to influence the actions of Prime Minister Benjamin Netanyahu."

Beyond the almost unlimited cash to purchase US weapons, Israel has access to some of the most advanced weapons systems in the

Pentagon's arsenal. Despite Israel's widely known nuclear arsenal, the US defends its refusal to sign the Nuclear Non-Proliferation Treaty, and has endorsed the principle of "strategic ambiguity" in which Israel refuses to officially acknowledge its documented nuclear capacity. Its arsenal of high-density nuclear bombs in the Dimona nuclear facility remains uninspected by the International Atomic Energy Agency.

During the Cold War, the US relied on Israel's military power as an extension of its own, with Israeli arms sales, military training, and backing of pro-US governments and pro-US anti-government guerrillas in countries from Mozambique and Angola to El Salvador, Chile, and Nicaragua. That "cat's paw" relationship consolidated the US–Israeli military ties that continue today. Most of the weapons Israel has used in the occupied territories since 1967, including Apache helicopter gunships, F-16 fighter jets, wire-guided missiles, armored Caterpillar bulldozers used to demolish Palestinian houses, and others are all made in the US, and purchased from US manufacturers with US military aid funds. Some of the weapons, such as the Merkava tanks, are joint products of Israel's domestic arms industry and US manufacturing technology.

Diplomatically, the US stands alone as it protects Israel in the United Nations, the International Criminal Court and other international arenas, and keeps it from being held accountable for its violations of international law. After 1967, the US patterns of opposing UN resolutions critical of Israel become more pronounced. The US cast its first veto in 1970—and from then until April 2024 it cast a total of 86 vetoes. Of those, 49 vetoes—57 percent of all US vetoes—were cast to protect Israel.

Where does US aid to Israel fit in the broader scheme of US foreign aid?

The US sends about $4 billion to Israel in regular military aid every year, in addition to tax-exempt contributions from individual and institutional US donors. About $3.8 billion is mandated directly from Congress. (The rest comes in smaller increments from specific US agencies.) In 2008 the longstanding US commitment to Israel to maintain its "qualitative military edge" was written into US law. According to the Obama White House, that is defined as "Israel's ability to counter and defeat credible military threats from any individual state, coalition of states, or non-state actor, while sustaining minimal damages or casualties." When that became part of US law, Washington was sending Israel about 60 percent of the entire Foreign Military Financing (FMF) program.

In 2001, Israel itself requested that the apportionment of its US aid be changed. Instead of a given year's balance of about $1.8 billion in military aid and $1.2 billion in economic assistance, the new plan called for a 10 percent reduction of economic aid each year, to be matched by a parallel increase in military aid. When Obama signed off on the 2016 agreement with Israel for an additional $8 billion over the ten years, totaling $38 billion, all of the US aid was in military assistance.

In 2022 the US was paying almost 17 percent of Israel's entire military budget. And when Israel launched its war against Gaza in 2023, the Biden administration announced, and Congress backed, a vast increase in support. Just in the first year of the war, the US provided Israel with $12.5 billion to buy warplanes, bunker-buster bombs, tank ammunition and more—amounting to 40 percent of Israel's military budget.

Does the US also provide aid to the Palestinians?

After the creation of the Palestinian Authority with the signing of the Oslo Accords in 1993, the US provided some economic aid to the Palestinians. But unlike European and Japanese aid to the Palestinian Authority, or US aid to Israel, US financial support for Palestinians was provided only to UN or non-governmental organizations working in the occupied territories—none went directly to the cash-strapped PA. While the PA, like so many fully sovereign governments that the US supports, certainly has had serious problems of corruption, bypassing it only ensured the PA's continued weakness and inability to even begin to function as a government. And the denial of economic aid continued to impact the civilian population significantly more than it affected PA officials.

After the election of Hamas to lead the PA's parliament and government in January 2006, the US orchestrated an international economic boycott of the PA. Despite the finding of the Carter Center and other international election-monitoring organizations that the Palestinian election was free and fair, the US decision collectively punished the entire Palestinian population and supported Israel's siege of Gaza, isolating its population as it grew to 2.3 million people by 2024.

The US has long used financial pressures against the Palestinians. In 2018, when then-President Trump visited Israel, he announced a series of actions designed to placate the most extremist wing of Netanyahu's government. Starting with the decision to move the US embassy to Jerusalem (in violation of international law and a host of UN resolutions), Trump also announced recognition of Israel's claimed annexation of the Syrian Golan Heights, that the illegal settlements in the West Bank and occupied East Jerusalem would now be considered legal, and more. He also announced a cut of $65 million budgeted for UNRWA, the UN agency tasked with supporting Palestinian refugees. Shortly after returning home, the Trump administration announced another cut of $200 million that would have gone directly to Palestinian programs in the occupied territories.

In 2024, just hours after the International Court of Justice ruled in favor of South Africa in its case charging Israel with genocide, Israel retaliated. It made a public announcement of a claim—showing no evidence—that twelve UNRWA staff, out of the 13,000 in Gaza (and a total of 30,000 across the region) had somehow participated in the attack on Israel of October 7, 2023. Despite the lack of evidence, within hours the United States announced a complete halt in its annual funding of UNRWA, quickly followed by a dozen US allies. Within a few days, eighteen countries had pulled their donations, leaving the most important UN agency supporting Palestinians—who were then facing famine across Gaza—on the verge of collapse. There was an immediate loss of $450 million, of which more than $300 million had been promised by the United States.

When no evidence was provided, all countries soon resumed payments to UNRWA—except for the United States. The UN's oversight office announced in August 2024 after their investigation that several of those accused in January 2023 may have entered Israel from Gaza on October 7, and two may have participated in a kidnapping—but they could not corroborate the evidence because they did not have direct access to it. The US still did not resume its funding—thus imposing a collective punishment on 2.3 million Gazans for what may or may not have been the illegal actions of two. In March, Congress passed, and President Biden signed a law prohibiting US funding of UNRWA at least until March 2025.

The impact of the US cuts was particularly dire because of Israeli actions that impoverish whole sectors of Palestinian society. Israel routinely prohibited West Bank Palestinian workers from traveling to their jobs in Israel. From the beginning of the October 2023 war against Gaza, tens of thousands of Palestinian workers were denied access to their jobs—and to their salaries.

Israel also continued to withhold millions of dollars in tax revenues that it collected from Palestinian workers on behalf of the PA. In February 2024, four months into the Gaza war, the PA announced it could pay public sector workers only 60 percent of their salaries, because Israel had been withholding $165 million since the beginning of the war in October. By May of that year, salaries were down to 50 percent—new cuts were imposed allegedly in response to Palestinian diplomatic efforts at the International Criminal Court. The US sometimes urged Israel to release those funds, but did not exert any actual pressure to make that happen.

Why is Israel so often criticized in the UN? Aren't other countries just as guilty of human rights violations?

Almost every country in the United Nations commits some kind of human rights violations—from absolute monarchies, military dictatorships, and elected authoritarians that make no pretense of human rights concerns, to ostensible democracies that routinely deny their residents the right to adequate housing, food, health care, or other rights guaranteed by international covenants. Israel is criticized by the international community more than many other countries because its violations of Palestinian human rights are also violations of international humanitarian law (the laws of war and occupation) and a host of specific UN resolutions. Further, in the twenty-first century, Israel is the only country supported by the United States and closely identified with the West—meaning it claims to hold itself accountable as a democracy—still expanding its settler-colonial practices of land theft, ethnic cleansing, and apartheid.

And in the United Nations, there is an understanding that the global institution itself has significant responsibility because of its role in creating the state of Israel with the partition resolution of 1947, and of the Israeli agreement to abide by international law and UN resolutions as a specific condition of joining the UN in 1948.

Only since about 2020 have broader Israeli violations—systems of apartheid and, by 2023, genocide—come directly before UN bodies. The Israeli violations most frequently targeted by UN resolutions—building settlements, demolition of Palestinian houses, military attacks on civilians, closures, and curfews, attacks on holy sites in Jerusalem, etc.—all take place in the context of the military occupation of the Palestinian territories seized in the 1967 war, an occupation that is itself illegal. Other countries—Saudi Arabia, Egypt, Uzbekistan, the Philippines, El Salvador, and many more, of course including the United States—commit massive human rights violations against their own people, but only Israel carries out those actions against a population that is supposed to be protected by the Fourth Geneva Convention, which guarantees safety for people living under occupation.

Finally, the seemingly repetitive resolutions challenging Israel's human rights violations against the Palestinians are most often passed in response to the success of consistent US actions designed to prevent implementation, and therefore protect Israel from the consequences, of its violations. If resolutions holding Israel accountable were allowed to be enforced, new resolutions covering old ground would be unnecessary.

To respond to the continued pattern of violations, the UN relies on a number of human rights systems, including the Human Rights Council, the Office of the High Commissioner for Human Rights, the appointment of experts as Special Rapporteurs or as part of commissions of inquiry or other Special Procedures, and special envoys of the secretary-general.

What is the role of the UN in the Middle East? Why isn't the UN in charge of the overall peace process?

The limitations on the UN's role in Middle East diplomacy, and the power of the US to impose those limitations, have been visible for a long time. One particularly blatant example emerged in 1991, when Washington issued invitations to countries participating in the Madrid peace conference. The US accepted Israel's demand that the United Nations be excluded from participation in the conference, allowing instead only the symbolic presence of a single representative of the secretary-general, who was explicitly prohibited from speaking. It was a powerful humiliation, but so consistent with US domination of the UN that few paid attention.

With the beginning of the Oslo peace process two years later, the US moved even further, forcing the United Nations to pull back from longstanding positions and sidelining the role of the global organization. Once the Oslo process took hold, the Clinton administration largely kept the United Nations out of the loop on Israel-Palestine diplomacy. In August 1994, then-US Ambassador to the UN Madeleine Albright sent a letter to all UN member states, outlining Washington's goals for that year's General Assembly. The overall thrust was essentially to remove the issues of Arab–Israeli relations, and especially the question of Palestine, from the UN's political agenda by claiming that the bilateral Israeli–Palestinian negotiations of the Madrid and Oslo processes had rendered UN involvement irrelevant except for economic and development assistance. Almost all past resolutions were identified as needing to be "consolidated ... improved ... or eliminated."

The Clinton-Albright campaign also demanded that any UN concerns over the fundamental questions of refugees, settlements, territory, and sovereignty, and the status of Jerusalem "should be dropped, *since these issues are now under negotiations by the parties* themselves." (Emphasis added). The sad irony, of course, was that under the terms of Oslo, those were the precise questions *not* under negotiation, because they were designated "final status" issues that would not come under consideration for five or seven years.

At the time of Israeli troops' reoccupation of Jenin in March 2002, the Security Council was able to convince US diplomats to accept a resolution calling for a UN investigation of the catastrophic assault that had laid waste to the city and killed fifty-two Palestinians and twenty-three Israeli soldiers. Israel initially agreed, but when Tel Aviv soon withdrew its approval of the fact-finding team, the US backed its rejection and refused to allow the council or the secretary general to enforce the resolution. The fact-finding team was disbanded. The General Assembly, however, responded to the developments by reconvening an emergency session to pass its own resolution calling for the secretary general to prepare a report based on other sources, primarily international human rights organizations.

In July 2002, at the height of Israel's violent reoccupation of Palestinian cities, the new US ambassador, John Negroponte, told a closed Security Council meeting that a proposed resolution condemning Israel was unhelpful and that the US would oppose it if it came to a vote. But he then went much further, telling the council that in the future the US would only consider resolutions concerning the Middle East that explicitly condemned Palestinian terrorism, and named and denounced several specific Palestinian organizations. There was no such demand that all future resolutions equally condemn Israeli military or settler violence, let alone a condemnation of Israel's illegal occupation.

But the General Assembly's response to the council's deadlock in March had raised the possibility of a broader role for the UN's most democratic component. Under longstanding UN precedent, if the council (which is the most powerful, but the least democratic, part of the UN because of the veto held by the five permanent members) is deemed deadlocked, the General Assembly may take up issues that would ordinarily be limited to council jurisdiction. That makes possible assembly initiatives on issues such as international protection for Palestinians living under occupation (something repeatedly vetoed by the US), or ultimately the creation of an entirely new diplomatic process, perhaps similar to that proposed by Brazilian President Lula in September 2006.

While those emergency procedures—known as the Uniting for Peace precedent—had been invoked repeatedly over the years, it had never gone as far as to actually call for direct measures such as calling for an arms embargo against Israel until it ends its violations of international law. Part of the reason was the lack of political will from enough countries, and the lack of clear leadership among them, to take on such an initiative. Part of it lay with fear—while Washington does not hold a veto in the GA like it did in the Security Council, threats and punishments for voting against US wishes were routine, and few countries were prepared to face those consequences. That changed in September 2024, when the General Assembly passed a resolution to implement the International Court of Justice's ruling on the illegality of the occupation—that included a call for an arms embargo and other sanctions on Israel until it ended its violations of international law.

On earlier rare occasions, the GA had tried to take independent positions critical of Israeli violations that went beyond the timid efforts of the Security Council. Some of them may have helped lay the groundwork for the General Assembly's 2024 decision directly challenging the US in the council. One of those came in response to the Israeli attack on Gaza known as Operation Cast Lead, which began the day after Christmas of 2008. While bombing raids and later full-scale wars against Gaza became routine parts of Israeli strategy in years since that time, Cast Lead was seen around the world as a shocking escalation. When the Security Council tried and failed to satisfy the United States in a resolution calling for a ceasefire (then-Secretary of State Condoleezza Rice had made clear that the US would not yet support a ceasefire), the president of the General Assembly, former Nicaraguan foreign minister Father Miguel d'Escoto, called the assembly into emergency session. In his opening speech Fr. Miguel told the assembled diplomats:

"Little analysis is needed to determine that the Council resolution has failed to bring about either a ceasefire or unimpeded humanitarian access. Obviously, it was never really meant to achieve those objectives. This is clearly not the fault of the majority of the Council members. It is due to the fact that there were some in the Council (and outside of it) bent on betraying their obligation to our Charter. Instead of supporting a strong, clear unequivocal demand for an immediate ceasefire, those forces succeeded in blocking such a demand, and instead allowing the military action to continue, which indeed seems to have been their purpose.

"All serious efforts to bring about an immediate ceasefire are urgently needed, and I support them all. ...People around the world—in the tens and hundreds of thousands—continue to take to the streets, including here in the Host Country of the United Nations as well as inside Israel, to demand an immediate ceasefire. We at the United Nations can do no less.

"The Council may have found itself unable or unwilling to take the necessary steps to impose an immediate ceasefire—but outsourcing these efforts to one or two governments or through the Quartet does not relieve the Council of its own responsibilities under the UN Charter. The Council cannot disavow its collective responsibility. It cannot continue to fiddle while Gaza burns.

"Passage of the Security Council resolution does not eliminate our responsibility. We in the General Assembly, who represent ALL the nations and peoples of the world, still have a corresponding individual and collective obligation of our own. And we will respond to that obligation."

Despite Fr. Miguel's efforts, disagreements among countries of the Non-Aligned Movement itself prevented the GA from acting. And since that time, while occasional GA meetings have been convened under the emergency terms of the Uniting for Peace resolution, none led to action by the General Assembly until 2024. Debates and speeches challenged the Security Council and ultimately the United States provision of impunity to Israel, but those discussions never actually led to GA action such as imposing an arms embargo against Israel, calling for sanctions, investigating avenues of protection for the Palestinians, or taking other actions to enforce UN positions.

The GA, as well as other UN agencies including the UN's educational and cultural arm, UNESCO, did support Palestine's longstanding bid for recognition as a state, by granting Palestine escalating levels of legitimacy within the United Nations. Since 2012, Palestine had had the status of a "non-member Permanent Observer State" in the UN, a designation of "statehood" that allowed Palestine to sign the Rome Treaty in 2015 to become a member of the International Criminal Court. In 2024, the US vetoed a Security Council resolution calling on the GA to vote on Palestine's full membership as a state. Unable by terms of the UN Charter to grant full membership on its own, the GA voted to assert Palestine's qualifications for membership, despite the US-driven Council refusal to recognize it.

In 2017, then-US President Donald Trump went to Israel and announced a set of new US policies that directly violated international law and longstanding UN resolutions, including recognizing Jerusalem as Israel's capital and moving the US embassy to Jerusalem. A nearly unanimous Security Council tried to condemn the actions, but the resolution failed with a US veto against the other fourteen members. Trump's UN Ambassador to the UN, Nikki Haley, called the United Nations "one of the world's foremost centers of hostility towards Israel." Two weeks later, the General Assembly voted overwhelmingly to condemn the action—with 128 votes to condemn, only 9 votes against, with 35 abstentions and 21 countries absent.

The longstanding pattern of US vetoes in the Security Council, and public or private pressure in the General Assembly to protect Israel from being held accountable, continued through Israel's war on Gaza that began in October 2023 following the Hamas-led attack in southern Israel. Urgent demands for a permanent ceasefire, for resumption of funding for UNRWA, and access to humanitarian aid at the scale required were vetoed or weakened in the Security Council and condemned or ignored by the United States. Israel's consistent military attacks on UN premises—including hospitals, clinics, and most frequently UN schools that were being used to shelter Gazans who had been forced out of their shattered homes under continual bombing, becoming refugees over and over again, for months on end—were in direct violation of international humanitarian law. UN meetings were held, powerful speeches condemned the actions, but again, until September 2024, almost a year into Israel's war, neither the council nor the assembly were prepared to call for action—such as an arms embargo. (Resolutions of the assembly are not legally binding—but as was true throughout the years of UN involvement in the anti-apartheid movement against South African apartheid, resolutions passed in the GA become powerful tools in the hands of national and global movements pressuring governments to do the right thing.)

It took the actions of the International Court of Justice to set new terms for what real accountability might look like. In the case brought by South Africa against Israel, the charge was violation of the Genocide Convention—an international treaty that defines and outlaws genocide, and obligates states to prevent and stop it. The initial finding of the ICJ in January 2024 was in favor of South Africa's claim, that Israel's actions in Gaza were plausibly genocide. The court also issued an initial, and then two later sets of provisional measures, obligations that Israel as well as other states that were parties to the convention, and the United Nations itself, were required to implement—the most important being that Israel should stop killing, injuring, or causing serious harm to people in Gaza and allow all needed humanitarian aid, and that other countries and the UN should do whatever is in their power to prevent or stop the actions that could constitute genocide.

Later that year, the court issued its advisory opinion, at the request of the General Assembly, on the overall legality of Israel's prolonged military occupation of the West Bank, Gaza, and East Jerusalem. Again, the court found against Israel, establishing that the presence of Israel in the OPT was illegal, that the settlements were illegal, and that the settlers should be evacuated from the occupied territory. It also determined that Israel was violating Article 3 of the Convention on the Elimination of All Forms of Racial Discrimination (known as CERD), which targets both segregation and apartheid—thus siding with the global movement against Israeli apartheid that by 2024 had been on the rise for ten years or more. And it called for all countries, as well as the Security Council and the General Assembly of the UN, to refuse to recognize or assist in any way, the illegal Israeli presence in the occupied territory.

The court's decisions in lawsuits between countries—such as South Africa vs. Israel—are binding, but they are not self-enforcing, and the ICJ itself does not have a military or police or even a process-serving force to ensure its rulings are followed. But it does have the credential, as the World Court, of being the UN's own judicial arm. The court's advisory opinions, such as its judgment on the legality of Israel's occupation, are not automatically binding, but it can, as this one does, include its analysis of what the relevant international laws require various countries or international institutions to do. So the UN and its agencies, from the Security Council and the General Assembly to the Human Rights Council, the secretary-general, and the secretariat itself, are all obligated to work to implement those judgments. The court gives the council and the assembly primary responsibility for determining what actions will work to that end—and it reminds all governments that they are obligated to follow the decisions of those agencies.

So when the assembly determined that one of the best ways to bring about an end to Israel's illegal occupation was an arms embargo to stop all arms trading to or from Israel, all countries, including those that provide arms to Israel and those that purchase military goods such as weapons or surveillance equipment from Israel, would be obligated to halt those actions. After the assembly's vote of September 2024, imposing, among other things, an arms embargo against Israel, the work of pushing governments to make good on those responsibilities remains the obligation of social movements around the world.

If not the US, then who else should be at the center of Middle East diplomacy?

Palestine-Israel diplomacy needs to be redefined. As the occupying power, maintaining a military occupation far longer than any other in modern history, Israel bears numerous obligations that international law requires it to implement unilaterally. That includes abiding by all the Geneva Conventions—which prohibit the transfer of people from the occupying power to the occupied territory (so all settlements are illegal), prohibit collective punishment of the occupied population (so bombing Gaza to "destroy Hamas" is illegal), prohibit the destruction of property in the occupied territory (so house demolitions are illegal), require the occupying power to ensure sufficient food and medical supplies (so stopping or diminishing Palestinian access to humanitarian assistance is illegal), and much more.

As of July 2024, the International Court of Justice determined that "the State of Israel's continued presence in the Occupied Palestinian Territory is unlawful; ...that the State of Israel is under an obligation to bring to an end its unlawful presence in the Occupied Palestinian Territory as rapidly as possible; ...that the State of Israel is under an obligation to cease immediately all new settlement activities, and to evacuate all settlers from the Occupied Palestinian Territory." The court imposed those obligations on Israel alone; they do not require additional negotiations to be implemented.

US-orchestrated diplomacy has failed. As President Luis Inácio Lula da Silva of Brazil told the opening plenary of the General Assembly in September 2006, "Middle Eastern issues have always been dealt with exclusively by the great powers. They have achieved no solution so far. One might then ask: is it not time to call a broad, UN-sponsored conference, with the participation of countries of the region and others that could contribute through their capacity and successful experience, in living peacefully with differences?"

The United Nations, not the US, should be the center of a process aimed at ensuring compliance with all existing requirements of international law and implementation of the rulings imposed by the International Court of Justice, as well as to consider protection for the occupied Palestinian population. The UN created the State of Israel; Israel's apartheid system and its occupation of the West Bank, Gaza, and East Jerusalem violate numerous UN resolutions; and the Israeli–Palestinian conflict has global significance and thus should be addressed by an international body.

Existing international law and UN resolutions—not a US-created "road map" or the Oslo agreement or any other text designed to replace international law with US-imposed frameworks equating the rights of the occupied population with the illegal occupying power—should be the basis for all diplomatic engagement on the issue.

Didn't the United Nations create the State of Israel? Why didn't it create a State of Palestine too? Why doesn't it now?

After World War II, with the British eager to give up their League of Nations Mandate over Palestine, the United Nations General Assembly took responsibility for the conflict-riven area. The local indigenous Palestinian population was angry about the influx of European Jewish settlers, whose numbers rose dramatically as the US and Britain refused to allow large-scale immigration of European Jews escaping, or later having barely survived, the Holocaust. For many of those refugees, British-controlled Palestine became their only possible refuge, whether it was their destination of choice or not. (Far more European Jewish refugees wanted to come to the US, where many had families.) Fighting escalated between the indigenous Palestinian population and the European settlers, and the British occupation soldiers became targets of both. The UN Special Commission on Palestine, or UNSCOP, recommended that Palestine be divided into two states, one Jewish and one Arab.

The November 29, 1947, resolution partitioning Palestine apportioned 55 percent of Mandate Palestine to the new State of Israel, leaving 45 percent for a future Palestinian state. The Zionist leaders accepted partition, though in private several indicated their intention to expand the new state to include all of Palestine. But Palestinians were opposed to the partition. At the time of the UN resolution, Jews in Palestine constituted just about 30 percent of the population while Palestinians were 70 percent, and the Jewish settlers owned only 6 percent of the land. Given those realities, it was seen by Palestinians, by many others in the Middle East, and by many around the world as a massive injustice for the Jewish population, almost all of them recent settlers, to be granted more than half the land. Over 450,000 Palestinian Arabs lived in the land the UN selected to become the Jewish state; the number of Jews in the area designated to become a Palestinian Arab state was tiny.

The Palestinian state never came into existence. The Israeli Jewish state did, of course, and by the end of the 1948 war it had taken over 78 percent of the land, far more than the 55 percent actually allocated to it by the United Nations.

In fact, no one seriously consulted the Palestinians themselves. While most of the indigenous population was strongly opposed to partition, the only opposition deemed relevant on the world stage came not from the Palestinians but from the Arab governments in the region. They were opposed also, for their own reasons, but in general they had little interest in defending the rights of the Palestinians. As soon as Israel declared its independence, several Arab armies, the strongest being those of Egypt and Syria, moved to oppose the well-armed Zionist militia. In the course of about eight months of fighting,

750,000 Palestinians were dispossessed of their homes and lands, and forcibly turned into refugees. Israel called it the war of independence; Palestinians called it the Nakba, or catastrophe.

Once hostilities ended, the UN recognized Israel as an independent state (though it still has never officially acknowledged its borders). Egypt and Jordan were in control of the now separate parts of Arab Palestine that remained, Gaza, the West Bank, and East Jerusalem, and Palestinian independence was not on any international agenda.

Since 1967, when the US-Israeli special relationship was solidified into a powerful military-economic alliance, the US has consistently protected Israel diplomatically, including keeping the question of Palestinian independence and an end to occupation for the most part off the enforceable agenda of the UN, especially the agenda of the UN Security Council. In 1975 the US promised Israel it would not recognize or negotiate with the PLO. The PLO was therefore excluded from the 1978 Camp David negotiations that led to the first treaty between Israel and an Arab state, whereby Israel agreed to return to Egypt the Sinai Peninsula it had occupied since 1967, but the treaty said nothing about Palestinian rights. The PLO implicitly recognized Israel in November 1988, when it declared independence as a state limited to the territories Israel occupied in 1967—the West Bank, Gaza, and East Jerusalem. The putative State of Palestine was soon recognized by scores of countries (by 2024 it was recognized by 145, more than 75 percent of UN member states) but not by the United States, which continued to prevent its full recognition in the United Nations.

In 1993, with the Oslo agreement, the PLO explicitly recognized Resolution 242 and Israel's right to exist in peace, while Israel only recognized the PLO as the representative of the Palestinians; it did not recognize Palestine as a state. Over the years, numerous UN agencies and departments and eventually the General Assembly did recognize Palestine as a state, but because of the US veto in the Security Council, it could not be considered a full member of the UN. From 2012, Palestine held the status of "non-Member state," but through 2024 it still lacked full status in the UN and, crucially, was not recognized by the US.

How was the PLO viewed in the Arab Middle East, the UN, and in the rest of the world?

When the PLO was created, the Arab governments viewed it largely as an instrument of their own interests. Only after the existing Palestinian guerrilla organizations became the major component of the PLO and Yasir Arafat became its leader in 1968 did it take on significant credibility among Palestinians themselves. During the early 1970s, political campaigns among Palestinian communities in the occupied territories and among refugees and exiles scattered throughout the world led to virtually unanimous support for the PLO as the sole legitimate representative and the voice of the still-stateless Palestinians.

In 1974, the United Nations invited Yasir Arafat, leader of the PLO, to address the General Assembly. Arafat spoke of bearing both a gun and an olive branch, and pleaded with delegates, "do not let the olive branch fall from my hand." That same year, the assembly identified November 29, anniversary of the day of the partition resolution years before, as an International Day of Solidarity with the Palestinian People. It also recognized the PLO as the "sole legitimate representative of the Palestinian people," and invited the PLO to become an official non-state "observer" at the UN, allowing it participation in all debates and welcoming a Palestinian ambassador.

While the PLO soon won diplomatic recognition in capitals across the world, Arab leaders were less than pleased at its independent stance. In Jordan in particular, King Hussein saw the rise of the PLO as a threat to Jordan's traditional influence in the West Bank and East Jerusalem. In 1982, when Ariel Sharon launched his "Jordan is Palestine" campaign, the king's opposition was seen as less than enthusiastic. Only with the first intifada, when virtually unanimous Palestinian rejection of Jordan's role became undeniable, did the king finally sever his kingdom's dominant links to Palestinian institutions. When the PLO declared Palestine independent in 1988, the new state, which still controlled no land of its own, quickly attained diplomatic relations with more governments than recognized Israel.

To the US, the PLO was nothing but a terrorist organization and Yasir Arafat an arch-terrorist. Some factions of the PLO had carried out plane hijackings in the 1970 that made international headlines and helped foster the image of terrorism. But the organization was always far broader than the acts of violence. The US used the same "terrorist" epithet to condemn Nelson Mandela and the African National Congress, and a host of other national liberation movements. (Mandela remained on a US terrorism watch list until 2008, nine years after finishing his term as South Africa's first democratically elected president.)

It was also the same accusation, ironically, that the British had hurled at Menachem Begin and other Zionist militia leaders in the pre-state period of Israeli history. In 1975, Henry Kissinger promised Israel that the US would never recognize or negotiate with the PLO.

When the UN again invited Arafat to address the General Assembly in November 1988, just after the Palestinian Declaration of Independence, the US refused to issue a visa, despite its obligations as host country of the United Nations. The entire UN—diplomats, security guards, interpreters, secretariat staff—packed up and flew to Geneva for one day to hear the PLO chairman. In that speech, Arafat again rejected terrorism and recognized Israel; the goal was to open a dialogue with the US. Word soon came from Washington that it wasn't good enough. A few hours later, the press corps was recalled to the auditorium in Geneva's Palais des Nations, and the revised speech was read out. In return, the US allowed a mid-level diplomat, then ambassador to Tunisia, to open talks with the PLO. But the talks languished and were soon canceled.

Only with the Oslo process, when the Palestinians had accepted Washington's centrality in the peace talks, did the US accept the PLO as a full-fledged interlocutor. During Bill Clinton's presidency, Yasir Arafat was one of the most frequent international visitors to the White House.

In the first two years of the George W. Bush administration, however, Arafat remained untouchable. President Bush refused even to speak with the Palestinian leader when their paths crossed at the United Nations, and by the spring of 2002 Bush called explicitly for the replacement of the PLO chairman and president of the Palestinian Authority. When President Arafat died in 2004, the US position was one of barely suppressed enthusiasm that in a "post-Arafat era" the PLO would prove far more malleable to US and Israeli interests.

Why is Israel isolated from Arab countries in the region?

Some of Israel's isolation reflects antagonism from neighboring countries, and some of it stems from Israel's own orientation and self-definition in the world. At the time the State of Israel was created, there was already widespread antagonism among Palestinians and in surrounding Arab countries toward the large and rapid influx of European Jews. While European Jewish settlement in Palestine had been going on since the 1880s, the numbers vastly increased in the 1930s and '40s, as Jews escaping the Holocaust, and those who survived it, were rejected by their first-choice countries of sanctuary, the US and Britain, where antisemitism and anti-communism combined into a basis for a cruel denial of refuge. Instead they turned (often out of necessity rather than choice) to British-ruled Palestine, where the UK kept the door mostly open. Significant loss of land and political power for the indigenous Arab population resulted. Arabs, both Palestinians and others, resented being forced to pay the price for European antisemitism and the Holocaust, in which they had played no significant role.

At the same time, the pre-state Zionist organizations and later Israeli government leaders viewed themselves as squarely part of the Western, Euro-American part of the world. Despite being located in the heart of the Arab Middle East, Israel positioned itself in the context of a colonial garrison, a "civilized," "Western," and presumably white outpost—explicitly so in early pleas of support sent to British colonial leaders such as Cecil Rhodes—in a foreign, "uncivilized" part of the world. From the beginning of their state-building settler-colonial project, Israeli officials oriented their economic, strategic, political, and cultural policies toward Europe and the US, rather than making efforts to cultivate ties with their neighbors.

After the 1967 war, when Israel occupied the last 22 percent of historic Palestine as well as occupying Syria's Golan Heights and Egypt's Sinai Peninsula, and later occupying a wide swathe of southern Lebanon, Arab anger increased still further. The view of Israel for an entire new Arab generation—Palestinians growing up under military control, Syrians dismayed at their government's inability to reclaim its lost territory, Egyptians outraged by their military defeat and the Israeli occupation of Egypt's Sinai Peninsula, and more—was shaped by the harsh reality of occupation and apartheid. And Arab anger toward, and rejection of, Israel increased.

In 1968, the Arab League voted to reject diplomatic and economic ties with Israel. Even earlier, Arab countries had put in place an economic boycott that prohibited trade with Israel. Egypt broke ranks with the rest of the Arab world in normalizing relations with Israel after the Camp David Accords of 1979, and faced years of ostracism within the Arab League as a result. The Arab boycott faded with the signing of the Oslo Accords in 1993, and Jordan and Israel agreed to full diplomatic and economic relations in 1994. Other countries, including Oman and Morocco, established various levels of trade and economic ties with Israel.

By 2020, numerous countries in the region had established various kinds of political and economic relations with Israel, though most of it remained covert—most Arab leaders were eager to trade with Israel, to buy its most-advanced-in-the-world surveillance equipment, and to normalize relations. But Arab public opinion remained staunchly pro-Palestinian, so an open embrace of Israel threatened unpopularity at best, widespread instability at worst.

When Donald Trump became US president, he took advantage of that reality and proposed a "new and different" approach to Middle East policy. Based on a purely economic cost-benefit assessment, Trump and his son-in-law, real estate developer-turned-White House advisor Jared Kushner, offered Arab leaders—including the most repressive absolute monarchs in Saudi Arabia, the UAE, Bahrain, and elsewhere, the king of Morocco who still illegally occupied Western Sahara, longtime Israel partners Egypt and Jordan, and other rulers—a wide range of trade and military advantages in return for normalizing relations with Israel. Saudi Arabia, for example, was offered a new security treaty with Washington, approval for an unprecedented new nuclear program, and a host of new trade perks if it joined what came to be called the Abraham Accords. Saudi Arabia had not signed on, but by 2024 the UAE, Bahrain, Sudan and Morocco had all signed on to various degrees of normalization with Israel. In return, the US gave Sudan a $1.2 billion loan, pulled Khartoum from its list of state sponsors of terrorism, and recognized Moroccan sovereignty for King Mohammed VII's colonial occupation of Western

Sahara. Other Arab governments had signaled their desire and/or intention to join Israel as well. But with Israel's genocidal assault on Gaza that began in 2023, enraging populations across the Arab world, little evidence of actual normalization was visible.

Since Jordan's population is about two-thirds Palestinian and there are twenty-one other Arab countries, why do the Palestinians insist on having a state of their own?

Palestine's origins, and its identity as a distinct region within the broader Arab world, go back thousands of years. Like that of most of the countries of the Arab world, Palestine's self-identity as a modern nation-state emerged only in the context of modern colonial rule. Post-World War I, British and French diplomats first set Palestine's modern borders, along with those of Syria, Lebanon, Iraq, Jordan, Kuwait, Saudi Arabia, and the small Gulf statelets, when they divided up the Arab portion of the defeated Ottoman Empire in 1922. Some of those newly identified states became independent; others remained under colonial, or later French or British Mandate authority. But in all of these newly created countries, new "national" identities emerged within the local populations. (Iraq and Egypt, whose national identities reach back to ancient Ur, Sumeria, and Alexandria, already had such a national consciousness.)

For Palestinians, national identity was first linked to the land itself. It was *their* land; their grandparents and great-grandparents and on to the incalculable past had farmed this same land, these same olive trees. It was very specific. National dialects, customs, cultural norms, etc., all developed in particular and identifiably Palestinian forms long before the construction of modern states. The notion of being transferred to another country just because they speak the same language, even before the beginning of the modern Arab nation-states, was unacceptable. The equivalent would be expecting seventh- or eighth-generation Americans to accept forcible transfer to Australia, or Britain, or even Canada, simply because they speak the same language. Perhaps a more exact comparison, taken from US history, was the forced transfer of Native American tribes from one shrinking reservation to another, on the theory that they could live anywhere just as well as in their indige-nous territory. The 4,000–6,000 deaths resulting from the Cherokees' forced removal from Georgia to what is now Oklahoma along the "Trail of Tears" in 1838–39 was only one such example.

In 1982, Israel's then-Defense Minister Ariel Sharon developed a "Jordan is Palestine" plan designed to legitimate the idea of forcible transfer of Palestinians out of the West Bank and Gaza, perhaps out of Israel itself, into "their" alleged homeland in Jordan. The campaign never took off, and by 1988, at the height of the first intifada, Jordan's King Hussein announced he was severing the formal sponsorship of West Bank institutions to ensure that there would be no confusion about the right of Palestinians to their own state in Palestine.

What many, perhaps most Palestinians in the twenty-first century want is not a new state, but new rights—specifically the rights of freedom, independence, and sovereignty, along with equality and human rights, in whatever part of their old nation they live. That means human rights and equality for all, regardless of how many states ultimately emerge: equality within all states, and between all states.

Is a two-state solution really fair, and is it still possible?

The notion of a "two-state solution" has been official US and interna-tional policy for Palestine-Israel for decades. Efforts towards creating a Palestinian state began years after the 1967 war brought the last 22 percent of Palestinian land under Israeli occupation, and Jewish settlers began to colonize much of the occupied territory. US-led negotiations officially to realize a Palestinian state began in 1991. The Palestine Liberation Organization's official acceptance of the notion of two states in 1988, recognizing the State of Israel and accepting that the Palestinian state would be limited to only the West Bank, Gaza, and East Jerusalem, had been an enormous concession, but was rarely recognized as such in the US or in Europe.

A two-state arrangement—dividing the total land of historic Palestine, now entirely under Israel's control—was never ultimately based on justice. United Nations resolutions call for two states, with the establishment of a Palestinian state on only 22 percent of the land of historic Palestine. And that 22 percent would include all of the West Bank, Gaza, and East Jerusalem. Limiting Palestine to such a tiny state, when even the 1947 UN partition resolution designated an already unjust 45 percent of Mandate Palestine as the Palestinian state (unjust because Palestinians were 70 percent of the population), would be profoundly unfair. Today, of course, only a small percentage of that 22 percent, in disconnected broken-up pieces, is even being considered for a Palestinian state.

Historical injustices sometimes do become permanent. They do not become just or fair because time passes, they remain unjust and unfair realities. The genocide that led to the dispossession and near-extermination of indigenous peoples during the early history of the United States is no less of an historic injustice now. But how that continuing injustice should be addressed did in fact change. In the year 1700, when the colonial population was 260,000, it might have been appropriate to advocate sending the European colonists back to Europe and returning all the land to the indigenous people; three hundred years later that is not possible and no one is calling for it. Combinations of national recognition, reparations, affirmative action, protection of remaining tribal-held lands are the new demands of Native Americans.

The Palestinian case bears some similarities and many differences. In 2024, the Nakba was seventy-five years ago—not 300 or 400 years past. A declining number of Palestinians around the world, now mostly in their eighties and nineties, still remember fleeing their homes. It is not something familiar only through history books or dusty engravings.

However, history has moved much faster in the last three-quarters of a century than in the many years before it. In its seventy-five years of existence, Israel has been consolidated as a highly technologically advanced, wealthy, militarily powerful and nuclear-armed Western-oriented society under the absolute protection of the United States. It is also an apartheid state, in which different social groups, separated by religion and ethnicity and where they reside within all lands controlled by the Israeli state, live under different legal systems. That means different—and unequal—sets of rights, privileges, and discriminations are imposed on or available to Israeli Jews; Palestinian citizens of Israel;

Palestinian non-citizen residents of Jerusalem; indigenous Palestinians in the occupied West Bank, Gaza, and East Jerusalem; Jewish colonial settlers in Jerusalem and the West Bank, and Palestinian refugees still not allowed to return to their homes.

The years of US-controlled diplomacy, supposedly aimed at achieving a two-state solution beginning with the Madrid talks of 1991 and continuing through the Oslo process and beyond, have failed. And major changes on the ground in the occupied territories during those years have made the creation of anything remotely resembling a just or even viable two-state solution impossible.

Over 750,000 illegal Jewish settlers are spread throughout the West Bank and East Jerusalem, most of them in large settlement blocs built on huge tracts of the best land. Israel has imposed hundreds of militarized checkpoints, built the Apartheid Wall, and claimed large amounts of West Bank land for military zones, nature reserves, and settlement expansion. Sixty percent of the West Bank (part of the 22 percent of historic Palestine that remained Palestinian until 1967) remains officially under complete Israeli control, making it virtually inaccessible for any Palestinian use. Alongside the hundreds of Jews-only settlements, some of them city-sized, built in the West Bank, thousands of olive trees have been uprooted, water sources are almost all in Israeli hands, thousands of Palestinian homes demolished, and tens of thousands of families forcibly separated. Palestinian towns and villages across the West Bank are cut off from each other and from the cities they historically linked to for health care, commerce, education, cultural life, and more. Gaza is besieged and cut off from both Israel and the West Bank.

From 1977 when they first came to power in the Knesset, the Likud Party stated clearly in its platform that "between the Sea and the Jordan there will be only Israeli sovereignty." In July 2014, Prime Minister Netanyahu said, "there cannot be a situation, under any agreement, in which we relinquish security control of the territory west of the River Jordan." When he was reelected the following year, he reaffirmed there would be no Palestinian state during his tenure. He based his right-wing extremist coalition on that commitment. Response from the Obama administration, already frustrated with Netanyahu's deliberate rejection of US diplomatic initiatives and deliberate disrespect of

President Obama, was to put aside efforts to negotiate a solution to the long-standing conflict.

In May 2024, at the height of Israel's lethal war against Gaza, then-US secretary of state Antony Blinken said that Israel would never have "genuine security" without a pathway to a Palestinian state. Netanyahu's answer was unequivocal rejection—claiming Israel "must have security control over the entire territory west of the Jordan River" even though "that collides with the idea of sovereignty."

One could imagine a two-state solution created in 1967 or 1968, made up of the entire territory that Israel had just conquered and occupied—all of the West Bank, all of Gaza, and all of East Jerusalem. But what has actually been discussed in the diplomatic debate since the late 1980s has been a far cry from that; what has been under discussion has been what tiny, unconnected scraps of land Israel might turn over to Palestinians for some modicum of local authority.

Despite decades of clear Israeli rejection of an independent Palestinian state, the call for a "two-state solution" remains a constant in US policy circles, in diplomatic engagements, at the United Nations, and beyond. It serves as a convenient excuse for not challenging Israeli intransigence. In the US, providing virtually unlimited weapons to Israel to enable its wars against Palestinians and consolidate the impossibility of a Palestinian state is often justified by "We're calling for a two-state solution."

Israel continues expanding settlements and seizing land, making the creation of any kind of state impossible because of lack of territory. The "state" of Palestine under discussion for more than three decades was in fact far from independent or sovereign. It was understood that "Palestine" would be forcibly disarmed and not allowed to have a military for self-defense, so the prospect of sovereignty would remain illusory. Israel would maintain control of Palestine's borders, entry and exit of goods and people, airspace, coastal waters, and electromagnetic spectrum. The Jordan Valley would see long-term or perhaps permanent Israeli military occupation, possibly with US or NATO troops supplementing the Israeli soldiers. Jerusalem would remain Israel's capital and would remain under complete Israeli control, forcing the creation of Palestine's capital to be located outside of the city, perhaps in Abu Dis or another village bordering Jerusalem. And Gaza would remain cut off, with no infrastructure created to link Gaza and the West Bank, despite long-ago promises for a land bridge or tunnel or another arrangement that would allow for a unified Palestinian state including both parts.

Without real sovereignty, without contiguity, and without control of borders and resources, Palestine would not be a state; it would be a series of truncated bantustans.

In response, the strategy for Palestinian freedom has been transformed. Instead of focusing on the arrangement-based demand for a "two-state solution," many Palestinian campaigners and human rights activists around the world are waging a rights-based struggle for freedom: for an end to occupation and apartheid, for human rights, and equality for all—regardless of whether the ultimate political arrangement encompasses one, two, or several states.

Do the Arab countries want to destroy Israel?

Unlike in Europe, antisemitism was not a long-standing component of either popular or elite culture in the Arab world. During the Spanish Inquisition, fleeing Jews famously found refuge in the Arab countries, particularly in North Africa.

In the period leading up to the creation of the State of Israel and the 1948 war that accompanied it, many Arabs both inside Palestine and in the surrounding Arab countries believed it would be possible to prevent the creation of a Jewish-dominated state, a self-proclaimed enclave of Europe and America in the heart of the Arab Middle East. Across the region, small Jewish communities had existed from time immemorial. But they were part of the indigenous communities of people, who had lived together for millennia. The European Jewish settlers who came in large numbers to settle in Palestine, beginning in the late 1880s and especially during and after World War II, who were trying to create a Jewish-controlled state, represented a very different situation. People opposed the creation of such a state, believing it unjust to the indigenous Palestinians, and governments in the region opposed it largely out of fear that a powerful, Western-backed Israel would represent a serious threat to their countries' own economic, strategic, and political interests.

The token Arab armies that entered Palestine in 1948 were soundly defeated by the smaller but far stronger Zionist militias and soon the official Israeli military. The Arab armies were defeated again in 1967 when Israel's first strikes destroyed the entire Egyptian air force, and soon that of Jordan, before either country could muster up a single plane. Since then, despite further wars, ongoing tensions, and continued occupation, Arab governments have largely come to terms with the existence of Israel in their midst; many are eager to consolidate business and financial links with the far wealthier, far more powerful, far better-positioned Israeli economy. If popular opinion were not so strongly against such normalization, there is little doubt that virtually all the Arab governments would be lining up to exchange ambassadors with Tel Aviv.

In its early years, the Palestinian national movement supported the call for a democratic secular state in all of historic Palestine: one person, one vote, from the river to the sea. It was the South Africa model—changing the power relations of the existing state structures, making sure refugees who had been forced out could come home. It wasn't about kicking people out. (For decades Israel has shown itself brilliantly capable of building new cities, new industries, and creating new jobs, for sometimes massive immigrant flows. In 1990–91, at the time of the collapse of the Soviet Union, more than a million Russians emigrated to Israel. Jobs, cultural centers, housing, language training, and more—all were made readily accessible to these new Israelis. There was space, there was knowledge, there were materials, and there was political will. (The claim that there was no more room was never true.)

By the 1980s, the idea of a separate Palestinian state was competing with the original call for a democratic secular state. There was resistance, certainly, since a "two-state solution" meant accepting a Palestinian state in (at that time) just 22 percent of historic Palestine—the territories occupied in 1967. But there was a clear appeal in the idea of a state just for Palestinians. Part of the reason had to do with the increasing oppression faced by Palestinians living in the OPT—including but not limited to house demolitions, checkpoints, and curfews. People had different ideas about what Israeli settlers—then "only" about 250,000 or so—in the occupied territories might do. Some, it was assumed, would want to leave and return to pre-1967 Israel; others would become citizens of the Palestinian state and live as everyone else did, without the armed protection and privileges currently available only to Jewish settlers; others might be bought out. But the understanding of creating a Palestinian state was rooted in human rights—including national rights—and settled international law, and that would be the basis of such a process.

Since the beginning of the first intifada in 1987, and especially since the collapse of Oslo negotiations and the beginning of the second intifada in 2000, regional anger toward Israel for its treatment of Palestinians living under occupation skyrocketed. The emergence in the mid-1990s of Arabic-language satellite television stations (most notably Qatar's al-Jazeera, along with Abu Dhabi's al-Arabiyya TV) transformed the level of outrage. While most Arabs long knew and opposed Israeli occupation, seeing televised coverage of the day-to-day humiliations, killings, and episodes of extreme violence that are endemic to military occupation brought that opposition to new and angry levels.

Israel launched a powerful propaganda campaign designed to convince Israelis, and even more, to convince supporters of Israel in the US, Europe, and elsewhere, that Israel was a beleaguered, endangered David standing up to the murderous Arab Goliath. The reality of course was quite different—from at least 1967 on, Israel's military capability, its US-guaranteed qualitative military edge, its global economic reach and technical (especially military-technical) prowess, and of course its officially unacknowledged but widely known nuclear weapons arsenal, all guaranteed economic, strategic and military superiority.

By 2020, or even before, there was a widespread view that a two-state solution was simply no longer possible—that there was no land left for anything remotely resembling a viable contiguous state. After decades of settlement expansion, the Oslo vision of a "two-state solution" was of small, disconnected parcels of land that together would make up perhaps 40 percent of the 22 percent of historic Palestine. For some Palestinians, that reality resulted in a return to the original call for a democratic and secular state in all of Palestine. For others, the focus shifted away from state-construction to focus on rights—international law, human rights, and equality for all. By 2024, opinion among Palestinians encompassed the whole range of political goals—from efforts to end Israel's occupation and apartheid system and create an independent Palestinian state, to building a single state, to fighting for human rights and equality for all in whatever states there are.

How does Israel see its role in the Middle East region?

The pre-state Zionist leadership deliberately crafted an identity for the new State of Israel that was oriented toward Europe, America, and the West. This was partly a tactical effort to win backing from one or another of the colonial powers; to do so, the putative Israelis had to convince would-be sponsors of their potential value as a surrogate for European, American, Russian, or Ottoman/Turkish interests. But it also reflected the personal worldview of those same leaders; while early Zionist colonies in Palestine were largely agricultural, most Jewish settlers would have been far more at home in Brooklyn or London than in the Middle Eastern hills or desert.

Throughout the Cold War, Israel deliberately shaped its position as a junior partner, or surrogate, for US military and strategic reach. Cynical remarks about Israel as the "fifty-first state" reflected the familiarity of the US–Israeli bond. For Washington, while Cold War–driven strategic considerations were the main force behind the US embrace of Israel, a powerful component was the sense that "Israelis are like us." There was more than a hint of racism in this assessment; it was designed to distinguish Israel from its neighbors. However close our ties with Egypt or Saudi Arabia, official Washington thinking went, they're still Arabs, they're not quite "like us"—part of that, crucially, was that the Arabs were not white. Official and other influential Israeli voices consistently promoted that racist view. The irony, of course, was that increasing numbers of Israeli Jews were also not white—they had immigrated or were descended from communities in the Arab world (or Iran or Turkey), despite the tendency of many to take on the widespread Israeli identification with Europe more than with their own Middle Eastern languages and cultures. But racism and history combined in Israel, with a clear racialized hierarchy within the Jewish community that ensured, at least through the 1970s, the continuing domination of Ashkenazi, or white European Jews among the leadership in Israeli government, business, and intellectual circles. That was particularly visible in the diplomatic corps of the new state for its first three decades or more, making it easier for US officials and business leaders, accustomed to dealing with Europeans far more than with Arabs, to relate to those Israelis.

Within Israel, the racialized hierarchy, reflected in relative access to wealth, power, and influence within the Jewish community, was maintained. With Ashkenazi Jews at the top, then came Russians, then the Mizrahim, or Arab/Turkish/Iranian Jews (with Yemeni Jews among the poorest of that sector), and finally the Ethiopian Jews at the bottom of the hierarchy. There were and are plenty of exceptions, of course, particularly in political power after the takeover of the government by the right-wing Likud Party in 1977, whose political base lay primarily among the Mizrahi Jews. But the color lines within the Jewish community remain—despite the much greater overarching divide between all Jews and Palestinians, when it comes to all economic, social, political, and national rights.

What role does the European Union play in the conflict? Why doesn't it do more?

Europe has generally maintained a nuanced position, preserving strong economic and political ties to Israel, while expressing opposition to Israeli settlements in the occupied Palestinian territories and recognition of how those settlements violate the Geneva Conventions, numerous United Nations resolutions, and other instruments of international law. The Euro-Israeli Association Accord, for instance, privileged European–Israeli trade by removing tariffs for all goods made in Israel. The accord was the basis of a challenge by the European Union to Israel's practice of labeling goods produced in Israeli settlements in the occupied territories as "made in Israel" and exporting them as tariff-free, in violation of the accord's provisions. But the unwillingness of some European countries, most notably Germany and the Netherlands, to criticize Israel openly prevented the EU from reaching the necessary unanimity to hold Israel accountable for those violations.

While Europe was invited to the 1991 Madrid peace talks, it was functionally excluded; the US alone set the terms, developed the agenda, and recruited the participants. During the Oslo process, the European Union was called on to pay much of the cost but remained excluded from serious involvement in the actual diplomacy. European governments throughout the Clinton era appeared to acquiesce to US domination over Middle East diplomacy, never demanding real influence in the negotiations. In the mid-1990s, the European Commission drafted a long critique of US policy toward the Israeli–Palestinian conflict, and especially of Europe's exclusion from the process. But the report concluded with the statement that nothing in it should be taken as a "challenge to US leadership" on the issue, thus largely vitiating the critique's impact.

When George W. Bush was elected, European diplomats were wary of the seeming disinterest of this oil industry-oriented administration in the explosive region. By summer 2001, the EU was already moving in to take some initiative in resolving specific on-the-ground crises that exploded in response to Israeli moves to expand settlements and dispossess Palestinians. Some European initiatives, led by the new Social-Democratic Party in Germany, seemed to be bearing fruit, but it was undermined by party leader Joshka Fischer's own approach when he began a new Israeli–Palestinian dialogue in Berlin with a careful bow to what he called "the American prerogative" in Middle East diplomacy. A few days later, the terrorist attacks of September 11 occurred, and Europe pulled back.

Only months later, when the post-9/11 global diplomatic impasse slowly began to crumble, did Europe begin to revive its cautious efforts. With Israel's violent reoccupation of Palestinian cities in the spring of 2002, most of the European-funded security infrastructure of the Palestinian Authority (police stations, police cars, etc.) was destroyed by Israeli soldiers. Israel made clear its expectation that Europe, not Israel itself, should be expected to cough up the funds to rebuild the shattered infrastructure.

In early 2006, Europe signed on to the US-orchestrated boycott of the Palestinian Authority following the election of Hamas as the dominant party in the PA. Many European parliamentarians, as well as large majorities of Europe's populations, expressed serious concern about the humanitarian consequences of such drastic actions, but US pressure won out. During the Israeli military escalation against Gaza that began that same summer, Europe criticized Israel's violations of the Geneva Conventions and other international covenants in its collective punishment of the Palestinians, and especially in the Israeli military's destruction of much of the Palestinian civilian infrastructure, such as Gaza's sole electricity-generating plant, which was destroyed in June 2006. But despite its criticism, Europe simultaneously began a pattern of paying for rebuilding infrastructure destroyed by Israeli bombings, but refusing to move politically to challenge the continued US military support that enabled the Israel's destructive actions in the first place.

That pattern continued into the 2020s. In the United Nations, European nations would often abstain on resolutions condemning Israeli violations, refusing to provide viable political support to Palestinian victims of the Israeli violations of international law that London's own diplomats acknowledged were continuing.

The extreme levels of violence in Israel's war beginning in October 2023 saw the strongest evidence of a beginning divide in EU positions. A number of European governments began to express criticism and soon outrage at the Israeli assault against civilians and at the destruction of so much of Gaza's infrastructure that Europe had rebuilt numerous times. In the UN, Europe voted in more significant numbers—including in the Security Council, where several votes for ceasefire resolutions (however weak) won support from all or nearly all of the European Council members.

The most visible occurred in September 2024, in the General Assembly vote on the resolution to implement the International Court of Justice's Advisory Opinion on the illegality of the occupation, Israel's violation of the crime of apartheid, and to impose a number of significant sanctions on Israel—including an arms embargo—designed to bring an end to the occupation. The vote was overwhelming—123 in favor with only 14 countries opposed, with 43 abstentions. But instead of the all-too-common practice of all the Europeans voting to abstain, the EU split—with a number of Washington's key European allies voting in favor. Those included Ireland, France, Spain, Portugal, Norway, Belgium, Finland, Greece.

The European votes shifting towards greater criticism of Israel and more support for Palestinian rights were particularly important because during the years that the Russian-Ukraine war had been raging, European militarism and military spending—especially focused on NATO and US leadership—were on the rise, right-wing populist parties were winning in a number of European countries, and the very notion that human rights was the central core of the EU project was under attack. Given all that, it was significant to see the European willingness to stand up to significant US pressure. The vote alone of course did not promise implementation of the sanctions, but the resolution itself provided a potentially powerful tool to be used by civil society and social movements across Europe to challenge their governments to go further.

What is Iran's role in relation to Israel and the Palestinians?

During the years of the US-backed shah's regime (1953–1979) in Iran, Israel and Iran developed close ties based on their centrality to US policy in the region and shared anti-Arab attitudes. When the shah was ousted in 1979, relations between the two countries turned hostile. Throughout the George W. Bush administration, escalating US antagonism toward Iran strengthened the US–Israeli "special relationship." Tel Aviv and the pro-Israeli lobbies in the US strongly backed the US invasion of Iraq, but Israeli security officials and public opinion had long claimed that it was Iran that posed an "existential" threat to Israel.

In January 2007, Israeli Prime Minister Olmert threatened a possible military strike against Iran. Later that year Israel acknowledged purchasing five hundred US-made bunker-buster bombs, aimed at destroying Iran's underground nuclear power facilities. In December, the US National Intelligence Estimate concluded that Iran did not have a nuclear weapons program. Israel rejected the assessment. On June 6, 2008, the Israeli newspaper *Yedioth Ahronoth* quoted a government minister claiming that an Israeli attack with US support on Iranian nuclear sites was "unavoidable" because sanctions (the US imposed harsh sanctions on Iran in response to its nuclear power program beginning in 2005) had failed. In February 2009 Israelis elected a right-wing government that continued threatening Iran.

In the United States, the intelligence community's increasing skepticism about Iran's alleged nuclear aspirations made a shift in the discourse possible. President Barack Obama repeatedly indicated his openness to negotiations with Iran; in a major foreign policy speech in Cairo in June 2009, Obama stated his willingness to negotiate with Iran without preconditions and based on mutual respect. Negotiations for a nuclear deal had begun back in 2006, but became much more serious when Obama took the lead in 2013. In 2015, the Joint Comprehensive Plan of Action (JCPOA), the Iran nuclear deal, was signed by Tehran and Washington, as well as the other four permanent members of the UN Security Council plus Germany. Iran had no nuclear weapons program, but the agreement called for Iran to significantly reduce its production of enriched uranium used in its civilian power programs and allow UN inspection of its nuclear facilities. In return, the US (and soon the UN) would lift all nuclear-related sanctions imposed on Iran.

The JCPOA held on both sides until early 2018, when then-President Trump unilaterally pulled out of the deal and escalated the economic sanctions. UN inspectors confirmed that Iran was in compliance with the deal's requirements, and for months Iran continued its (then self-imposed) limitations on nuclear enrichment. The other signatories promised to provide economic and other support to Iran to take the place of the agreements Washington had abandoned. But that plan didn't work, and eventually Iran began gradually to increase its enrichment capacity.

By 2024 Israel remained the only nuclear weapons state in the Middle East. While it continued to produce some highly enriched uranium that could theoretically be used in a future weapons program, Iran still was not producing nuclear weapons.

But Israel continued to refer to Iran as an existential threat to its existence, and continued to demand military support and weapons from the US aimed at a potential war with Iran. The rise of two competing regional blocs—one made up of Iran and several non-state militias it supported in Lebanon, Iraq, Syria, Yemen, and Gaza, and another led by Israel and including wealthy Gulf Arab monarchies and other Arab countries all backed by the US—escalated.

Iran has provided military support to Hezbollah in Lebanon for many years. But the organization was created in response to the Israeli invasion of Lebanon in 1982, and it has long defined itself in the context of opposing Israeli opposition of Lebanese territory. Its political wing leads one of the largest political blocs in the Lebanese parliament, and while it collaborates closely with Iran (and shares Iran's majority-Shi'a demographic), its strategic decisions reflect its own priorities as well. The northern border of Israel—also the southern border of Lebanon—has long been the site of regular Hezbollah-Israel rocket-fire exchanges. That erupted again on October 8, 2023, as Israel began its assault in Gaza following the October 7 attack. The on-again, off-again exchanges continued at least through the first eleven months of Israel's war, and Hezbollah made clear it would not stop until a ceasefire ended the attack on Gaza. (A temporary ceasefire was declared in Lebanon in November 2024.)

Iran has also provided military and financial support to militias in Iraq (which early on challenged the US occupation and later the US-backed government there) and in Syria (largely supporting the government in Damascus against the opposition movements). In Yemen, civil war broke out in 2014 between the government and the Houthis, an indigenous political/military organization that had long fought for a bigger share of political power in the country. Only after Saudi Arabia, long Iran's biggest Arab challenger in the region, led a US-backed coalition in a massive bombing campaign against Yemen in 2015 did Iran provide large-scale military support to the Houthis. At the time, Iran made clear it had opposed the Houthi escalation, and had urged the leadership in Yemen not to go forward with their attacks on shipping in the Red Sea, but the Houthis had ignored the Iranian advice.

All of this led to a consolidation of the notion of Israel standing against the so-called axis of resistance, led by Iran and backed by the various militias, allegedly constituting an existential threat to Israel and

Israelis. The US embraced this narrative, and it underlay the efforts by both Trump and Biden to create a process of an anti-Iran normalization of relations between Israel and Arab states across the region (see pages 173–176).

Iran's support for Hamas has also been overstated and used to justify huge transfers of additional US weapons to Israel throughout the war against Gaza. There is no question that Iran has provided financial support to Hamas, as well as even some limited military support, although how significant that support may be remains unclear. But Hamas, an overwhelmingly Sunni-based organization, does not share the Shi'a connection that binds Iran more closely to Hezbollah, the Iraqi and Syrian militias, and somewhat to the Houthis. And Hamas publicly broke its relationship with Iran in 2011 during the first year of the Syrian civil war, when Hamas supported the largely Sunni-led opposition movements. Some of that relationship was rebuilt, as evidenced during Israel's war against Gaza, but the level of Iranian support is often certainly exaggerated in the Western media.

There is no question that the view many in Washington share with Tel Aviv, that Iran represents a fundamental, even existential threat not only to Israel but to the West as a whole, played a huge role in the escalation of military threats and provision of ever-more-powerful weapons to Israel, as well as the deployment of US aircraft carriers and nuclear-capable submarines to the region following Israeli assassinations of Hezbollah and Hamas leaders in June and July 2024, and the threat that brings of a major regional war.

What kind of nonviolent campaigns have Palestinians engaged in?

As the second Palestinian uprising wound down in 2004–05, many Palestinians recognized that the armed nature of the mobilization had led to significantly reduced popular involvement. At the same time, political momentum, strategic leadership, and legitimacy were shifting from the longstanding political factions, especially Fatah and Hamas, to Palestinian civil society.

For years Palestinians had been mobilizing nonviolent protests against the Israeli occupation. Across the West Bank, especially in the villages, they challenged the separation wall that expropriated land and divided Palestinians from their own agricultural land and separated villages from cities. They built movements opposing the pervasive checkpoints, house demolitions, lack of water, travel restrictions, and other aspects of the occupation. The nonviolent movements engaged large numbers of Palestinians across geographic, generational, gender, class, and other lines. Outside supporters, both Israelis and internationals, joined the protests, some of which became institutionalized with weekly vigils in villages such as Bil'in, Bani Naim, and many more.

International supporters of the Palestinian nonviolent movements traveled frequently to the occupied territories to participate in and bring back information from the continuing anti-occupation mobilizations. Creation of the International Solidarity Movement and later the Free Gaza Movement, the global protests that answered the Israeli blockade and assaults on Gaza, the flotilla movements challenging the blockade—all reflected the widening international support for Palestine's nonviolent activism. United Nations reports, traditionally limited to the role of states and intergovernmental organizations, began to address the need for international support for and protection of global civil society's work in defense of Palestinian rights.

Palestinian refugee communities—particularly in the camps of Lebanon and Syria, as well as second and third-generation refugees in Europe, North America, and elsewhere—increased their mobilizations as well. And inside Israel itself, Palestinian citizens were increasingly active in demanding equality and supporting demands of other Palestinian sectors.

The protest movement, which challenged Israeli occupation and apartheid as whole systems even while targeting specific aspects in specific campaigns, claimed its legitimacy from international law and human rights. In 2004, the International Court of Justice issued an advisory opinion at the request of the UN General Assembly, determining the building of the separation wall on Palestinian land, as well as key aspects of the settlement project, to be illegal. The ruling sparked significant expansion of the nonviolent actions in the OPT and around the world.

What is the global movement known as "BDS"?

In 2005, a coalition of more than 170 Palestinian civil society organizations issued a global call to supporters around the world to "impose broad boycotts and implement divestment initiatives against Israel similar to those applied to South Africa in the apartheid era. We appeal to you to pressure your respective states to impose embargoes and sanctions against Israel. We also invite conscientious Israelis to support this Call, for the sake of justice and genuine peace."

The non-violent economic and cultural pressure of the boycott, divestment, and sanctions campaign (BDS) would be maintained, "until Israel meets its obligation to recognize the Palestinian people's inalienable right to self-determination and fully complies with the precepts of international law by:

Ending its occupation and colonization of all Arab lands and dismantling the Wall;

Recognizing the fundamental rights of the Arab-Palestinian citizens of Israel to full equality; and

Respecting, protecting and promoting the rights of Palestinian refugees to return to their homes and properties as stipulated in UN resolution 194."

BDS soon became central among Palestinians and to the movements around the world supporting Palestinian rights. It was powerful because it identified a unified global strategy for ending Israel's violations of international law and human rights, while recognizing that conditions and movements differ between countries. Consumer boycotts might be the centerpiece in some European countries where Israeli produce and other goods were widely available, while divestment campaigns in the US targeting corporations, banks and universities might be most successful, and in countries purchasing significant military goods from Israel (such as India or Argentina), pressure for government sanctions might make the most sense.

The UN-based International Coordinating Network on Palestine, a consortium of 400+ civil society organizations working for Palestinian rights around the world, endorsed the coalition's call the day after it was released. In the US, the BDS call was quickly endorsed by organizations such as the US Campaign for Palestinian Rights (formerly the US Campaign to End the Israeli Occupation), a coalition of several hundred groups working to change US policy. The campaign had already been working on boycott and divestment efforts against corporations that profited from Israel's occupation, such as Caterpillar, but becoming part of the global BDS movement significantly strengthened the campaign's US work and its global ties.

From 2005 on, BDS campaigns arose on campuses and in communities, with perhaps the most important taking shape in mainstream churches, such as the Presbyterians and Methodists, where years-long efforts for social responsibility in investments, and ultimately calls for divestment, took on new urgency. Local efforts to mobilize city council resolutions supporting BDS took shape, and longstanding campaigns against US military aid to Israel fit easily into a BDS framework.

Over the next decade, BDS expanded in breadth and depth of participation, and in impact. BDS successes in Europe included Veolia—a French corporate giant that lost $24 billion in canceled or rejected contracts between 2006 and 2014 in response to global campaigns against its involvement in Israeli settlement projects. By 2015, Veolia announced it was selling off almost all of its Israeli operations, admitting that BDS campaigns had cost the company "important contracts." Elsewhere in Europe, opposition to Israeli banks' support for occupation led large pension-fund management companies in the Netherlands and Luxembourg to cut ties with five Israeli banks, Denmark's largest bank to blacklist Bank Hapoalim, and Norway's state investment fund to boycott Israeli construction companies involved in building settlements. Numerous other campaigns in France, Spain, and elsewhere brought further economic pressure to bear on Israel to end its violations.

In the United States, BDS played a huge role in education and advocacy campaigns, and by 2010 or so was starting to show some real, though still largely symbolic, economic impact. The role of faith-based organizations in building BDS campaigns remained strong, and mainstream churches reflected that. The United Methodist Church passed a strong boycott resolution in 2012 and took up a move to divest from the G4S Israeli security company operating in West Bank and East Jerusalem settlements as well as in the private prison industry in the United States.

The Presbyterian Church passed boycott and divestment resolutions, including decisions to divest funds from Caterpillar, MotoSolutions (Motorola), and Hewlett-Packard because of those companies' role in supporting Israeli repression in the occupied territories.

Beyond the churches, BDS campaigns became common on campuses across the United States, including demands for both divestment of university funds from corporations profiting from occupation or Israeli apartheid and boycotts of specific Israeli products. They also included calls to join the global academic and cultural boycotts, which did not target individual Israeli academics or artists, but rather aimed at ending the institutional ties between US and Israeli academic or cultural institutions funded and supported by the Israeli government.

In October 2014, Stephen Hawking, probably the most famous scientist in the world, announced he was withdrawing from participation in a high-profile Israeli conference, saying that he had decided "to respect the boycott, based upon his knowledge of Palestine, and on the unanimous advice of his own academic contacts there." Academic organizations, including the American Studies, Asian-American Studies, and Native American Studies Associations all passed resolutions supporting the academic boycott.

And in the world of popular culture, numerous US and global artists publicly rejected performing in Israel or the occupied territories, linking their decision to the legacy of the "Don't play Sun City" campaigns of the South African anti-apartheid years. Sometimes, decisions not to support BDS brought consequences. US film star Scarlett Johansson made commercials for SodaStream drink machines, manufactured in an illegal West Bank settlement, and as a result was forced to step down from her position as an ambassador of Oxfam when the British charity made clear its opposition to SodaStream's role in the occupied territories.

The Israeli government, backed by the pro-Israel lobby in the US, tried to portray the BDS campaign as antisemitic or racist. In fact BDS was, from its origins, precisely the opposite: a nonviolent strategy against the systemic discriminatory policies of Israel, and explicitly opposed to racism and all forms of discrimination, including antisemitism. The 2005 BDS call made clear that the goal was not a permanent boycott or effort to isolate Israel, but rather the use of BDS as a means of bringing nonviolent economic pressure to bear on Israel to end its three specific areas of violations of international law and human rights: the occupation of the 1967 territories, the legal discrimination against Palestinian citizens of Israel, and the refusal to reach a just solution for Palestinian refugees denied their right to return home. In that context, compared to Israel's own policies, the BDS campaign was an explicitly anti-racist, equality-for-all challenge.

As BDS campaigns became more frequent, and won more victories, the strategy also became the centerpiece of growing efforts to shut down work supporting Palestinian rights by using false claims of antisemitism to discredit and undermine campaigns and campaigners. Led by parts of the pro-Israel lobbies, components of the US government including the Department of Education and the State Department worked towards discrediting BDS, including by weaponizing false claims of antisemitism among its adherents. More than thirty US states, and numerous cities and other jurisdictions, followed suit, passing or trying to pass laws criminalizing BDS or denying access to state or municipal contracts to anyone who refused to sign a McCarthy-era-style pledge that they were not then and never would boycott Israel. The longstanding US laws and Supreme Court decisions holding that boycotts are a First Amendment-protected form of political speech, seemed not to apply when the target of the boycott was Israel.

PART II:
THE CHRONOLOGY–
What Happened, Who Did It, and Why?

Did the Palestinians demand national rights and an independent state before the 1967 war?

Like most parts of the Arab world, national consciousness in Palestine grew in the context of demographic changes and shifts in colonial control. During the 400 years of Ottoman Turkish control, Palestine was an identifiable region within the larger empire, but was linked closely with what was then known as Greater Syria (also part of the empire). With World War I and the end of the Ottoman Empire, it was taken over by the British Empire. But even before that, beginning in the 1880s, the increasing influx of European Jewish settlers brought about a newly articulated national identity—reflecting a distinctly Palestinian consciousness—among the Muslims and Christians who were the overwhelming majority of Palestinian society. There was widespread unease about, and sporadic organizing campaigns against, the influx of Zionist European settlers, who were viewed as a threat to indigenous land ownership. But nation-states mostly did not yet exist in the Arab world.

In 1922, when the French and British divided up the Arab world they had taken over from the defeated Ottoman empire, Palestine was demarcated with specific borders and turned over to Great Britain to rule as a Mandate territory under the approval of the League of Nations. It was in that period, in the context of rising anti-colonial struggles around the world, that national consciousness turned into the demand for national rights and independence among Palestinians. As more European settlers arrived, and the British made contradictory promises to the Arabs on one side and the Zionist leaders on the other, conflict escalated. Palestinian Arabs challenged the new settlers' claims to Palestinian land, as well as the legitimacy of the British overlords protecting the immigrants; the Zionist settlers saw the indigenous Arabs (they denied for decades that there was an identifiable Palestinian people) as an impediment to their full settlement of the land and resisted the British efforts to restrict the numbers of immigrants allowed in to Palestine.

That conflict, and the armed clashes that accompanied it, eventually led to the British decision that Palestine was ungovernable, which led them to turn Mandate authority over to the new United Nations. When the UN voted to partition Palestine in 1947, opposition was heard from the Arab states—but the only survey taken of Palestinian opinion to determine what they themselves wanted was ignored in the international debate. The Palestinians were given no voice. For many years the popular sentiment among Palestinians was a desire to reverse partition—to create a democratic and secular state for all its citizens in all of what is now Israel and all the rest of Palestine.

The period after the 1967 war, when Israel occupied the last remnants of Palestine, corresponded with the rise of the PLO as a popular guerrilla organization. (It had originally been created largely as a tool of Arab governments in 1964.) The initial strategic approach of the PLO was the call for Palestinian national rights in the context of a democratic secular state in all of historic (Mandate) Palestine. By the mid-1970s, debate was underway within the organization about recognizing Israel and shifting to a two-state approach. In January 1976, the PLO, with support from Egypt, Syria, Jordan, and the Soviet Union, introduced a resolution in the UN Security Council calling for a two-state solution. The US vetoed that resolution, the first of many times it would veto the very proposed solution it claims to support.

In 1988, at the height of the first intifada, the PLO's parliament-in-exile, the Palestine National Council, voted to accept a two-state strategy, while declaring Palestine an independent state in the 1967 territories.

What was the Six-Day War in 1967 and how did Israel come to be in control of the West Bank, Gaza, and East Jerusalem?

The 1967 Six-Day War began with Israel's attack on the Egyptian air force, which was wiped out within a few hours. Some argue that Israel's first strike was justified because Egypt, Syria, and Jordan were massing armies near Israel's borders. Certainly the tensions on all sides were on the rise. Egypt's nationalist president, Gamal Abdel Nasser, had demanded that the UN withdraw the emergency forces stationed on Egyptian territory since the 1956 Anglo-French-Israeli attack on Egypt. Although Israel had refused to grant the UN the right to station forces on its side of the border in 1956, it considered the withdrawal as a justification to go to war against Egypt.

But war still might have been prevented; just before Israel struck, Nasser had agreed to send his vice president to Washington for negotiations. Israel's attack was at least partly to prevent Nasser from using his Washington trip as a face-saving way to pull back his forces; such a move would have undermined what Israel saw as justification for its own attack. Israeli and US military officials agreed that the war had been Israel's decision. Menachem Begin, Israel's right-wing Likud bloc leader and later prime minister, told the Pentagon's Army War College in 1982 that "in June 1967 we again had a choice. The Egyptian Army concentrations in the Sinai approaches do not prove that Nasser was really about to attack us. We must be honest with ourselves. We decided to attack him."

Whatever one thinks about how Israel's war began, it is clear that although it was aimed at the Arab states surrounding Israel, it was the Palestinians who paid the highest price. Even after the ceasefire, Israeli troops moved into Syria and captured the Golan Heights; 90,000 Golani Syrian Arabs were expelled from their homes. By the end of the war, Israel occupied Syria's Golan Heights, the Egyptian Sinai Peninsula, and the Palestinian West Bank, including Arab East Jerusalem, and Gaza Strip. Two hundred fifty thousand more Palestinians were dispossessed of their homes and forced into exile, and over a million more were now under Israeli military occupation. Israel now controlled all the land—and all the people on that land—from the Jordan River to the Mediterranean Sea.

What was the international community's response to the 1967 war?

For the United Nations, the 1967 war provided the organization with an opportunity to articulate, for the first time, a clear rejection of the long-accepted practice of victorious nations simply keeping, as colonies or to expand their existing territory, the lands and nations they conquered and occupied in wartime. This colonial practice was finally deemed unacceptable, and Security Council Resolution 242, passed just six months after the June war, asserted "the inadmissibility of the acquisition of territory by war." It was an unequivocal position, on which most future Israel-Palestine negotiations would be based.

Other parts of the resolution turned out to be less precise. While almost every nation agreed that Israel should return all of the captured territories it was occupying, there was some diplomatic wrangling with the US. The final result was a linguistic dodge, made possible by the UN rule at the time that the working languages of the Security Council were English and French. The French version called for return of "des territoires," or "the territories," implying all the captured land Israel held. But the English version, whose grammar doesn't require the article before the noun, called for the "withdrawal of Israel [sic] armed forces *from territories* occupied in the recent conflict" leaving open the argument that perhaps return of only some of the territories might fulfill the requirement.

From that moment, Israel adopted the position that it was not obligated to return all the territories. With its return of the Sinai Peninsula to Egypt after the Camp David Accords of 1979 between Israel and Egypt, Israel claimed that since the barely populated Sinai desert represented the largest percentage of land it had occupied in 1967, its return to Egypt should be sufficient to meet the UN's demand. Any further return of occupied land, to Palestinians or Syria, would be at Israel's choice and on Israel's terms.

From 1967 until today, the UN has passed numerous resolutions calling for an end to Israel's occupation of the "Occupied Palestinian Territory," which is routinely defined in UN documents as constituting the West Bank, including East Jerusalem, and Gaza. But those resolutions remain unfulfilled.

How did the US respond to the 1967 war and occupation?

At the time of the Six-Day War, US relations with Israel were friendly and supportive, but not anything close to the "special relationship" that has defined US–Israeli ties since that time. In 1967, the Pentagon predicted that the balance of forces was so one-sided that no matter who struck first, no combination of Arab forces would overcome Israel's superior strength. But nonetheless, on May 25 the Pentagon sent battalions of Marines to the Sixth Fleet, then cruising the Mediterranean, in case they were needed to bolster Israel. By June 2, the date was set for Israel to teach Syria and Egypt the long-awaited "lesson." But first Israel needed permission from the US. On June 4, even as Nasser was negotiating with the US representative in Cairo, President Lyndon Johnson telegraphed Defense Minister Moshe Dayan and gave Israel the final green light. The next day, Dayan ordered the attack.

After the war, relations between the US and Israel became much closer. Most important was the new recognition in the Pentagon of Israel's strategic value. It was the middle of the Cold War, after all, and Israel's military prowess had showed US policymakers how valuable an ally it could be as the regional policeman for US oil and security interests in the Middle East. Soon Israel's junior partner role in the region would be expanded to include other Cold War battlefields much farther afield—such places as Angola, Mozambique, El Salvador, Chile, Guatemala—where Israeli military assistance, training, and arms bolstered politically unsavory, but strongly anti-Soviet, US allies.

In the US, the Six-Day war was presented as evidence of a heroic Israeli David triumphing over the aggressive Arab Goliath. Public support skyrocketed for closer US ties to Israel led by, but not limited to, traditional pro-Israel institutions. Fundraising by Zionist organizations, blood drives, and volunteer campaigns all soared. During the six days of the war, the United Jewish Appeal sold $220 million worth of Israeli bonds; private American contributions for Israel in 1967 totaled $600 million (equal to about $5.6 billion in 2024).

But the biggest gain was not from those individual contributions.

Just ten days after the Six-Day War ended, a State Department memo noted "Israel has probably done more for the US in the Middle East in relation to money and effort invested than any of our so-called allies and friends elsewhere around the world since the end of the Second World War. In the Far East, we can get almost nobody to help us in Vietnam. Here, the Israelis won the war singlehandedly, have taken us off the hook, and have served our interests as well as theirs."

The reward for Israel was a flood of sophisticated weapons, including advanced Phantom jets. In the four years after the 1967 war, Israel would receive $1.5 billion in US arms—ten times as much as the total sent during the previous twenty years.

Given all of that, Israel's occupation of Palestinian land, and the degree to which that occupation was violating international law and UN resolutions, were of little concern for Washington. Over the years, different US presidents criticized the settlements in the occupied territories, variously describing them as "unhelpful," "obstacles to peace," or, briefly, "illegal." But little action matched the words. America's presumed strategic interests outweighed humanitarian and legal concerns in the Middle East—and the "special relationship" prospered.

What was the 1982 Lebanon war all about? What was Ariel Sharon's role?

In 1970, after a bitter battle with the Jordanian military, the PLO moved its headquarters from Jordan to Lebanon. Hundreds of thousands of Palestinian civilians followed, and the existing camps in Lebanon were soon crowded with more refugees. Lebanon became a key focal point in the Israeli–Palestinian conflict.

With hundreds of thousands of Palestinian refugees living in Beirut and southern Lebanon, much of the governance, from running schools and hospitals to licensing and legal systems, was taken over by the PLO. From 1975, Lebanon was stuck in a bloody civil war, pitting sectarian and religious factions against each other. Palestinian guerrillas and Israeli troops also continued to trade rocket fire across the Israeli–Lebanese border.

In March 1978, Israel invaded and took over a strip of southern Lebanon, and continued to occupy it in defiance of UN Resolution 425, passed just a few days later, which called for Israel to immediately and unconditionally withdraw. Instead, Israel sponsored an anti-Palestinian Christian-led militia called the South Lebanon Army, arming, paying, training, and supporting it in the occupied zone. Israel eventually partially pulled back from the territory it was occupying in Lebanon, but continued to support the SLA against the PLO.

Israel's real goal was to destroy the PLO infrastructure—social as well as military—in Lebanon, and to put in place a compliant, pro-Israeli regime in Beirut. In 1982, when it appeared Lebanon's civil war might drag on forever without achieving those goals, Israel decided to move on its own towards a full-scale invasion. But first it needed to be sure its allies in Washington would approve.

Ensuring US support was a little bit tricky. After all, the US-brokered ceasefire between Israel and the PLO in south Lebanon had held for quite a while. There wasn't an obvious provocation on which to claim that a direct Israeli invasion was "necessary for self-defense." In May 1982, Israeli Defense Minister Ariel Sharon went to Washington to meet with President Reagan's secretary of state, Alexander Haig. Former President Jimmy Carter said later, after a national security briefing, that "the word I got from very knowledgeable people in Israel is that 'we have a green light from Washington.'"

Once US backing was assured, a new provocation was created. On June 3, a renegade anti-PLO Palestinian faction attempted to assassinate Israel's ambassador in London. The British police immediately identified Abu Nidal's forces as responsible, and revealed that PLO leaders themselves were among those on the would-be assassins' hit list. The PLO had nothing to do with the London attack. But Israel claimed the attack (the ambassador remained unhurt) as justification for war against the PLO.

Three days later, on June 6, 1982, the Israeli army invaded Lebanon in "Operation Peace for Galilee," crossing the Litani River and moving almost as far north as Beirut, destroying the feeble resistance from local villagers and from the United Nations peacekeeping troops swept aside in the assault. Israel remained in virtually uncontested control of the air, and maintained overwhelming military superiority on land and sea. Beirut was besieged and subjected to merciless bombing for two months. Casualties were enormous, totaling more than 17,000 Lebanese and Palestinians, mostly civilians. Hospitals were hit, and the Palestinian refugee camps were leveled in massive bombardment. General Ariel Sharon, then minister of defense and later prime minister of Israel, was at the center of planning and executing the Lebanon invasion.

Israel relied overwhelmingly on US-supplied planes, bombs, and other military equipment in the offensive. But despite existing laws mandating that US military supplies be used only for defensive purposes, no one in Washington complained. The *New York Times* said,

"American weapons were justly used to break the PLO." The Reagan administration and Congress both tried to outdo the other in calls to raise the levels of US aid to Israel. Throughout June and July the siege of Beirut continued, with inhabitants in the city in constant danger and many deprived of adequate food, water, and electricity. The bombing intensified in early August, culminating on August 12 with eleven solid hours of bombing in one day. Condemnation poured in from around the world, and even the US issued a mild criticism. A ceasefire was eventually achieved.

The US brokered the terms of the ceasefire, which required the PLO to leave Beirut: its guerrillas, its doctors, its civilian infrastructure, its officials, everyone and everything would board a ship heading for Tunis, almost as far from Palestine as one could get and still be in the Arab world. The US promised to serve as guarantor of Israel's promises to withdraw, and as protector of the Palestinian civilians—primarily women, children, and old men—left behind. US Marines were deployed as the centerpiece of an international force with a thirty-day mandate to guard Beirut during and after the withdrawal of the PLO fighters.

What was the Sabra-Shatila massacre in Lebanon?

On September 1, 1982, President Reagan announced his plan for a new peace initiative between Israel and the Palestinians. It included a freeze on new settlements, limited autonomy for Palestinians in the West Bank and Gaza, and some version of a "Jordanian solution," plus lots of new economic and military aid for Israel. But Israel rejected the Reagan plan, and the initiative remained stalled; in the West Bank, Israel immediately launched several new settlements. At the same time, Israel was having unanticipated difficulties with the new president of Lebanon, Bashir Gemayel. Israel had expected Gemayel to be "their man" in Beirut, but unexpectedly he was emerging as a Lebanese nationalist instead.

On September 11, two weeks before the end of their official mandate, the last US Marines were withdrawn from Beirut. Three days later, Gemayel was assassinated. Within hours, Israel responded by invading Muslim- (and formerly Palestinian-) dominated West Beirut. The invasion completely violated the guarantees of protection the US had negotiated with the PLO.

After a few hours, Israeli Defense Minister Ariel Sharon announced that the Christian Phalangists, the most anti-Palestinian of all the Christian militias, would actually enter the Palestinian camps, rather than the Israelis themselves. According to the CIA, the founding of the Phalangist party in 1936 was inspired by Hitler and European fascism, and the group was armed and trained by Israel from the 1970s on. The senior Israeli commander in Lebanon met with the top Phalangist leaders and told them, Sharon said, "to act humanely, and not to harm women, children, and old people."

On Thursday, September 16, Israeli troops lit flares to light the way for their Phalangist allies to enter the Sabra and Shatila refugee camps, on the outskirts of West Beirut. The massacre that followed, of unarmed children, women, and old men, went on for three days. It resulted in the deaths of between 2,000 and 3,000 Palestinians, most left piled up or hastily buried in mass graves. The Red Cross later said it would be impossible to know exactly how many died.

There was no question that the Israeli soldiers knew what was going on inside the camps—it was visible even without their high-powered binoculars, and the sound of machine-gun fire continued throughout the days and nights. Finally, the US pushed Israel to withdraw the Phalangists. The Los Angeles Times reported that US Special Envoy Morris Draper told the Israeli officers, "You must stop the massacres. They are obscene. I have an officer in the camp counting the bodies ... They are killing children. You are in absolute control of the area and therefore responsible for that area."

Israel's Kahan Commission, convened to investigate the massacre, found Sharon "personally responsible" for it, having allowed the Phalangist militia to enter the camps and refusing to prevent or stop the massacre as it was carried out by Israel's allies. Sharon was forced to step down as defense minister but remained in the Israeli cabinet.

Israel would continue occupying a large strip of south Lebanon until 2000, when the mounting deaths and injuries of young Israeli soldiers there at the hands of Hezbollah resistance forces (a Lebanese organization created in response to the 1982 Israeli invasion) brought about a political outcry inside Israel. The occupation was finally ended unilaterally, implementing most of the requirements of Resolution 425, twenty-two years after it was passed. But a small piece of land on the Lebanon-Syrian border known as Sheba'a Farms—under Israeli occupation since 1967 as part of the Syrian Golan Heights—remained contested, and the Lebanon–Israel border remained tense and militarized, leading to Israel's widely condemned Lebanon War of 2006.

What were conditions like in the occupied territories before the first intifada?

In some ways, it was surprising that the uprising did not erupt earlier. Israel's military presence was everywhere, although the crippling closures and curfews that became commonplace later during the intifada were rare. The PLO was outlawed, and expressions of support for it, let alone membership, could land one in prison. Arrests, indefinite detention, and even expulsions from the territory were common. Israel tried and failed to create a compliant leadership to compete with the PLO. Nationalist political figures, such as the popularly elected local mayors, were targeted by Israelis. In one incident, three mayors were attacked, killing one and leaving two badly maimed.

Economic and social conditions were dire, jobs few, money scarce. Education was central to Palestinian families, and many young university graduates headed abroad for professional training or to find work as doctors, engineers, and other professions. For most families, particularly the half of the population who lived in the refugee camps, meeting the most basic needs was a daily struggle.

An international consensus on ending the occupation and creating a Palestinian state emerged, but there seemed to be no way to implement that view. The UN was powerless to enforce its resolutions because the US protected Israel's occupation. Arab governments talked of liberating Jerusalem and supporting Palestinian rights, but it remained all talk. International law seemed irrelevant.

What was the first intifada all about?

In the twenty years after Israel first took over the West Bank and Gaza in 1967, a new generation, half the population, grew up knowing nothing but military occupation. Unlike their parents, many of whom still dreamed of returning to their homes inside what had become Israel in 1948 (a dream that would later be reclaimed by the third generation of refugees and exiles), many of these teenagers and young adults built their future hopes around the creation of a Palestinian state in the West Bank, Gaza, and East Jerusalem.

Repression, despair, and, for some, passivity all grew. Then, on December 8, 1987, near the densely crowded checkpoint at the entrance to the Gaza Strip, an Israeli truck swerved, and struck and killed four Palestinians: a doctor, an engineer, and two laborers. Some said it was deliberate, though no one knew for sure. What made the incident extraordinary was not that it happened; such incidents were common. It was the consequence. Palestinian outrage sparked an uprising that swept across the Gaza Strip, spread to the West Bank and occupied East Jerusalem, and set into motion a blaze of nationalist resistance to occupation.

The uprising soon came to be called the *intifada* in Arabic, a word whose roots refer to rising up or shaking off. It began with spontaneous actions, stone-throwing children and young people challenging the troops and tanks of Israel's occupying army. But soon it became more structured, as existing grassroots groups, most of them linked to various factions of the PLO, mobilized to respond to new conditions and to answer the needs of the population as Israel's increasingly repressive response made new kinds of organizing necessary.

Organizations of all kinds—women's, workers', medical, student, agricultural, and community groups—took on new tasks: growing food in home and community gardens to replace the Israeli goods now being boycotted; guarding village streets at night with whistles to warn of approaching soldiers; deploying mobile clinics to provide emergency medical help to villages or towns under curfew; boycotting taxes. A daily commercial strike was soon declared that shut down Palestinian businesses at noon in a sign of unity and resistance. What came to be called the UNLU—Unified National Leadership of the

Uprising—emerged clandestinely, distributing leaflets overnight that provided protest calendars and information about coming strike days, special commemorations of the intifada, or particular constituencies to be mobilized at particular times.

But throughout, there was a unified view that only the PLO, with its leadership in exile in Tunis, could speak for the Palestinians. Every international envoy who showed up in East Jerusalem or Ramallah or Gaza City was told the same thing: our address is in Tunis. We're glad to see you here to witness what Israeli occupation looks like and to see our nonviolent response. But if you want to engage us diplomatically, talk to the PLO. The UNLU itself included representatives of all the major PLO factions.

The call for recognition of the PLO as the sole legitimate representative of the Palestinian people had been in place for decades; the intifada renewed and strengthened that call. For twenty years, since the 1967 occupation, that PLO-led diplomacy had gone on at the UN and in capitals around the world. With the intifada, the voice of the Palestinian people and the centerpiece of Palestinian identity shifted back to the occupied territories—even as the residents of the West Bank, Gaza, and East Jerusalem pointed to the PLO in exile as their leaders.

While there were some diplomatic gains, by far the major advance of the intifada was visible internally, within Palestinian society itself. The opening up of new ideas, new empowerment of women and young people, the strengthening of grassroots organizing and new levels of community involvement and participation, all would last beyond the intifada itself.

It was only with the exaggerated enthusiasm that greeted the signing of Oslo's Declaration of Principles, in September 1993, that the first intifada began to wind down. For the next seven years, Oslo, rather than intifada, would be the buzzword on everyone's tongue.

What happened to Israel and Palestine during the 1991 Gulf War?

Iraq's invasion of Kuwait opened a huge rift in an Arab world once unified, at least rhetorically, in support of Palestinian rights. Viewed as siding with Iraq, the Palestinians were quickly ostracized by many Arab governments, particularly in the wealthy US-aligned Gulf states. The rift grew as more Arab states succumbed to US pressure to join the US-led anti-Iraq coalition. Palestinian abandonment and isolation grew more severe.

In Israel, the threat of attack by Iraq grew. Rumors of Iraqi chemical or biological weapons fed the fears among Israelis; gas masks were distributed, and citizens were instructed to create sealed rooms in their homes to protect them from chemicals. Palestinians living under Israeli occupation were largely denied gas masks, engendering fury across the occupied territories, to the degree that some Palestinians actually cheered the prospect of incoming Scud missiles. In order to maintain Arab participation in the coalition, the US demanded that Israel not retaliate even to a direct Iraqi strike. In return, the US agreed to protect Israel.

When fighting began, Iraq did indeed fire several dozen missiles on Israeli cities. None were armed with chemical or biological weapons, and none did major damage. Casualties included two Israelis killed in the attacks, along with some who died from stress-related heart attacks and from misuse of gas masks. Israel acquiesced to the US demand and did not respond militarily to the Iraqi strikes.

The end of the war, with Iraq qualitatively defeated, weakened, and facing crippling economic sanctions, left Israel in a very strong position. It used its elevated influence in Washington to shape the terms of the post-war Madrid conference—including functional exclusion of the United Nations and severe restrictions on the nature of Palestinian participation.

The major concession the Palestinians had made in 1988, when they accepted a two-state solution and declared an independent state on only 22 percent of their historic territory, was largely ignored after the Gulf War. The intifada that began in 1987 had brought new credibility and political power to the Palestinians and the PLO; by the end of the Gulf crisis, between Israel's increased clout in Washington and PLO isolation in the Arab world, most of that short-lived influenced was lost.

What was the Madrid peace conference in 1991?

When the Gulf War ended in 1991 with the defeat of Iraq, the Soviet Union was on the verge of collapse and the US marched triumphant and unchallenged across the Middle East. Washington then turned toward redrawing the political map of the region. The goal reflected a continuation of the US rationale for the war itself: Iraq's illegal invasion of Kuwait had provided a convenient pretext for the US to lead the world to war, to prove it remained a military superpower even as the Cold War ended. Now it aimed to prove it could orchestrate a regional peace the same way.

It would do so at a moment of terrible division in the Arab world, division rooted in Iraq's invasion of a fellow Arab country. Palestinian leaders had opposed the US war buildup, as did public opinion in the Arab world, and supported earlier attempts to bring about a joint Arab solution, but together with Jordan, they refrained from supporting the US war effort against Iraq. One result was the erosion of long-standing support for Palestinian national rights from Arab governments that supported Kuwait, evident in the expulsion of thousands of Palestinians from Saudi Arabia and other Gulf states, and the significant weakening of the Palestinian diplomatic position in the Arab world and beyond.

The Madrid peace conference opened on October 30, 1991. It was ostensibly convened by joint US-Soviet invitation, but with the Soviet Union about to disintegrate, there was no question that Washington was in sole charge. Madrid was designed to look like the long-sought international peace conference—invitations were sent to the European Union, Japan, many Arab countries, and beyond—but the glittering gala provided only the ceremonial opening to the actual negotiations. And those were—as Israel had long demanded—in the form of separate talks between Israel and each of its Arab interlocutors, Syria, Lebanon, and Jordan.

It was only within the confines of the Jordanian diplomatic team that the Palestinians were even included; they were denied the right to participate as an independent delegation. The US allowed Israel to control who negotiated on behalf of the Palestinians, so no members of the PLO, no one from East Jerusalem or Israel, and no Palestinians who were not from the West Bank or Gaza were allowed to participate—thus disenfranchising the millions of Palestinian refugees outside of the West Bank and Gaza as well as their internationally recognized legitimate representatives (although PLO officials played a significant role behind the scenes). Washington also accepted Israel's demand that UN participation be essentially excluded; the one UN representative allowed to be present was denied the right to speak.

Madrid was very much an American initiative. President George H.W. Bush, opening the conference, said its aim was to achieve a "just, lasting, and comprehensive peace" in the Middle East, not simply to end the state of war and replace it with a state of non-belligerency. Bush identified his goals as peace treaties, security, trade, economic relations, investment, "even tourism." Significantly, he did not speak of justice, ending occupation, or Palestinian independence or statehood as goals to be fought for or protected in the Madrid talks.

Bush's plan called for five years of Palestinian "self-government," in the third year of which negotiations would begin for a final resolution of the status of the occupied territories—very close to the Oslo formula that would later replace the Madrid process. He claimed that this "self-government" would "give the Palestinian people meaningful control of their own lives," while "taking into account Israeli security." Bush appropriated Israel's own formula, describing how Palestinians under "self-rule" would be allowed to control their own lives, but there was no change in maintaining Israel's control of the land. The Soviet president, Mikhail Gorbachev, focused primarily on the international context for the peace conference, and described Middle East peace in words that evoked Dr. Martin Luther King—defining peace as "not merely the cessation of war, but of moving towards justice." His country, however, would disappear from the map less than two months later, and his words would have little relevance.

What kind of diplomacy followed the Madrid conference?

After the ceremonies in Madrid, Israeli diplomats met with representatives of Syria, Lebanon, and Jordan (which included the Palestinian diplomats as a subset of the Jordanian team), the countries that had participated in the conference, and began talks mostly based in Washington and under US leadership. A parallel set of multilateral talks on issues such as refugees, water, and economic development brought together much broader participation, including Russia (the Soviet Union had collapsed just weeks earlier), Canada, Japan, and the European Union, first in an opening conference in Moscow in January 1992, and later with separate meetings in scattered capitals.

The various sets of talks plodded along in fits and starts for the next eighteen months or so. Little progress was made on the Israeli–Palestinian front, and frustrations grew higher. The impasse involved two principal issues: Israel's refusal to acknowledge its role as occupier or to make any commitment to stop building the illegal settlements. As months passed, and Palestinian and Israeli diplomats returned to Washington, DC, hotels and State Department conference rooms for round after round of fruitless diplomacy, a growing realization emerged that Madrid was failing.

The PLO leadership in Tunis faced the task of simultaneously orchestrating the work of the officially non-PLO diplomatic team in the Madrid process, while trying to provide international grounding and leadership to the continuing intifada still going on at home in the occupied territories. Developments were getting dire, and it was in that period of Madrid's stalemate that the secret back-channel Oslo talks began.

The urgency of the PLO may also have been rooted in the organization's growing clarity on the US role. Round ten of the Madrid talks collapsed over the issue of Jerusalem. Prior to that round, some hope had lingered among at least some of the Palestinian diplomats that the Clinton administration would stake out a position reflecting its claimed commitment to human rights—rather than in its well-known close ties to Israel. When Secretary of State Warren Christopher not only accepted the legitimacy of Israel's position (that the interim Palestinian authority would have no jurisdiction in occupied Arab East Jerusalem) but also demanded that the Palestinians sign a "joint statement of principles" based on that position, the Palestinians realized they could not hope for an even-handed sponsor in Washington, and the talks collapsed. The loss of that hoped-for US role, and the resulting recognition that

Madrid was a failure, helped set the stage for a new level of Palestinian urgency in the Oslo talks.

What was the Oslo process? How did the Oslo process start?

The Oslo process began while the official, public negotiations that followed the 1991 US-sponsored Madrid peace conference were still going on. But after ten sessions, those talks had stalled again in the spring of 1993, this time over the status of Jerusalem, and it was becoming clear they weren't going anywhere. Madrid's failure increased interest among the highest-level officials on both sides in the still-secret talks already underway in Oslo.

Those talks, initially involving Israeli academics and mid-level Palestinian officials brought together by Norway's foreign minister, had gone much further than the Madrid talks. They culminated in September 1993 with announcements that the parties had agreed to letters of mutual recognition and a Declaration of Principles. The US quickly moved in to take over sponsorship of the process, and the White House signing ceremony finalized the agreement.

Oslo's DOP separated the various issues that divided Israelis and Palestinians into two types: easy and hard. The theory was that the "easy" issues—such things as release of prisoners, economic cooperation, construction of Palestinian sea and airports, security considerations, etc.—would be dealt with first, during a five-year interim period. Discussion of the "hard" or final status issues—including borders of a Palestinian state, settlements, the status of Jerusalem, and the rights of refugees—would not even begin until the third year, and their resolution would be delayed till the end of the interim period (which was eventually extended from five to seven years).

While the structures created by Oslo—the Palestinian Authority, the division of the Occupied Palestinian Territory into disaggregated pieces of land with different levels of authority, and the continuation of Israel's military occupation throughout the territory—remained in place, the sense of Oslo as a process headed towards statehood disintegrated.

Why didn't the Oslo process work?

From the beginning, Oslo was rooted in the understanding that negotiations between the two sides—between the occupying power and the occupied population—however unequal, would be the basis for all decisions. While UN Resolution 242 was mentioned in the opening paragraph, it never appeared again, and the actual requirements of international law, most of which impose unilateral obligations on the occupying power regardless of any agreements they might reach with representatives of the occupied population, were ignored. The words "occupation," "occupying power," "Geneva Conventions," and "international law" do not appear in the text. The entire premise of Oslo was rooted in maintaining Israeli domination over Palestinians, and denying the authority of international law as the necessary basis for resolving the longstanding occupation and apartheid system.

Thirty-one years later, with Gaza withering under a then nine-month-long Israeli assault with tens of thousands dead, 90 percent of the population forcibly displaced, and virtually the entire Strip devastated, with the West Bank facing escalating settler and IDF killing of more than 600 Palestinians, the International Court of Justice acknowledged that Oslo was indeed over.

As noted on page 55 of the ICJ advisory opinion on the illegality of the Israeli occupation, the court reminded governments and the UN itself that legally, under the Geneva Conventions, the protected population "shall not be deprived" of the benefits of the Conventions, "by any agreement concluded between the authorities of the occupied territories and the Occupying Power." In case it wasn't clear enough, the court went on to state that, "For this reason, the Oslo Accords cannot be understood to detract from Israel's obligations under the pertinent rules of international law applicable in the Occupied Palestinian Territory." In other words, nothing agreed to by the Israeli government and the Palestinian representatives could overrule the requirements of international law—which among other things, required Israel to end its occupation and evacuate its settlers as soon as possible.

Beyond those fundamental challenges, the supposedly "easy" interim issues proved to be too difficult, and most were never resolved.

As a result, no one ever even got around to discussing the final status questions. And no one—meaning the US, which remained the sponsor of the diplomatic process—was prepared to weigh in on the side of the Palestinians in the hope of balancing the extraordinary disparity of power that characterized relations between the two sides, let alone to try to enforce international law.

The Oslo process began under a Labor government in Israel. In November 1995, Prime Minister Yitzhak Rabin, who had signed the Oslo Declaration of Principles with Yasir Arafat two years earlier, was assassinated by an extremist Jewish Israeli. By May 1996, the right-wing Likud bloc had won the new Israeli elections, bringing to power Benjamin Netanyahu as prime minister. Netanyahu had campaigned against the Oslo Accords, and when elected he reneged on almost all of the Israeli troop redeployments his predecessor had agreed to. He continued the construction of settlements and bypass roads in the occupied territories that the Labor Party had also encouraged, and consolidated the most nationalistic settlers as a core component of his constituency.

When the Labor Party returned to power in 1999, another hard-line general, Ehud Barak, became prime minister. He escalated the pace of settlement-building even beyond that of Netanyahu, resisted troop redeployments, increased closures of Palestinian territory and house demolitions, and raised the government subsidies to settlements in the occupied territories.

For Palestinians, things went from bad to worse, and diplomatic exchanges between the two sides ostensibly aimed at implementing Oslo's "interim" issues dwindled. Economy, health, education, and security all deteriorated for ordinary Palestinians, and the hope that many Palestinians had placed in the Oslo process faded.

So in the summer of 2000, nearing the end of his presidency, having invested a huge amount of personal prestige in figuring out a solution to the conflict, Bill Clinton summoned the top Israeli and Palestinian leaders to Camp David for a summit to jump straight into the final status issues. It was a go-for-broke plan, and like earlier diplomatic efforts, it failed.

What were Oslo's "final status" issues? Why were they so difficult?

There were four key issues discussed in Oslo: the nature and borders of a Palestinian state, the status of Jerusalem, the right of return for Palestinian refugees, and Israeli settlements in the occupied territories. They were the most difficult, individually and collectively, because they represented the fundamental issues of Israeli control and domination versus Palestinian national aspirations. Further, although they were all subject to international law and specific UN resolutions, Israel (backed by the US) rejected international jurisdiction and even the relevance of international law and international actors other than the United States.

What happened to Israeli settlements and settlers during the years of the Oslo process?

Construction of new settlements and expansion of existing settlements in the occupied territories were already increasing by the time the Oslo process began in 1993. The settler population was growing by about 10 percent a year, during both Labor and Likud governments. (In fact, the years that Labor Prime Minister Rabin's government was in power saw the largest expansion of the settlements since they began in 1968.)

In 1998, Israel began construction on a new settlement named Har Homa, on a West Bank hillside known as Jabal Abu-Ghneim, lying between Jerusalem and Beit Sahour. It caused enormous opposition because it was the final link in a ring of settlements surrounding East Jerusalem that together served to cut off Arab East Jerusalem from the rest of the West Bank. It led to new UN debates about the settlements as a violation of the Geneva Conventions. But the protests led nowhere, building continued, and by mid-2002 Israeli Jewish residents were filling the gleaming white stone, ultra-modern settlement apartments.

From the beginning of Oslo until 2002, the settler population almost doubled. While the US-backed road map of 2003 called for a freeze in settlement construction as an Israeli "confidence-building measure," the expansion continued. In 2024, the Israeli settler population in the occupied territories topped 723,000—about 500,000 in the West Bank and 223,000 in Arab East Jerusalem.

The continued existence and expansion of the colonial settlements make ending the occupation enormously difficult. All the settlements—whether huge city-settlements like Ma'ale Adumim or the small "outposts" established outside Israeli government procedures—violate the Geneva Conventions, which specifically prohibit the transfer of anyone from the occupying country to the occupied territory; they constitute a war crime.

Further, the settlements, and the settlers-only or "bypass roads" that connect them and link them to cities inside Israel, and especially the Apartheid Wall built on West Bank land, all serve to divide the territories into separate cantons surrounded by Israeli troops and prevent the creation of a contiguous Palestinian state. These roads, and much of the settler infrastructure, mostly built during the Oslo period, have been constructed on confiscated Palestinian land and funded with United States tax money. By the 2020s, settlement construction and expansion had made the possibility of a viable, contiguous Palestinian state virtually impossible.

What would a Palestinian "state" as determined by Oslo/Camp David have looked like?

In October 1995, a year after winning the Nobel Prize for Peace for ostensibly agreeing to a two-state solution in the Oslo Accords, Israeli Prime Minister Yitzhak Rabin declared Israel would not return to its 1967 borders as required under international law. He said Jerusalem would remain unified under exclusive Israeli sovereignty, and that most of the settlements would remain. Further, he described the Palestinian "entity" to be created as something "less than a state."

What Israel proposed at Camp David in August 2000 (the first occasion when final status issues were directly negotiated) was a Palestinian "state" in something approaching 80 percent of the West Bank plus Gaza. The capital would not be in Jerusalem, although some limited municipal authority in Palestinian neighborhoods might be granted.

The 20+ percent of the West Bank that Israel would keep would be made up of the settlements, military bases, and, crucially, the bypass roads that divide the West Bank into separate regions. It was as though a family's house had been occupied against their will for many years, and they were suddenly told that they could have most of the rooms back, but the occupier was going to keep control of the hallways between the rooms and would control who or what was allowed into or out of every room. How much of a home would that be?

Israel proposed maintaining control of two major east–west highways, which would cut the West Bank into three completely separate, noncontiguous areas. Key water sources and underground aquifers would remain under Israeli control, as would external borders and air space. About 20 percent of the West Bank settlers, primarily from small isolated settlements, would be resettled inside Israel; the other 80 percent, including the large settlement blocs, would remain under Israeli jurisdiction and under the protection of the Israeli army; the Palestinian state would have no authority over the settlers. Newer versions of this Sharon plan, agreed to by Sharon and Bush in the April 2004 letter exchange and later known as the "convergence" plan of Sharon's successor, Ehud Olmert, remained official Israeli policy until the summer 2006 war in Gaza and Lebanon changed the political equation. The Israeli version of a solution was not for two states: it was for one state and one diminished, non-sovereign, non-state entity made up of dozens of small noncontiguous pieces of land all under the control of the existing state.

What happened at Camp David? Why did it fail?

The Camp David summit reflected an almost desperate effort by President Clinton in 2000 to salvage the failing Oslo peace process before the end of his second term. Although Oslo was not a US diplomatic initiative, Washington had taken on sponsorship of the process, and the September 1993 Rabin-Arafat signing ceremony remained the high point of Clinton's presidency. There is little question that by the end of 2000, the president was eager for a new photo op to burnish his scandal-tarnished place in history. Ehud Barak, Israel's then prime minister, whose lackluster term was also coming to an end, persuaded Clinton to convene the ill-prepared summit.

Camp David reflected the failure of Oslo's seven-year-long "peace process." Palestinian lives had deteriorated, unemployment was up, incomes were down, military checkpoints, house demolitions, and dispossession had all increased, and the euphoria that had greeted the White House handshake seven years earlier had turned into bitter resentment and rising anger. Until Camp David, Israeli and Palestinian negotiators had never even opened talks on the difficult final status issues. Clinton's view was that by leapfrogging over the "interim" issues and going straight to the fundamentals—state and borders, settlements, Jerusalem, and refugees—it might be possible to rescue the process and, in the process, his legacy.

But that would have been possible only if the US was prepared to demand serious concessions from Israel, its longstanding ally and the holder of all the cards. It would have required the US to negotiate on the basis of international law, not on the basis of maintaining the power of the occupier. Instead the Clinton administration continued the Oslo assumptions as though the talks were between two equal partners who bore equal power and responsibility to make compromises and concessions, instead of between an occupying power obligated to abide by international humanitarian law, and an occupied population entitled to protection under that same legal system.

In fact, the problem at Camp David was precisely that the disparity of power that had long characterized Israeli–Palestinian negotiations remained unchallenged; President Clinton did nothing to try to balance the thoroughly lopsided playing field. The talks persisted for two weeks, through sleepless nights and intense days, through Bill Clinton's hasty departure for the G8 summit in Okinawa and his hurried return. The official post-summit statement issued jointly by the Palestinian, Israeli, and American sides called the talks "unprecedented in both scope and detail." But in the end, they failed anyway.

Didn't Israel make the most generous offer in history to the Palestinians? Why did they reject it?

President Clinton had promised both parties that he would not blame either side if the talks collapsed. But when the talks broke down, he pointed his finger squarely at Yasir Arafat and the Palestinians. Perhaps the most widely repeated claim after Camp David was that of Palestinian rejection of Barak's "generous offer." It was, we were told over and over again, the most generous offer any Israeli official had ever made.

That statement, technically, was true. It was also, however, absolutely irrelevant. The standard against which any serious diplomatic offer made by a country illegally occupying another must be judged is not how well it compares to earlier offers made by that same occupying power; it must be judged against the requirements of international law. And from that standard, Barak's offer was far from generous. The "generous offer" was, as one of Clinton's negotiators at Camp David, Rob Malley, put it in the *New York Times*, "a myth."

More important than the comparison to earlier Israeli offers was the fact that, according to Malley, it was simply not true that "Israel's offer met most if not all of the Palestinians' legitimate aspirations." That was the reason Palestinians rejected the offer. One can certainly question the wisdom of a diplomatic tactic that did not provide an immediate counter-proposal to an unacceptable offer. But there should be little difficulty in understanding why Palestinian negotiators would reject an offer of disconnected pieces of territory amounting to only 80 percent of the remaining 22 percent of historic Palestine; a network of roads, bridges, and tunnels accessible only to Israeli settlers and permanently guarded by Israeli soldiers; permanent loss of water resources; no shared sovereignty in Jerusalem; the right of return for refugees not even up for discussion; and with 80 percent of the illegal settlers to remain in place.

What would a real, comprehensive peace have looked like at Camp David?

A comprehensive peace would have called for an end to Israeli occupation—all the occupation, withdrawing Israeli troops from all of the West Bank and Gaza, returning Israel's borders to those of June 4, 1967. It would have called for an independent Palestinian state in the entire West Bank and Gaza Strip, with the Palestinian capital in East Jerusalem and the entire city of Jerusalem open between the two countries. "Independent Palestinian state" would have meant actual, not symbolic sovereignty, control of water resources and borders, control of its own economy, and the right to a military force. It would have announced the closure of all settlements as Israeli military enclaves, with settlers given the option of moving back to Israel or remaining in their settlement towns as ordinary citizens of the new Palestinian state: equal, with no privileges. It would have recognized the Palestinian right of return and opened negotiations on how best to implement that right. It would have created security guarantees for both the Israeli and Palestinian peoples, perhaps including international assistance in monitoring borders. As called for in the 2002 Saudi-Arab League peace proposal, normalization of relations between Israel and all the Arab countries would follow the end of Israel's occupation.

Then, the hard work of rebuilding a shattered economy and shattered society in Palestine, and rebuilding shattered lives in both Palestine and Israel, could have begun.

Wasn't the famous 1993 handshake on the White House lawn supposed to end the conflict between Israel and the Palestinians?

The handshake between Israeli Prime Minister Yitzhak Rabin and Palestinian leader Yasir Arafat, at the urging of President Bill Clinton who presided over the ceremonies, accompanied the signing of the first part of what became known as the Oslo Accords. The Declaration of Principles (DOP) outlined a new relationship between the two sides, following more than a year of secret negotiations held in the Norwegian capital under the auspices of its government.

The agreement signed September 13, 1993, between the PLO and Israel did not bring an independent Palestinian state into being; it did not call for an end to Israeli occupation or even use the word occupation. But it did transform the terrain on which the diplomatic and political efforts to end the conflict would be waged.

For the Palestinians, the DOP brought about two important goals. First was recognition of the PLO as the representative of the Palestinian people. Although the weakness of the PLO is widely discussed, the importance of this recognition should not be forgotten: It reversed a longstanding Israeli policy that rejected the PLO because it represented the Palestinians as a separate and whole people, including all those inside and outside Israel and the occupied territories; therefore, it meant Israel's recognition that the solution to the conflict could not be limited only to those Palestinians living under occupation in the West Bank and Gaza—it had to include the rights of refugees. It also called for redeployment of Israeli troops out of the Palestinian cities and population centers.

But it did not call for an end to military occupation, or even a withdrawal of troops (the troops remained throughout the occupied territories, on the roads, surrounding towns and villages, etc.). But for a while, until the re-occupations of Palestinian cities in 2002, it represented a major security improvement in the lives of ordinary Palestinians, who could now go to work or send their children to school without worrying about Israeli soldiers camped on their roofs or in the road in front of their houses. The DOP, however, did not include Israeli recognition of the Palestinian right to freedom, equality, or an independent state.

For the Israelis, the DOP brought official recognition by the Palestinians of Israel's right to exist, and a renunciation of terrorism and armed struggle. It opened the door to an end to the Arab boycott and the beginning of normalization of Israel's relations with Arab neighbors. That meant the opening of trade relations with surrounding countries, a potentially huge boon for Israel's high-tech advanced economy. It also allowed Israel to renege on its responsibility, as the occupying power, for the economic and social needs of the Palestinian population—all without ending actual Israeli control over the occupied territories.

Didn't the US support the creation of the Palestinian Authority? Why did the US treat it differently than the PLO, which Washington usually tried to undermine or sideline?

The Palestinian Authority was a product of the Oslo process, which began with the signing of the Israeli–Palestinian Declaration of Principles on the White House lawn in September 1993. While Oslo grew out of a secret, initially unofficial diplomatic track initiated by Norway, the US quickly took over as the main sponsor, acting as overseer of the process and, tacitly, patron of the Palestinian Authority itself.

The US saw the PA as a useful tool for accomplishing a key US goal: stability and normalization in the occupied Palestinian territories. The PA's authority was limited politically and geographically, and derivative ultimately of Israeli power. Israel viewed the PA largely as an agency that would be responsible for organizing social and economic life in the Palestinian territories, including schools, health, welfare, etc., thus alleviating Israel's obligation under the Geneva Conventions to take care of the lives of the occupied population, but without allowing any real power to devolve to the Palestinian Authority that might have made that possible. Later, when Palestinian armed resistance to the occupation escalated around 2002, and especially with the emergence of suicide bombing attacks inside Israel, both Israel and the US began to view the PA as a security agency, whose job would not be to protect the lives and safety of Palestinians living under occupation but to prevent any attacks on Israel. It was as though the Palestinian Authority was to serve as a surrogate for Israel's own power—assigned the job of keeping Palestinians under control.

Unlike the PA, the PLO was a product of the Palestinians themselves. While it initially operated under the influence of Arab governments, the PLO was from the beginning made up of indigenous Palestinian resistance organizations, and its own history was that of a nationalist movement fighting against an occupying power. Its means of fighting, both military and diplomatic, were similar to those of many other liberation movements, particularly during the anti-colonial wars of the 1960s and '70s.

The US, as was true in so many other cases of liberation movements fighting against US allies, identified the PLO as a "terrorist" organization, the same brush that the US used to tar the African National Congress and its leader, Nelson Mandela.

As a result, despite UN and widespread international recognition of the PLO as the sole legitimate representative of the Palestinian people, the US refused until late 1988 to recognize or negotiate with the organization. Instead, the US backed Israeli efforts to anoint various non-PLO Palestinian leaders and notables as the "acceptable" Palestinians, and US-led diplomatic efforts failed.

Why did violence break out again in 2000? What was the second intifada, and how was it different from the first intifada of 1987–1993?

By the late 1990s, Palestinian hopes that the Oslo process would finally lead to an end to occupation and creation of an independent Palestinian state had pretty much collapsed. Israeli repression was escalating.

The second uprising, or intifada, began in September 2000. While the immediate spark was General Ariel Sharon's deliberately provocative walk across the Haram al-Sharif, the third holiest site of Islam, in occupied East Jerusalem, the uprising's real origins had far more to do with the failed peace process and the dashed hopes and deteriorating lives of Palestinians living under occupation than with any particular incitement.

Israel had increasingly escalated the weapons it deployed against the Palestinians. Numerous respected human rights organizations, including Amnesty International, Human Rights Watch, and Physicians for Human Rights documented Israeli soldiers employing excessive force in their suppression of Palestinian demonstrators. Their reports cited the use of live ammunition against unarmed civilians, attacks on medical personnel and installations, the use of snipers with high-powered rifles, and attacks on children.

In September 2000, President Bill Clinton's end-of-term effort to reach a Palestinian–Israeli agreement at a Camp David summit ended in failure. The second uprising, was sparked on September 27, 2000, by then Israeli Prime Minister Ariel Sharon's decision to walk, accompanied by about a thousand armed Israeli troops, on the Haram al-Sharif, or Noble Sanctuary, the Muslim holy site in East Jerusalem. (The complex is also known as the Temple Mount, the holiest site for religious Jews because the most sacred temple in Judaism was once located here—and some Jews believe the Western Wall, which borders the Haram al-Sharif, is a remnant.) The next day, Israeli troops opened fire on Palestinian protesters, killing several, some on the steps and inside the doorway of the al-Aqsa Mosque. What came to be called the "al-Aqsa Intifada" began that day.

Unlike the first intifada, in which they were unarmed, this time Palestinians used small arms, mainly rifles, against Israeli soldiers, tanks, and sometimes settlers. They also fired Qassam rockets that hit both military and civilian targets inside Israel. As the situation became more desperate, some young people acted as suicide bombers, attacking either military checkpoints in the occupied territories or civilian gathering spots inside Israel itself. As the level of violence escalated, the widespread, society-wide mass participation of Palestinians that characterized the first Intifada, largely ended.

As the al-Aqsa Intifada ground on, Israel escalated to the use of tank-mounted weapons, helicopter gunships firing wire-guided missiles on buildings and streets to carry out targeted assassinations, and finally F-16 fighter bombers, which dropped 2,000-pound bombs in refugee camps and on crowded apartment buildings, resulting in significant civilian casualties.

The second intifada began seven years after the first ended with the signing of the Oslo accords in 1993. Oslo did not realize the actual goals of the first intifada—the end of occupation and creation of an independent Palestinian state—but for a while it did hold out the hope that the new diplomatic "peace process" might actually lead to such a result. So the nonviolent uprising—the mass mobilizations, daily commercial strikes, widespread tax resistance, and children throwing stones at Israeli tanks that characterized the first intifada—largely came to a halt with the signing of Oslo's Declaration of Principles on the White House lawn.

In the seven long years that followed, the so-called peace process ground on with little result. Especially after the collapse of the Israeli–Palestinian summit sponsored by President Bill Clinton at Camp David in August 2000, Palestinians faced the unfortunate reality that Oslo's diplomacy had been much more about process than about peace. Palestinians' living conditions and economy had all seriously deteriorated throughout the Oslo years. Israel's military occupation had become increasingly harsh: closures preventing Palestinians from entering Israel were expanded to prevent travel within and between the West Bank and Gaza; military checkpoints proliferated throughout the maze of Israeli control and partial limited Palestinian authority; house demolitions continued; and settlement construction nearly doubled throughout the occupied territories after Oslo.

The second intifada was the response to those lost hopes. Initially it took similar forms to the first intifada—mass protests in the streets against Israeli military checkpoints surrounding Palestinian cities characterized the first weeks' mobilization. But the Israeli response was far more brutal than it had been during the first intifada; young stone-throwing protesters the day after Sharon's provocative visit to the Haram al-Sharif were met with withering fire, killing four and wounding hundreds on the steps and even inside the mosques. The Israeli military immediately began using live fire and tank-fired weapons where once tear gas and rubber bullets might have been used first, and soon helicopter gunships and US-supplied F-16 fighter bombers became regular parts of the Israeli arsenal in the occupied territories.

By March 2002, Amnesty International reported that over a thousand Palestinians had been killed; more than 200 of them were children.

In response, Palestinians changed their tactics. The mass street demonstrations largely ended as the lethal price exacted by the Israelis for marches and stone-throwing rose. Instead, small armed Palestinian factions took over in challenging the Israeli military occupation forces. Since the Oslo process had created the Palestinian Authority, there were now armed Palestinian police and security forces, and they used their arms both to protect Palestinian demonstrators and civilians, and sometimes to challenge directly the checkpoints and Israeli soldiers. One result was that killing on both sides escalated—but the deaths and injuries were disproportionately Palestinian (about four times as many), and initially the Israeli victims were almost all soldiers and settlers inside the occupied territories. Small numbers of young Palestinians carried out suicide attacks against Israeli military and in some cases civilian targets.

As the intifada settled into a kind of war of attrition, twenty-four-hour shoot-to-kill curfews were imposed on Palestinian cities and villages for long periods, imprisoning people in their homes. That reality, along with the escalating violence and the increasing role of the small armed factions, largely ended the mass public participation in the streets that had characterized the first intifada.

What was the George W. Bush administration's Middle East policy all about?

Immediately after the September 11, 2001, attacks on the World Trade Center and the Pentagon, the Bush administration appeared to distance itself from Israel. Bush's need to maintain active support from Arab and Islamic governments in the "global war on terror" briefly usurped the usual intensity of the US's warm embrace of Israel, although the economic and strategic backing of Israel remained quietly unchanged. Fearing even greater distancing, Israeli spokespeople launched a near-frenzied campaign, claiming unparalleled unity with Americans as common victims of terrorism and common Arab/Muslim enemies. For a while that pressure campaign didn't change the rhetoric, and in November 2001 both Secretary of State Colin Powell and President Bush himself, at the UN General Assembly, paid significant attention to words the Palestinians and—more strategically—Arab governments and their restive populations, wanted to hear. Bush's call for a "state of Palestine" and Powell's "the occupation must end" appeared to herald a new, maybe even close-to-even-handed, approach for US diplomacy.

But that relative evenhandedness was not to last. As it became less important to maintain the pretense of an international military coalition in Afghanistan (since major cities under Taliban rule were already falling to the US and its allies), the tactical pendulum swung back, and Washington returned to a more public embrace of Israel and Prime Minister Ariel Sharon. This took the form of an announced intention to "reengage" in the "peace process." The first messenger was General Anthony Zinni, whose two brief visits to the Middle East at the end of 2001 ended in failure. For a while, the administration appeared unconcerned with the escalating violence, appearing to believe, against all evidence, that Palestine could burn, the supply of desperate young suicide bombers heading into Israel could remain unending, and yet the crisis would somehow stay contained.

But then, by about February 2002, Iraq reemerged as a central feature of US regional efforts. The stakes were rising; a new round of regional shuttle diplomacy was required to lay out the requirements and lay down the law to Washington's Arab allies regarding the need for them to support a US attack on Iraq. General Zinni wasn't quite high enough in the administration hierarchy for this one, so into the breech stepped Vice President Dick Cheney, an experienced Middle East hand from his years as secretary of defense in the elder Bush's administration. (Actually, Cheney's oil-driven loyalties were clear long before: as a member of the House of Representatives, Cheney supported the 1981 sale of AWACS planes to Saudi Arabia, despite powerful Israeli opposition, and in 1979, he voted against the windfall profits tax on oil company revenues.)

In the wake of September 11, with dependent and already compliant Arab regimes virtually falling over each other to climb on board the Bush "anti-terrorism" train, the administration seemed to anticipate that Cheney's job would be effortless. Sure, there might be some unease in the palaces over how to deal with Arab populations already raging about the rapidly deteriorating crisis in the West Bank and Gaza, but it was assumed that however much they twitched and weaseled, the US's Arab allies would eventually stand—however reluctantly—with Washington against Iraq.

As it turned out, it wasn't quite so easy. The Israeli–Palestinian conflict stood in the way. While there was little doubt that at the end of the day the Arab kings, emirs, princes, and presidents would indeed do as their patron ordered, public opinion throughout the Arab world had hardened not only against Israel and its occupation, but against Israel's global sponsor, the United States. Arab governments from Egypt to Jordan to Saudi Arabia and beyond, already facing severe crises of legitimacy, might do as they were told by the Bush administration, but they would pay a very high price domestically for their alliance with Washington. Israel's escalation in the occupied territories offered what seemed to provide an easy dodge for the Arab royals: "How can you even talk to us about supporting your invasion and overthrow campaign against Iraq when Palestine is burning and you are doing nothing?"

Shortly before Cheney's Air Force Two plane took off, someone in Washington realized what was about to happen, so to avoid embarrassment to the vice president, General Zinni was sent back to the region first. His mandate for Israel-Palestine had not changed, and there was virtually no chance he would "succeed," however that elusive word might be defined, but that was OK. His real goal had far more to do with developments in Arab capitals than those in Tel Aviv and Ramallah, where he began a shadow shuttle. Zinni was Cheney's political cover. The vice president could now point to Zinni's shuttle diplomacy to refute claims that the US was doing nothing to solve the Israeli–Palestinian crisis.

The goals of Washington's diplomatic "reengagement" in the region had far more to do with war in Iraq than with peace in Israel-Palestine. As it turned out, of course, the Iraq-focused plan didn't work either; dependent Arab rulers were simply not willing to concede prematurely and risk further destabilization or even potential threats to their regimes. Cheney's trip fizzled, and the Bush spin operation focused on convincing audiences inside and outside Washington that the vice president's trip had never been intended to consolidate support for an attack on Iraq.

Then it was Secretary of State Powell's turn. Following Cheney's failed trip, the Bush administration called a brief time-out in the new game of diplomatic engagement. The press focused largely on the problems of the messenger. Was General Zinni simply too far down in the hierarchy to have the requisite clout with Sharon and/or Arafat? Would Bush send General Powell, ratcheting up the four-star factor?

But what was largely left out of the debate was the reality that it was not the messenger but the mandate that would determine the success or failure of the mission. Zinni failed not because he wasn't of high enough rank, but because he had no mandate to seriously dictate terms to Israel. As it turned out, neither did Powell. Two suicide bombings in late March, killing dozens of Israeli civilians inside Israel, raised the stakes; Washington clearly was going to respond.

But before any new US decision was announced, March 29, 2002, brought an unprecedented Israeli military offensive across the West Bank, carried out with mostly US-provided tanks, helicopter gunships, armored bulldozers, and F-16s punching into Ramallah, Bethlehem, Nablus, Jenin, Tulkarem, and tiny villages in between. On the Israeli side at least, it looked like what UN Secretary General Kofi Annan called "a conventional war," even though it was the world-class Israeli army operating against civilians; Palestinian resistance, where there was any, was largely limited to small arms and homemade explosives.

At that point, Bush himself jumped into the fray. In a major speech in the White House Rose Garden on April 4, he announced he would send Secretary of State Powell to the region, and outlined a vision, if a bit skimpy and more than a bit blurry, of what a peaceful settlement might look like. "The outlines of a just settlement are clear," he said, "two states, Israel and Palestine, living side by side, in peace and security."

For long-term thinking, the words were all there: Israel must stop settlement activity, and "the occupation must end through withdrawal to secure and recognized boundaries …" Four days later, Bush said he had told Sharon, "I expect there to be withdrawal without delay." The words were strong. The key action, though, was limited to sending Powell back to the region. There was no real pressure on Israel: no cut in the billions in military aid, no brake on the pipeline of military equipment being used against civilians, no reversal of the Israel-backing veto in the Security Council preventing the deployment of international protection or even observer forces. Bush talked the talk of serious pressure, but he refused to walk the walk. (The contradiction would be repeated two decades later when President Joe Biden would repeatedly send his secretary of state and other officials to Israel, and make phone call after phone call to the Israeli prime minister, each time requesting a ceasefire, or urging more humanitarian aid to Gaza—all while continuing to send unlimited shipments of warplanes, bombs, tank ammunition, and more. Like Bush's talk, Biden's failure to walk the walk would lead to failure.)

The real limits of Bush's intentions were made clear in the timetable. Powell would go to the region, but he would take his time getting there. When Powell arrived first in Morocco, the young king greeted him by asking, "Why are you here, why aren't you in Jerusalem?"

Powell's languid pace, from Morocco to Madrid, to Jordan, to Egypt, before arriving almost a week later in Jerusalem, provided what amounted to a weeklong green light for Sharon's assault on the cities, villages, and especially refugee camps of the West Bank. Yet, when Powell returned from his fruitless shuttle, President Bush welcomed him home with the claim that US goals had been met, that the trip was a success, that all was well with the world. It was an upside-down, Alice in Wonderland moment, with Bush then announcing straight-faced that "I do believe Ariel Sharon is a man of peace."

Israel's assault gradually wound down in some of the West Bank refugee camps, even as tensions mounted around Bethlehem's besieged Church of the Nativity and Arafat's tank-encircled presidential compound in Ramallah. But the stated goal of the Bush administration, the aim of Zinni's, Cheney's, and Powell's shuttles, as well as those of the underlings who took over when the top officials went home, had failed. That objective, to stabilize the region sufficiently so that Arab regimes could safely endorse a US military strike against Iraq without fearing domestic upheaval, had not been reached.

And at home, the Bush administration faced its first serious foreign policy challenge from the right. Christian fundamentalists and other components of the Republican Party's hard-right edge moved into an even tighter embrace of Ariel Sharon's government, rejecting even Bush's rhetorical pretense of concern for Palestinian rights. Paul Wolfowitz, an ardent pro-Israel hawk and Bush's deputy chief of the Pentagon, was booed by tens of thousands of Christian "We stand with Israel" demonstrators when he had the audacity to mention in a brief aside that Palestinian children might be suffering too. The danger of a serious split within the Republican Party—with its farthest right wing and neoconservatives backing Israel, while the "moderates" clung to their traditional ties to big oil and the Arab regimes—loomed as a Texas-sized nightmare for the president.

By midsummer, Iraq war fever was epidemic in Washington. Competing battle plans for diverse military operations were leaked by competing administration factions to competing newspapers. Powerful Republicans in Congress, the pages of the *New York Times*, the State Department, former Republican officials, even the Joint Chiefs of Staff hesitated about or even rejected the increasingly belligerent war cries of the Pentagon's civilian leadership. But as the debate about Iraq wore on, supplanting most other international stories on the front pages and the news shows, the crisis in Israel-Palestine continued with no end in sight. There was no US effort to craft new peace talks—let alone taking direct US action such as cutting military aid—aimed at making real the president's rhetorical commitment to ending the occupation and creating an independent Palestinian state.

What was the Middle East "Quartet" created on the eve of the Iraq war, and what chance did it have to end the Israeli–Palestinian conflict?

As a US-British war against Iraq loomed, the US called together a diplomatic foursome—the US, Russia, the European Union, and the United Nations—known as the Quartet, in August 2002. The crisis resulting from Israel's reoccupation of Palestinian cities in the West Bank and Gaza Strip was at its height, and there was a global outcry demanding a solution. The Quartet, dominated by the US, created what it called a road map, ostensibly designed to be presented to the Israelis and Palestinians in a more or less take-it-or-leave-it fashion, to impose on the two sides an internationally sanctioned resolution of the conflict.

But just a few months later, the Bush administration began its attempt to redraw the map of the Middle East through its invasion of Iraq. The overthrow of the regime in Baghdad, the sacking of Iraq's cities, destroying much of its ancient history, and the devastation brought to the civilian population of the country dramatically reshaped regional politics, in ways still not fully apparent. Despite the Bush administration's claims of victory in Iraq, the new Middle East remained occupied and violent. The road map's goals were largely sidelined.

There were numerous serious problems and deficiencies in the road map. From its first phase on, it failed to achieve any of its major objectives, and certainly did not make any progress toward an end to the occupation and the establishment of an independent, sovereign, and viable State of Palestine.

The road map's failure was predictable. The most significant problem was that it was based on maintaining Israeli dominance over Palestinian rights, rather than being rooted in the requirements of international law. Beyond that, the so-called Quartet was not really a four-part partnership, but more like a solo act with three backup singers; US power easily dominated the other three. And because the rules of the Quartet dictated that decisions were made by consensus, the US had what amounted to a veto. It was particularly unfortunate that the United Nations was coerced into providing political cover to the US through its participation in the Quartet, a move that seriously discredited the global organization.

On March 14, five days before invading Iraq, Bush announced his personal commitment to the road map. That same day, US National Security Advisor Condoleezza Rice convened a meeting with US Jewish leaders to reassure them that American support for Israel was not in danger. "We will lead the process and not the Europeans," she told them. "We know you are worried about the Quartet, but we're in the driver's seat," she said. She was right. By early April 2003, General Sharon's government announced that Israel had fourteen "reservations" on the terms of the road map, and if they were not accepted, Israel would walk away from the negotiations. With war in Iraq raging, the road map dropped off the agenda.

Neither the United Nations nor any of the other Quartet members were even invited to attend the June 2003 Aqaba summit heralding the road map. And the "international monitoring team" announced at the summit was solely an American creation, to be staffed by CIA and Pentagon officers and headed by a Bush administration official.

How did the US war in Iraq impact the Palestinian–Israeli conflict?

In the run-up to the 2003 US invasion of Iraq, the Bush administration failed to win international backing or legitimacy for the war in the UN Security Council; there was widespread global recognition that the war would be illegal. But the US did not give up hope that other governments—particularly that of Britain's Tony Blair—would join its "coalition of the willing." Italy, Japan, Spain, and others were prepared to endorse the US-UK war despite broad public opposition in virtually every country, but they wanted a political trade-off too. In response, Bush and Blair announced the text of a new "road map" for Middle East peace, at a moment timed and orchestrated for maximum global visibility, highlighting the links between Iraq and Israel-Palestine just days before the Iraq war was launched. But actual diplomacy remained stalled.

In March 2003, the US, backed by the British, invaded and occupied Iraq; less than two months later, the UN Security Council recognized the US and UK as "occupying powers" in Iraq, with all the accompanying obligations under international law.

Under the Fourth Geneva Convention, the Palestinians of the West Bank, Gaza, East Jerusalem, and in 2003 the people of Iraq all constituted "protected" populations, living under foreign occupations. Throughout its years of occupation since 1967, Israel has engaged in practices that constitute serious violations of international law, including torture, extrajudicial assassinations, extended curfews and closures, house demolitions, the destruction of agricultural land and civilian property, expulsions, illegal imprisonment, and other forms of collective punishment. Even before the US invaded Iraq, the Pentagon and other US government agencies were looking to the Israeli occupation as a model for a future US occupation of Iraq—long before the Bush administration even admitted its plan to invade Iraq. Increasingly, the two occupations came to resemble each other, as the occupiers actively collaborated to consolidate their control over angry populations.

In April 2002, more than a year before the US invaded Iraq, Israel sent troops to fully re-occupy the West Bank, in complete violation of the terms of the Oslo agreement. The Israeli military's attack on the Palestinian refugee camp in Jenin led to the killing of dozens of Palestinian civilians, including seven women and nine children. According to Human Rights Watch, "Israeli forces committed serious violations of international humanitarian law, some amounting prima facie to war crimes." But the US viewed the Jenin attack as a model for its planned invasion of Iraq, and US military officials met with the Israeli military to learn the urban warfare techniques that Israel had used in Jenin. Two years later, in April 2004, the US used those same tactics in the attack on Fallujah in Iraq, including the widespread killing of women and children. In a reversed version of collaboration, Israel admitted using white phosphorous munitions during its 2006 war in Lebanon; the US military used white phosphorous, a weapon banned for use against civilians, in Iraq and had long been condemned for its continued use of it since the Vietnam War.

Further, the torture scandals involving US prisons at Abu Ghraib in Iraq, Guantanamo Bay, and in CIA "black sites" elsewhere reflected many of the same techniques Israel had long used against Palestinian prisoners. The Israeli High Court banned torture in 1999, but the Israeli Public Committee Against Torture documented 58 percent of Palestinian detainees reporting they had been subjected to the same techniques the US troops used against prisoners in the "global war on terror": beatings, being forced to remain in painful positions, being hooded for long periods, sleep and toilet deprivation, sexual humiliation, and more. The US general in charge of Abu Ghraib in the first months of the US occupation of Iraq told the BBC that Israeli agents were assisting US interrogators throughout the US-run prison system in Iraq.

The US military certainly did not need Israeli help to occupy another country. But Israel's years of occupation allowed it to provide the Pentagon with advice and training in tactics designed to take advantage of specific cultural, religious, and national Arab traditions. The US claims that its occupation of Iraq was somehow "democratizing" the entire Middle East, was countered by what people on the ground throughout the region actually saw: the expansion of occupations. Instead of new democracy, the US war and occupation in Iraq were viewed throughout the region as a parallel occupation to the US-backed Israeli occupation of Palestine.

By the time of the 2006 Israeli war against Hezbollah and Lebanon, an even clearer connection had emerged. The Israeli goals of attempting to wipe out all resistance to its control and domination of the region matched almost word-for-word the US goals being fought out on a global level in Iraq. In fact, the strategies had similar origins. In the early 1990s, a group of neoconservative American analysts and former policymakers collaborated on a strategic vision for US foreign policy, which became known as the Project for the New American Century, or PNAC. After the terrorist attacks of September 11, 2001, many of their ideas gained dominance, being included in the 2002 National Security Strategy document of President George W. Bush, which set the terms for the invasion and occupation of Iraq. But before that, back in 1996, several of the PNAC authors had traveled to Israel at the request of Benjamin Netanyahu, then a conservative and US-oriented Israeli politician making his first run for prime minister. Their strategy paper, called "Making a Clean Break: Defending the Realm," proposed an almost identical recipe for Israeli foreign policy: focus on military power rather than diplomacy, let all of Israel's neighbors know that force rather than negotiations would be the new basis for relationships, and make a "clean break" with all earlier peace processes, most notably the Oslo process, then in its third year. When Israel went to war against Lebanon in 2006 at the height of the US war in Iraq, many saw the "clean break" strategy coming to bloody life.

What is "transfer"? Why did talk of "transfer" of Palestinians increase during the build-up to war in Iraq?

Beginning in the spring of 2002, as war fever against Iraq began to heat up in Washington, the threat of "transfer" became a much more serious concern for Palestinians, and moved into the forefront of political discussion. The goal of controlling maximum territory with minimum numbers of Palestinians had been central to Israeli strategy since its founding. But it had long been deemed inappropriate in polite discussion in Israel to call openly for "transfer," Israel's prim euphemism for ethnic cleansing. Featured prominently in the Israeli media, the subject of at least one high-profile academic conference at one of Israel's most prestigious universities, "transfer" moved into the mainstream of political discussion.

Ethnic cleansing had long been a feature of Israeli policy in the occupied West Bank and Gaza Strip. Land expropriation, house demolition, denial of residency, and other practices all resulted in large numbers of Palestinians being forced out of their homes, many into permanent exile. Besides the massive expulsions that forced more than one million Palestinians into exile during the 1948 and 1967 wars, Israel had relied on official forced "transfer" as recently as 1994. At that time, Israeli troops arrested 415 Islamists from the occupied Palestinian territories, forced them into military helicopters and flew them into the hills of south Lebanon. There, without documents, without permission, and despite explicit rejection of the action by the Lebanese government, they were abandoned on the snow-covered hillsides.

The specific threat reflected in the newly aggressive public embrace of "transfer" was that, in the regional chaos resulting from the US war in Iraq and its aftermath, Israel might again forcibly expel large numbers of Palestinians. No one was sure what it might look like—perhaps it would be in the form of a punishment against a whole village from which an alleged suicide bomber came. Perhaps 500 or 1,000 targeted Palestinian individuals—political leaders, intellectuals, militants, or those Israel claimed to be militants—would be bused over the river into Jordan or flown over Israel's border into Lebanon.

General Ariel Sharon, elected prime minister of Israel in January 2001, had initially created the "Jordan is Palestine" campaign in 1981–82 that called for expelling all Palestinians out of the occupied territories and pushing them into Jordan. In 1989, soon-to-be Israeli Prime Minister Benjamin Netanyahu told students at Bar-Ilan University: "Israel should have exploited the repression of the demonstrations in China [referring to the Tiananmen Square protests], when world attention was focused on that country, to carry out mass expulsions among the Arabs of the territories." In 2002 polls showed that more than 40 percent of Israelis were in favor of such ethnic cleansing.

Since that time, explicit calls for "transfer" have become normalized in Israeli political life. Transfer—or ethnic cleansing—as a key component of Israeli policy of control of Palestinians in the interest of continued Jewish domination of the land has been a reality for decades. By July 2024, the International Court of Justice ruled that "Israel's policies and practices are contrary to the prohibition of forcible transfer of the protected population under the first paragraph of Article 49 of the Fourth Geneva Convention."

What was Israel's "convergence plan" for the West Bank, and why did President George W. Bush endorse Israel's unilateral 2004 plans to annex much of the West Bank?

In April 2004, President George W. Bush signed off on Prime Minister Ariel Sharon's unilateral plan to annex the major West Bank settlement blocs and repudiate the internationally recognized Palestinian right of return. The agreement, formalized in an exchange of letters, was a quid pro quo for Israel's decision to unilaterally withdraw the illegal Israeli settlers and redeploy the Israeli troops from the Gaza Strip.

In rejecting the Palestinian right of return and accepting the permanence of Israeli occupation of Palestinian land, Bush banished any claim that US policy aimed to achieve a serious and comprehensive solution to the Palestinian–Israeli conflict based on international law. The "new status quo" of US-recognized permanent Israeli occupation, no right of return, and no viable Palestinian state, set the terms for the next period.

The US backing of Israel's unilateral decision-making also returned Middle East diplomacy officially to its pre-1991 position, in which Palestinians were excluded from all negotiations. Israeli-US meetings become the substitute for Israeli–Palestinian talks, with the US free to concede Palestinian land and rights. As one PLO legal advisor told the New York Times, "Imagine if Palestinians said, 'O.K., we give California to Canada.' Americans should stop wondering why they have so little credibility in the Middle East."

The US endorsement reaffirmed Washington's willingness to violate international law, ignore the United Nations Charter, and undermine UN resolutions (including the often-cited Resolution 242, which unequivocally prohibits the acquisition of territory by force), to continue providing diplomatic and political protection to Israel. It violated the terms of the US-imposed but internationally endorsed "road map," which stipulated that Israel must freeze all settlement activity; to the contrary, Sharon stated explicitly that the six major settlement blocs should continue to grow and be strengthened.

What was the significance of Yasir Arafat's death?

Yasir Arafat, the long-time Palestinian leader who had become synonymous with the struggle and the movement he led, died on November 11, 2004. Whatever his weaknesses, and they were many, Arafat had played a crucial role in building a national identity and a movement that kept intact and unified the three disparate components of the Palestinian people: those living under Israeli occupation in the West Bank, Gaza, and East Jerusalem; those who remained as second-class citizens inside Israel; and those millions of refugees and exiles who languished in impoverished camps or lived scattered across the globe far from their homeland. He had been elected chairman of the Palestine Liberation Organization in 1969, and in 1996 was elected president of the Palestinian Authority, the quasi-governing structure in the West Bank and Gaza created by the 1993 Oslo peace process.

Throughout his political life, Arafat proved far more willing to shift and compromise his position than most international observers gave him credit for. After years of holding to the goal of establishing a democratic, secular state in all of Palestine, he led the PLO to its historic 1988 concession of recognizing Israel and accepting as a goal the creation of a Palestinian state limited to the West Bank, Gaza, and East Jerusalem—together comprising only 22 percent of the land of the historic British Mandate Palestine. He managed the transition from a liberation movement to the forms of governance, despite the lack of any real power or independence for the Palestinian Authority.

Perhaps his most important contribution was keeping the question of Palestine at the top of the global agenda to a degree unprecedented by any national liberation movement since Vietnam. Arafat went to the United Nations to demand recognition in 1974, and quickly won an observer seat in the global organization for the PLO. And when he declared a putative Palestinian "state" in 1988, in the context of recognizing Israel and accepting a two-state solution, Arafat's action was quickly followed by a diplomatic initiative that led to full diplomatic relations for Palestine with over 110 countries.

His death followed more than two years of an Israeli-orchestrated and US-backed campaign to isolate and marginalize Arafat in an effort to force even greater political concessions from the Palestinians. During Israel's spring 2002 offensive, which included massive assaults by ground troops reoccupying most West Bank cities, Arafat's presidential compound in Ramallah was attacked and largely destroyed by the Israel military. The compound remained besieged for ten days. Although Israeli officials claimed they did not intend to attack Arafat personally, they made clear that if he left the country, he would not be allowed to return. As a result, Arafat spent the next two years in his crumbling compound, leaving only to seek treatment in Paris in the last weeks before his death.

Despite relentless criticism from his own constituents as well as from international leaders, no Palestinian leader ever came close to Arafat's hold on the emotional loyalty of Palestinians of every political stripe. His last two years focused on ultimately failed efforts to maintain political and organizational coherence among the various PLO and Palestinian Authority security and political agencies, with Arafat's longstanding goal of leading a truly independent and viable Palestinian state giving way to the reality of presiding over an authority reduced to squabbling over crumbs of derivative power.

Many world leaders, particularly those in countries that had faced their own struggles for independence from colonial control, issued powerful statements of respect and shared grief at the news of Arafat's passing. But for Israel, the US, and other powerful countries, pro forma expressions of condolence quickly gave way to barely concealed statements of happiness that Arafat was gone from the scene. Only now, Western leaders claimed, could what was quickly anointed the "post-Arafat era" result in a chance for an Israeli–Palestinian peace— based on the assumption that any post-Arafat leader would be even more compliant to US–Israeli demands.

Didn't Israel's occupation of Gaza end with its withdrawal of settlers and redeployment of soldiers in 2005?

In 2002, Israel's prime minister, Ariel Sharon, announced his intention to "disengage" from the Gaza Strip, removing the 8,000 or so Israeli settlers and all soldiers from the territory and removing all settlement infrastructure. As the occupying power, Israel certainly had the unilateral obligation to end its occupation. That meant it was obligated to remove its soldiers and its illegal settlements (all the Gaza settlements, as well as all those in the West Bank and in occupied East Jerusalem, were and are illegal, built in violation of the Geneva Conventions), and stop the illegal acts such as the demolition of over 3,000 Palestinian houses since 2000.

But ending occupation does not mean only pulling out settlers, closing down colonial settlements, and redeploying occupation soldiers off Gaza's land. In international law, occupation is defined as effective control by an outside ruling force, regardless of numbers of troops or settlers on the ground. Sharon's action in Gaza was not designed to actually end Israel's occupation. It changed the nature of the occupation—from an armed presence on the ground to a siege, in which Gaza was sealed off by a militarized wall and soldiers who were redeployed from inside Gaza to surround the territory.

Following the Israeli military redeployment, Gaza's territory was free of Israeli soldiers and settlers, but remained under complete Israeli control: Israel continued to control Gaza's economy, withholding $50 million of Palestinian monthly tax revenues, prohibiting Palestinian workers from entering Israel, and controlling the Israeli and Egyptian border crossings into and out of Gaza to restrict all goods and people. Israel forcibly limited the range of Gaza's fleet of fishermen. It controlled Gaza's airspace and coastal waters, and continued to prohibit construction of a seaport or the rebuilding of the Gaza airport Israel had destroyed in a bombing raid in 2002. And after the election of the Hamas-led government in January 2006, Israel continued its air strikes and ground attacks on people and infrastructure throughout Gaza, and its almost nightly barrage of sonic sound-bombs across Gaza's population centers. Under international law, such a siege constitutes a continuation of occupation.

The redeployment was part of a strategically calculated plan to end Israeli–Palestinian negotiations, and to impose instead what Sharon called a "long-term interim solution," in which the Israeli occupation would be retooled to remain in place without ever reaching "final status" negotiations. Further, it would get rid of Israel's costly occupation of the impoverished and thirsty Gaza Strip, while gaining crucial US support for permanent annexation of huge swathes of territory in the far wealthier, more strategic, and water-rich West Bank.

The carefully planned removal of Gaza settlers in the summer of 2005 showed a powerful picture of grieving families being forcibly—if gently—removed from their homes. Israel offered each settler family hundreds of thousands of dollars in compensation, and new homes were quickly made available in Israeli towns or, ironically, in equally illegal West Bank settlements. Groups of settler families wishing to remain together were assured of neighboring homes wherever they wished to move. It was a humane response to the human cost of forcible relocation (although all the settlers knew they were living on occupied territory in violation of international law). And it was a far cry from the get-out-with-whatever-you-can-carry-in-fifteen-minutes warnings that had accompanied most, and the complete lack of compensation in all, of Israel's expropriations, expulsions, and house demolitions of Palestinians throughout the West Bank, East Jerusalem, and Gaza Strip.

Conditions in Gaza rapidly deteriorated; by early 2006, around the time of the Palestinian elections, UN and other humanitarian agencies were reporting widespread hunger. Unemployment spiked over 60 percent in many areas, and long-term Israeli closures of the border crossings meant virtually no Gazan produce could reach the market. The rate of absolute poverty—of people living on less than $2 per day—rose to 78 percent, an unprecedented level.

In June 2006, Israel responded to a border skirmish in which an Israeli soldier was captured, with a full-scale armed assault on Gaza, including air, sea, and ground attacks. Israeli commandos carried out midnight raids in Gaza (as well as many West Bank cities), kidnapping Hamas legislators and cabinet ministers of the Palestinian Authority. The *New York Times* quoted Prime Minister Ehud Olmert saying that despite the earlier claims of "disengagement," Israel would continue to act militarily in Gaza as it wished: "We will operate, enter, and pull out as needed."

The Gaza settlements, while economically valuable for Israel (not surprising given that the 8,000 settlers controlled 40 percent of the land and 40 percent of the water of the then 1.4 million Palestinian residents of the Gaza Strip), were still costly, because the small number of settlers depended on significant numbers of Israeli troops for protection. So giving up the Gaza settlements was a small price to pay for consolidating Israeli control over the much more valuable land of the West Bank, and guaranteeing permanent US support for Israeli annexation of the huge West Bank settlement blocs and even more land encompassed within the Apartheid Wall.

This strategy of giving up Gaza settlements to annex West Bank land and settlements became known as the "convergence plan" when Ehud Olmert took over as prime minister in March 2006, after the stroke that had ended the political career of Ariel Sharon. Following Israel's serious defeat in the Lebanon war that summer, Olmert's popularity quickly declined, and his plan to evacuate tens of thousands of West Bank settlers, while leaving 80 percent of the 240,000 settlers in place, evaporated. Israelis no longer seemed willing to envision even a small-scale symbolic withdrawal to provide political cover to its much larger-scale annexation of prime Palestinian land. Instead, a potentially indefinite continuation of the unstable status quo loomed.

Why did the Palestinians choose Hamas in the January 2006 elections?

The January 2006 Palestinian elections were an imperfect exercise in democracy, since they were held under conditions of military occupation. However, it is clear that the results represented a reasonably accurate assessment of public opinion. International observers like former President Jimmy Carter, representing the US-based Carter Center—offered praise, calling the election "peaceful, competitive, and genuinely democratic."

There are strong indications that the huge turnout for Hamas was not entirely or even primarily a statement of support for an Islamist social agenda or for their prior military attacks. (Hamas had initiated and maintained its own unilateral ceasefire from early 2005.) Rather, it was a call for change in the Palestinians' untenable situation, a rejection of the status quo. In his report immediately after the election, Carter recognized that "Fatah, the party of Arafat and Abbas, has become vulnerable because of its political ineffectiveness and alleged corruption." At the time, many Palestinians said that they could have accepted the existing leadership even with its corruption, if only Fatah had any success in ending the occupation, and could have accepted its political failures if only it were not so corrupt. But the combination of corruption and failure was simply too much, and Hamas reaped the electoral results.

Israeli leaders immediately responded with claims that they now had "no partner for peace," stated that they would not negotiate with a Hamas-led Palestinian Authority, and called for an international boycott of the new government. But those claims were a red herring—Israel had not been negotiating with the existing (Fatah-led, non-Hamas) Palestinian Authority for more than two years, having chosen instead a strategy of unilateral action to redraw borders and impose an Israeli "solution" to the conflict.

The US, having already accepted the unilateral, no-negotiations approach of Prime Minister Ariel Sharon, including Israel's rejection of the US-backed "road map," also promoted the Israeli call for an international boycott and sanctions against the Palestinians. And it was US pressure on Europe, Arab states, and many other US allies to accept the boycott that was largely responsible for the humanitarian crisis that soon hit the occupied territories, especially Gaza. For example, when some Arab banks announced plans to transmit humanitarian assistance donated to beleaguered Palestinians, the US announced that the US branches of those banks would face serious sanctions. Not surprisingly, the banks withdrew their plans, and the Palestinians did not get the funds.

The result was a dramatic rise in the already dangerous humanitarian crisis. In a rare joint statement in July 2006, UN agencies stated that they were "alarmed by developments on the ground, which have seen innocent civilians, including children, killed, brought increased misery to hundreds of thousands of people, and which will wreak far-reaching harm on Palestinian society. An already alarming situation in Gaza, with poverty rates at nearly eighty percent and unemployment at nearly forty percent, is likely to deteriorate rapidly, unless immediate and urgent action is taken."

The UN's overall coordinating body, OCHA (Office for Coordination of Humanitarian Affairs), called on Israel to allow UN deliveries of emergency supplies, but recognized that "humanitarian assistance is not enough to prevent suffering. With the [Israeli] bombing of the [Gaza] electric plant, the lives of 1.4 million people, almost half of them children, worsened overnight. The Government of Israel should repair the damage done to the power station. Obligations under international humanitarian law, applying to both parties, include preventing harm to civilians and destroying civilian infrastructure and also refraining from collective measures, intimidation and reprisals. Civilians are disproportionately paying the price of this conflict."

All of this was occurring for years before the October 7, 2023, Hamas-led attack from Gaza into southern Israel and the genocidal attack Israel launched in retaliation.

What were the reasons for and consequences of the Hamas-Fatah divide in 2007 and beyond?

From its origins, the Palestinian national movement has been composed of diverse, often-feuding factions. From the 1960s through the 1990s, the Palestine Liberation Organization, itself a coalition long dominated by the Fatah organization, was the centerpiece of Palestinian national life (see pages 23–26). Hamas, which emerged in Gaza in 1987 simultaneously with the first intifada, was never part of the historically secular PLO.

The PLO was ostensibly the official partner in all negotiations with Israel and the US, but in fact it was largely sidelined by the Palestinian Authority created in 1993 by the Oslo Accords. Until his 2004 death, Fatah leader Yasir Arafat served simultaneously as PLO chairman and PA president, as has his successor, Mahmoud Abbas. At least since

2000, Fatah lost support as it was widely viewed as having failed to end the occupation and faced widespread accusations of corruption. Over time the PLO's secular left parties largely lost much of their vision and strategic direction for the movement as a whole and became less influential. Inside the occupied territories and among Palestinian refugees in the diaspora, new civil society organizations emerged with new approaches to national and global strategy. Most of those organizations and strategies did not focus on broad "final status" positions, such as the one-state/two-state debate, but rather various rights-based approaches including the Boycott, Divestment, and Sanctions (BDS) campaign. But the Fatah-led PLO-PA has continued to control most Palestinian diplomacy, largely excluding both Hamas and much of civil society.

After Hamas won parliamentary elections in both Gaza and the West Bank in 2006, the Islamist organization formed a government dominated by independent technocrats. However, Israeli-US demonization and increasing Israeli repression made real governing power impossible. The Israeli-US position, backed by Europe, was to isolate the Palestinians, particularly Hamas, until they explicitly agreed to recognize Israel as a Jewish state, implement all earlier agreements, and renounce violence. There were no matching demands that Israel implement earlier agreements, recognize a Palestinian state, abide by international laws, or cease its "targeted assassinations" in Gaza and military attacks in Gaza and the West Bank.

In February 2007, Palestinians formed a national unity government, but Fatah-Hamas tensions continued to mount. A short, brutal civil war broke out in June 2007, leading to the routing of Fatah supporters from Gaza, the dissolution of the unity government, and a greatly tightened boycott and Israeli siege of Hamas-controlled Gaza.

The Western media widely described this as a "Hamas coup," but the situation was much more complicated. *Vanity Fair* documented a covert action approved by President Bush and implemented by Secretary of State Condoleezza Rice and Bush's Middle East adviser Elliott Abrams to provide millions of dollars of US weapons and military training to Fatah. When Congress balked at the spending, the Bush administration turned to key Arab allies for funds and weapons. In a confidential report, the UN representative to the so-called Quartet, Alvaro de Soto, stated that "the US clearly pushed for a confrontation between Fatah and Hamas." He added that the US envoy twice declared, "I like this violence."

Shortly after the Hamas victory, the Bush administration signed a 10-year, $30 billion military aid package for Israel, 75 percent of which would go to US arms dealers. President Obama agreed to implement the deal.

What were Israel's attacks on the Gaza flotillas all about?

Israel's siege of Gaza was first imposed in 2006 after Hamas won Palestinian elections, and then tightened in 2007 after it took up its authority in Gaza. The borders of the Gaza Strip were closed to all exports; imports of food and medicine were severely limited; construction, electrical repair, educational, and cultural materials were almost entirely cut off; and most Palestinians were prohibited from entering or leaving. The siege created a serious and escalating humanitarian crisis (see pages 128–130). The US backed the Israeli action, and the United Nations was unable to respond, so Palestinian and international civil society took the initiative to try to break the blockade. Beginning in August 2008, the flotilla movement's international activists began sending ships filled with humanitarian goods to the besieged and isolated Gaza Strip, whose coastal waters were patrolled by the Israeli military, which prohibited Gazans from leaving and all international traffic from entering.

The ships and passengers were unarmed and were inspected to prevent contraband by authorities at the various European ports from which they set sail. The first few ships, carrying food, medicine, and other humanitarian supplies as well as human rights activists, were allowed to reach Gaza. Later flotillas were surrounded, the ships forcibly boarded by the Israeli military in international waters, the ships, passengers' possessions and cargo confiscated, and passengers arrested, often beaten, and expelled from Israel.

But on May 31, 2010, the Israeli response to a new flotilla escalated. In the dead of night, heavily armed Israeli commandos, in speedboats and assault helicopters, attacked one of the boats, the Turkish-flagged *Mavi*

Marmara, bearing several hundred unarmed activists, in international waters of the Mediterranean. They killed nine activists, eight Turks, and one American, and wounded scores more. The *Mavi Marmara* and the other boats of the flotilla were commandeered by Israeli forces and brought to Israel, where the passengers were held in custody for days.

International media attention, which had been negligible regarding earlier flotillas, was riveted on the story. Despite Israeli efforts to portray its military assault as legal or even self-defense, international outrage grew. The attack created a major rift between Israel and its longtime ally Turkey. Thousands marched from the Israeli consulate to Istanbul's main square in the first hours after the attack, while thousands more took to the streets in Ankara, demanding international accountability and immediate action to end Israel's blockade of Gaza. President Abdullah Gul of Turkey stated that "from now on, Turkish-Israeli ties will never be the same. The incident has left a deep and irreparable scar." Turkey issued three demands to Israel as the price for restoring normal relations: apologize for the raid, organize an independent investigation, and, significantly, lift the blockade of Gaza. Israel refused, and faced the serious consequences of weakening its longstanding relations with NATO's only Muslim-majority country, ties that included Israeli access to water, a popular destination for Israeli tourists, joint military exercises, and a ready market for military exports.

The attack—especially the killing of unarmed non-Palestinians—increased global public and governmental anger towards Israel. The UN Security Council, pressured by the US, refused to condemn the Israeli attack, instead issuing a presidential statement, which does not carry the force of law, condemning the acts but without specifying Israeli responsibility. In September 2011, the UN commission established to investigate the flotilla attack issued its report. It made clear that Israel's use of force on board the *Mavi Marmara* and the treatment of those detained from the ship was excessive and unreasonable; acknowledged that forensic evidence indicated at least seven of the nine killed were shot in the head or chest, five of them at close range; recognized Israel's refusal to provide any accounting for the nine deaths; and called on Israel to compensate the families of those killed and seriously injured during and after the incident.

Israel responded to the outcry with an announcement that it was "easing" the siege of Gaza, allowing slightly more food, medicine, and building supplies into the beleaguered Strip, but the humanitarian crisis continued, and Gaza's residents remained effectively imprisoned.

The loss of Israel's alliance with Turkey and diminishing support from Europe were among the most visible consequences, along with a major spike in global activism challenging the blockade. Overall, Israel's flotilla attack represented a key loss for Israel in its campaign to legitimize its illegal occupation.

What was the basis for Israel's wars against Gaza from 2008–09 to 2021?

In 2006, all the European, US, and other international observers agreed that the Palestinian election in the OPT had been free and fair. But Hamas won the election, and in response, Israel closed all borders with the Gaza Strip.

An Israeli wall encircled the entire Gaza Strip, with the Israeli military in complete control of the air space, coastal waters, and all border crossings including the one into Egypt. Israel determined whether and how much food, fuel, parts for water treatment systems, medicine, and medical equipment reached Gaza. Under the siege, the situation for Gaza's already impoverished 1.5 million residents, 56 percent of whom were under the age of eighteen, quickly became even more dire. In spring 2008, a coalition of British humanitarian agencies called the crisis "worse than at any time since the beginning of the Israeli military occupation in 1967." And that was *before* the military assault that began in December 2008.

Israel also continued its military raids, air strikes, and "targeted assassinations" in Gaza. All of those actions violated the Geneva Conventions, which set out the obligations of an occupying power to the protected population of the territory it occupies. Air strikes violate the prohibition on collective punishment; assassinations are illegal; denial of food, medicine, etc., is prohibited. The military wing of Hamas resumed rocket fire against Israel, some of which violated international laws governing the right to resist (which limit resistance to military targets, not civilians).

Egypt took the lead in negotiating between Israel and Hamas, and in June 2008 a ceasefire was declared. For the next five months, the ceasefire largely held on the Palestinian side. As illustrated in a bar graph on the website of Israel's own Ministry of Foreign Affairs, earlier averages of up to 200 rockets per month fired into Israel dropped to an average of only two during the ceasefire. During the ceasefire, not a single Israeli was injured or killed. But during that same ceasefire, Israeli forces killed at least eighteen Palestinians in Gaza and ignored their commitment to open the border crossings.

On November 4, 2008, Israel effectively ended the ceasefire, killing six Palestinians in Gaza. The ceasefire officially expired December 26; Israeli air strikes and ground attacks in Gaza followed. Israeli officials claimed that the attack was an urgent response to the rocket fire. But former Mossad head Ephraim Halevy admitted that if protecting Israelis from rockets had really been the motivation, "opening the border crossings would have ensured such quiet for a generation."

On December 31, senior Israeli defense officials admitted to *Ha'aretz* that their government had "instructed the Israel Defense Forces to prepare for the operation over six months ago, even as Israel was beginning to negotiate a cease-fire agreement with Hamas." Rather than urgent necessity, the article identified "long-term preparation, careful gathering of information, secret discussions, operational deception and the misleading of the public" as the components of Israel's war strategy.

Israel's assault, named Operation Cast Lead, violated a range of international laws. According to the UN's Special Rapporteur on Human Rights in the Occupied Territories at that time, Professor Richard Falk, the attack itself was illegal because Israel had a viable nonmilitary alternative available to protect its people—returning to the ceasefire. The vastly disproportionate use of force was a separate violation of Geneva—a war crime.

According to the widely respected Palestinian Center for Human Rights in Gaza, during the twenty-two days of the assault, Israeli forces killed 1,417 Palestinians, of whom 926 were civilians, including 313 children and 116 women. Thirteen Israelis were killed, of whom only three were civilians; four of the Israeli soldiers were killed by friendly fire. Israeli forces directly attacked individuals, some waving white flags, as well as schools, hospitals, mosques, and—in a separate violation—attacked UN facilities and personnel. Israel's use of collective punishment, penalizing 1.5 million civilians for the actions of a small group of militants, violated Article 33 of the Fourth Geneva Convention. And Israel's use of certain weapons—including white phosphorous bombs and fléchette-filled bomblets—in civilian areas violated international prohibitions.

Israel's assault on Gaza could not have happened without Washington's direct support, then including approximately $3 billion a year in military aid, plus parts for attack planes and helicopters, and additional weapons contracts. The assault violated the US Arms Export Control Act, which prohibits US arms from being used for any purpose other than security inside a country's borders or for legitimate self-defense purposes. Israel's attack did not meet those limitations, and the US government confirmed it was fully aware of Israel's plans before the assault.

The UN Security Council addressed the attack only reluctantly, and its resolution (with the US abstaining) was narrow and limited. The General Assembly's position, despite efforts by Miguel d'Escoto, the GA president, and others to pass a much stronger resolution, echoed the weak Security Council approach (see pages 47–53). By using or threatening its veto and other pressures to protect Israel from being held accountable in the United Nations, the US was also complicit in Israeli violations.

A similar war erupted in December 2012. As it had done previously, Israel launched the attack shortly after the US elections and before the inauguration of President Obama, this time for his second term. Four days into the assault, Defense Minister Ehud Barak of Israel said, "this effort could not have been concluded without the generous and consistent support of the American administration led by President Obama." Once again, Israel used US-made and US-funded fighter jets and attack helicopters, so once again the US was complicit. As had been true in earlier Israeli assaults, and would continue right through the long Israeli war against Gaza that began in October 2023, one of Israel's targets of direct assassination in 2012 was a Palestinian negotiator, Ahmed Jabari, who was killed while overseeing Hamas's negotiations with Israel for a long-term truce.

And like before, the 2012 assault was not a response to some Palestinian action—it had been long planned. A year earlier, in 2011, the Israeli chief of staff had announced that Israel would soon need to launch another "swift and painful" attack on Gaza, that it must be "initiated by Israel" to restore what he called Israel's power of "deterrence." These Gaza offensives were long planned; they were not responses to Palestinian rockets.

Five days into the assault, Gilad Sharon, son of former Israeli prime minister Ariel Sharon, described in a *Jerusalem Post* op-ed what Israel should do before any ceasefire was considered: "We need to flatten entire neighborhoods in Gaza. Flatten all of Gaza. The Americans didn't stop with Hiroshima—the Japanese weren't surrendering fast enough, so they hit Nagasaki, too ... There should be no electricity in Gaza, no gasoline or moving vehicles, nothing. Then they'd really call for a ceasefire." It was almost a prediction of what the Israeli assault on Gaza that began October 2023 would look like.

The impact of the 2012 attack on Gaza was not far from what Sharon called for. But that assault took place while the uprisings of the Arab Spring were at their height, and one effect was that Israel at that time was far more isolated than the Palestinians. Tel Aviv could no longer count on US-backed dictatorships in the Arab world to provide secret support. Hamas broke its ties with the Syrian regime and reduced its ties with Iran as its strategic connections to the new Islamist-dominated government in Egypt as well as to Turkey took hold. And Hamas's new supporters in Cairo and Ankara were, for the moment, the same governments Washington most urgently needed to keep close. During the Israeli assault, Egypt's prime minister, the Tunisian foreign minister, the emir of Qatar, and foreign ministers of a number of other countries traveled to Gaza to stand with the Palestinians.

At the end of the week of fighting, the United Nations had documented at least 168 Palestinians killed by the US-backed Israeli military action, of whom 101 were civilians, including thirty-three children. Six Israelis were killed, four of whom were civilians. Gaza was once again devastated.

A year later, in 2013, analysts at the Begin Sadat Center for Strategic Studies, an influential Israeli think tank, wrote a paper about the

Gaza attacks titled "Mowing the Grass: Israel's Strategy for Protracted Intractable Conflict." The paper described these "occasional large-scale operations" as a "strategy of attrition ... not intended to attain impossible political goals." As Israel's summer 2014 war in Gaza was just beginning to escalate, the *New York Times* quoted Israeli officials breezily describing Israel's lethal attacks on Gaza as "mowing the grass." According to Yoav Gallant, a former military commander of Israel's southern district, which abuts Gaza, and defense minister during the 2023–24 war, "this sort of maintenance needs to be carried out from time to time, perhaps even more often." (Netanyahu fired Gallant in November 2024 for urging a ceasefire.)

Israel launched Operation Protective Edge in July 2014. According to the United Nations, during fifty days of Israeli air and land bombardment, at least 2,131 Palestinians were killed, of whom at least 1,473 were civilians, including 501 children. During the same period 71 Israelis (and one Thai guest worker in Israel) were killed, of whom 66 were soldiers.

As is always the case, the timeline and immediate origins of the one-sided war remained disputed. In the US, most mainstream voices claimed the run-up to the 2014 war began when three Israeli teenagers were kidnapped and killed in the West Bank on June 12. Without putting forward any evidence as to who was guilty of the crime, the Israeli government immediately blamed Hamas and launched an almost three-week-long series of raids against Palestinians across the West Bank. Israeli troops arrested more than 1,300 Palestinians, including children and twenty-eight members of the Palestinian parliament. None were charged with anything, but many remained in prison for months or longer. Hundreds of homes were raided, many destroyed. During that period, Israeli troops killed eleven Palestinians.

Even before the teenagers' bodies were found, egged on by ultra-right-wing elements within the Israeli parliament and government, racist calls for vengeance and cries of "death to the Arabs" exploded across Israel. Israeli planes carried out air strikes over Gaza for six nights beginning on June 13, the day after the teenagers went missing. Another casualty was sixteen-year-old Palestinian Mohammed Abu Khdeir, kidnapped in Jerusalem and burned to death on July 2 by a group of young Israelis.

In starting the clock with the kidnapping of the three young Israelis, most of the media coverage left out what was happening prior to that criminal act. Just a few weeks before, Israeli troops had killed two Palestinian teenagers in the West Bank. Virtually no media coverage ensued. There was also little coverage of the significant continuing violations of international law inherent in Israel's siege of Gaza. Hamas's primitive rockets fired into Israel also violated international law, since they cannot be aimed at military targets. There should have been accountability for all those violations.

However, Israel's violations of its obligations as the occupying power in Gaza were far deeper and broader. Israeli claims of self-defense could not hold, since Israel had an obligation to use nonmilitary methods of protecting its own population if feasible. If Israel's real goal was to protect its civilian population from the fear of Palestinian rockets, it would have called for an immediate ceasefire at the beginning of what would become a fifty-day war, because history showed very clearly that Israelis were safe during ceasefires. In the course of the ceasefire that began after Operation Cast Lead in January 2009 and lasted until the November 2012 Israeli assault on Gaza, 271 Palestinians were killed by Israeli air strikes, drones, planes, and helicopter attacks. No Israelis were killed by Palestinian rockets. Ceasefires protected Israelis, even if they didn't protect Palestinians very well. So the 2014 Israeli attack itself, launched by the occupying power obligated by the Geneva Conventions to protect the occupied population, was entirely illegal.

US support for Israel continued, and even escalated (along with the $3.1 billion in 2014 military aid, the US added $351 million extra military support right in the middle of the Gaza war). In complete violation of US law—including the Leahy Law prohibiting military aid to forces known for patterns of human rights violations—Washington continued to provide Israel carte blanche to use US-made weapons to attack Gaza: F-16s fighter jets, Apache helicopters, armored Caterpillar bulldozers, and more, all produced in the United States and purchased with US tax dollars.

And beyond the US support for Israel, Gaza and the Palestinians in general faced a return to international isolation. During the 2012 attack, with the Arab Spring at its height, Hamas had found powerful allies in Turkey and Egypt. Turkey's foreign minister traveled to Gaza during the bombing and pledged support for the people of Gaza, while the newly elected Muslim Brotherhood-backed government in Cairo kept the Rafah crossing between Gaza and Egypt open most of the time, helping Gazans survive the Israeli siege.

But by the time of the 2014 attack, all that was over. The Arab Spring was in crisis. The overlapping civil wars in Syria were broadening across the region, Iraq teetered on the precipice of a new civil war, and Libya had collapsed into violence and chaos in the wake of the NATO intervention. The 2013 coup in Egypt overthrew the elected government and installed a military regime once again, with a US-backed general with strong ties to Israel, as president. Egypt turned against Hamas, against Gaza, and the Rafah crossing remained closed. Once again Gaza remained besieged and alone.

The siege of Gaza continued. And the next major Israeli attack came seven years later. In May 2021, another Israeli assault began. First came major escalations in Israeli police and settler attacks against Palestinians in Jerusalem and across the West Bank. House demolitions forced Palestinians out of their homes in Sheikh Jarrah in East Jerusalem. In a deliberately provocative move, Israeli police raided the al-Aqsa Mosque, the third-holiest site in Islam, firing rubber bullets, tear gas, and stun grenades at worshipers praying around and even inside the mosque itself. Rocket fire from Gaza answered the assault, and Israel's major assault against Gaza took place while major attacks continued across the West Bank.

In Gaza, over eleven days of fighting, 232 Palestinians were killed, sixty of them children. The direct provocations on both sides were only a part of why Israel launched another full-scale raid. One reason was that Israel's military and strategic leaders believed the time was right to "mow the grass" again, to remind Palestinians just who was in control. Prime Minister Benjamin Netanyahu had another, more personal reason: as long as he was leading his country in war, he was safe from being recalled or defeated in an election. And once he was no longer prime minister, he would be back in court in four separate corruption trials, any one of which was likely to result in conviction and imprisonment—the frequent wars served as "get out of jail free" cards for him. And finally, for Israel's arms industry, the Gaza attacks provided big profits—because, as the Israeli bureau chief for Defense News put it, "combat is like the highest seal of approval when it comes to international markets." For the editor of *Israel Defense*, the 2021 assault on Gaza "was an outstanding thing for the defense industries."

What was the Goldstone Report and why was it so important?

Following Israel's twenty-two-day war on Gaza in December 2008 and January 2009, organizations ranging from Amnesty International and Human Rights Watch to the Arab League to the UN's Office for the Coordination of Humanitarian Affairs all issued human rights reports. The most eagerly awaited was that of the UN Fact-Finding Mission on the Gaza Conflict, led by the renowned South African jurist and former UN prosecutor Justice Richard Goldstone. He and his team of experts in international law had been appointed by the UN's Human Rights Council with a mandate to investigate the violations of human rights and international humanitarian law, or the laws of war, committed in Gaza by all sides during and prior to the war.

The 575-page analysis was by far the most comprehensive and detailed of all the reports. On its release on September 9, 2009, Goldstone described the report in the context of challenging the world's history of impunity for war crimes. The report reflected a balanced approach and recognized that the primitive rockets Palestinians fired into Israel against non-military targets had also violated international humanitarian law.

But by far the most numerous and most serious violations identified were carried out by Israel. The UN report found that Israel's blockade amounted to collective punishment and recognized that more than 1,400 people were killed during the military operation. The UN itself noted that the report called Israel's action "a deliberate policy of disproportionate force aimed at the civilian population" and that it states that "Israeli acts that deprive Palestinians in the Gaza Strip of their means of subsistence, employment, housing and water, that deny their freedom of movement and their right to leave and enter their own country, that limit their rights to access a court of law and an effective remedy, could lead a competent court to find that the crime of persecution, a crime against humanity, has been committed."

The Goldstone team called on the Security Council to refer the situation to the International Criminal Court for further investigation and prosecution, urged the General Assembly to act, and urged a meeting of the signatories of the Geneva Convention to consider other actions to hold Israel accountable. It called for the creation of an escrow fund to pay reparations for the vast destruction in Gaza, and urged governments to use universal jurisdiction to assure accountability. In an innovative move for official UN positions, the Goldstone report called directly on civil society to press governments to hold Israel accountable.

In response to the findings that Israel had illegally used weapons known to be provided by the US, activists in the US demanded that Congress investigate military aid and arms sales to Israel for possible violations of the US Arms Export Control Act. Several European and other countries initiated campaigns to identify and keep out of their borders potential Israeli perpetrators. Pressure mounted on the Security Council to act on the Goldstone recommendations and on the International Criminal Court to initiate criminal investigations.

But the pushback was fierce. The US backed Israel's rejection of the report, dismissing its conclusions even before the official text was released. Israeli and US pressure even led the Palestinian Authority to urge the Human Rights Council to delay consideration of the report—a position it soon reversed under even more powerful pressure from Palestinian human rights activists.

Israelis and supporters of Israel in the US, Europe, and elsewhere launched personal attacks on Goldstone's character, honesty, and his history. In South Africa, pressure from the Board of Jewish Deputies led to Justice Goldstone, who is Jewish, being told he would be unwelcome at his own grandson's bar mitzvah.

It was almost unprecedented for a UN human rights report to so broadly identify obligations and responsibilities under international law, not only of the alleged perpetrators but for virtually all relevant UN agencies, as well as for individual governments and even civil society. Endorsed by both the Human Rights Council and the UN General Assembly, the report remains a powerful indictment of and call for international action in response to war crimes and crimes against humanity committed in Gaza.

What was the effect of the Arab Spring on Israel and Palestine?

The Arab Spring began at the end of 2010, when a young Tunisian fruit seller, in a desperate response to disempowerment, humiliation, and despair, immolated himself in the streets of a small town, sparking an uprising against dictatorships across the region.

The Arab Spring was very much a product of a particular political moment, but the origins of its form can be traced directly to the first Palestinian intifada, the nonviolent, society-wide mobilization that transformed Palestine's national struggle from the late 1980s. For Palestine and Palestinians, that shake-up included a major challenge to US-dependent Arab regimes whose commitments to Palestinian rights were always limited to a few dollars and the rhetoric useful for distracting their own populations from state repression and lack of rights.

By the time the Arab Spring began, civil society had become the most important component of the Palestinian national movement—and not only because of the twenty years of failure of the US-controlled "peace process." Inside the occupied territories, Palestinian activists built nonviolent movements protesting the Apartheid Wall, the checkpoints, and the occupation itself, as well as issuing the global call for boycotts, divestment, and sanctions. Those nonviolent mobilizations, while underway for years without significant attention in the US, were empowered and strengthened, and became more visible because of the Arab Spring. People around the world began to view the nonviolent popular character of the Palestinian movement through the prism of the much newer but far more visible actions in Egypt, Tunisia, Bahrain, and elsewhere.

Initially, the victories of the Arab Spring created new possibilities for achieving Palestinian rights. In Egypt, the popular mobilization led directly to the overthrow of the longtime US-backed dictator Hosni Mubarak. The first post-Mubarak government remained largely controlled by the military, but still had to pay far more attention to public opinion than the old repression-dependent regime ever did. The new government faced divided loyalties: the military needed to keep on Washington's good side to continue getting the $1.3 billion in annual US military aid, but the civilian face of the government was concerned about the possibility of losing public support and perhaps being overthrown by a new Tahrir Square mobilization. The dispute resulted in a modicum of improvement for Gaza's people with the reopening of the Rafah crossing from Egypt, allowing in some medicine, food, and humanitarian goods, but Gaza remained isolated under Israel's siege.

In the United States, the first year or so of the Arab Spring transformed popular perceptions of Arabs, including Palestinians. It challenged anti-Arab racism and Islamophobia by showing images of Palestinians and other Arabs who "look just like us." Despite longer-term dangers (the notion that Arabs were suddenly OK because they are "like us" still reflected racism and American exceptionalism), the recognition that Arabs wear blue jeans, speak colloquial English, and are addicted to cell phones, Facebook, and Twitter played a significant role in changing popular perceptions and discourse in the US on the Middle East.

For Israel, the Arab Spring created new and serious challenges. Tel Aviv could no longer rely on the US-orchestrated relationships with Arab regimes that had never needed to take into account the views, wishes, or demands of their people. The overthrow of dictatorships in Egypt and Tunisia, and what looked like serious threats to regimes from Yemen to Syria to Bahrain and beyond, meant that kings and emirs and presidents could no longer simply ignore popular will and assume that repression would suffice. (Libya's NATO-dependent defeat of the regime of Muammar Gaddafi around the same time remained largely outside this indigenous democratic process.)

Turkey's emergence as the most popular government in Arab public opinion, largely because of Ankara's embrace of the Arab Spring's uprisings and its responses to Israeli assaults, particularly the lethal 2010 Israeli attack on the *Mavi Marmara* aid flotilla in international waters, severely weakened Israel. For years, the quiet partnership between Israel and Turkey, including major collaborations on water, military sales, joint military exercises, and Israeli tourists flooding Turkey, had given Israel a friendly non-Arab Muslim partner and a link to NATO to supplement its US connection. As the Arab Spring took hold, that connection collapsed, leaving Israel more isolated than ever.

Many in the US claimed that the protesters' core demands for jobs and dignity somehow meant that the people of the Arab world no longer cared about Palestine and about Israeli occupation. But they were wrong. While the uprisings shared a priority commitment to democracy and dignity, the rights of citizenship, and the basics of economic, social, and political rights, there is no question that just barely beneath the surface support for Palestinian rights and outrage at Israeli treatment of Palestinians remained intense. The Arab Spring's revolutionary processes shook up the Middle East and transformed the relative power and options for both Israel and Palestine like nothing in a generation.

Washington's reliable strategy of forcing US-dependent Arab governments to move towards normalization with Israel wasn't working any longer, as once-compliant dictators suddenly faced loud, vociferous, and mobilized public opposition—not the silent, sullen public acquiescence of the past.

But then came enormous setbacks. Across the region, these diverse and democratic, largely nonviolent movements were suppressed by brutal militarized responses from resurgent dictatorships, violent extremist elements of all kinds, and the return of direct US and NATO military intervention in the region.

In Egypt, the military government allowed the country's first free and fair election—which chose the Muslim Brotherhood-backed Mohamed Morsi as president. During his year in office, Morsi largely kept the Rafah crossing to Gaza open and hosted unity talks between Palestinian factions, but he was overthrown in a military coup in July 2013. The new military government led by General Abdel Fattah al-Sisi quickly reaffirmed its close ties with Israel, closed the Rafah crossing, and ended its support for Hamas and for Palestinian unity. Crucially Sisi also ordered the destruction of the network of smuggling tunnels between Egypt and Gaza that had provided access to basic food, consumer goods, medicine, hospital equipment, construction materials (and arms as well), to the 1.8 million Gazans living under Israel's siege.

With the closing of the brief democratic moment and the return to absolute control, repression and detention, the stage was also set for the renewal of Washington's campaign for Israel's normalization with Arab governments. When Trump abandoned the Iran nuclear deal in 2018, and moved to mobilize a region-wide Israel-led coalition against Iran, the Arab regimes were ready to join him. When that campaign, known as the Abraham Accords, continued under Joe Biden, the Palestinians would continue to pay the price.

What was the impact on Israel and the Palestinians of the civil war in Syria and the US anti-terrorism war?

Neither Palestinians nor Israelis were the main players in the civil war in Syria, the US-led war against ISIS or the Islamic State, the militarized chaos in Libya, or the other components of the new war on terror that took shape in 2014. But there were direct political, regional, and ideological connections.

War-related crises affected Palestinian refugees in and around Syria most seriously, particularly those who lived in refugee camps in and around Damascus, some of whom had been made refugees four or five times. Some Palestinians had fled to Syria during the *Nakba*, the forced expulsion and dispossession of Palestinians from their land during the 1947–48 war of Israeli independence. Others escaped the Nakba into the West Bank or Gaza, and then were forced out again in 1967, perhaps ending up in a refugee camp in Jordan, only to be expelled in 1970 during Jordan's anti-Palestinian campaigns. Maybe they ended up in one of the Palestinian refugee camps in Lebanon and were expelled from there during the 1982 Israeli invasion and occupation and ended up in Syria.

When the Arab Spring uprising broke out in Syria in 2011, most of the Palestinian refugees there tried to avoid taking sides, fearing the consequences. As the popular uprising shifted to a lethal, multifaceted civil war, the situation for Palestinians, like others in Syria, became much worse. In July 2012 the United Nations agency responsible for providing basic survival services to Palestinian refugees, UNRWA, issued a statement of direct concern, particularly for the more than 100,000 refugees living in

Yarmouk camp in Damascus: "UNRWA views with increasingly grave concern the situation in Syria, particularly as regards the implications for the stability and protection of 500,000 Palestine refugees across the country," the agency said. "The current situation in the Damascus neighborhood of Yarmouk and in rural Damascus, home to both Syrian and Palestinian communities, is especially worrying .... UNRWA has appealed to the Syrian authorities to safeguard the security of Palestine refugees wherever they reside in Syria."

But safeguarding the security of refugees was not a priority for the Syrian military, nor for any of the myriad of opposition forces. Many thousands of Palestinian refugees in Yarmouk and elsewhere in Syria were forced to flee their homes once again. Israel continued its post-1948 denial of the refugees' right of return to their homes, forcing many to seek refuge in already overcrowded camps in Lebanon and Jordan, neither of whose governments were particularly welcoming of the newest refugee population.

In December 2012, Syrian military jets bombed areas of Damascus including Yarmouk, hitting a mosque and a school inside the camp. The already-severe humanitarian crisis in the camp turned dire. It was perhaps the bitterest of ironies that of the Palestinians fleeing Yarmouk who managed to get to Lebanon, many found refuge, of a sort, in the decrepit Beirut-area refugee camps known as Sabra and Shatila—the site of the brutal 1982 massacre by Lebanese Christian extremists armed and backed by the Israeli military (see pages 91–93).

The situation in Syria did not improve. By July 2013, the 18,000 Palestinians left in Yarmouk were fully under siege by the Syrian regime, and water was cut off in September 2014, meaning residents had to rely on untreated ground water or open wells, carrying cans of water since there was no electricity to fill tanks. On February 25, 2015, UNRWA spokesman Chris Gunness issued a statement tracking UNRWA's inability to distribute humanitarian assistance, its assessment that no successful aid distribution was possible because of the escalation of fighting, and that an immediate cessation of hostilities would be needed to protect the Palestinian civilians in Yarmouk.

UNRWA issued the same statement, word for word, every day for almost three months. By April 2015, Yarmouk's destruction was virtually complete. While the 18,000 people still inside (3,500 of them children) had already suffered through months of the Syrian government's siege, they now faced an attack by ISIS forces who invaded the camp. Fighting escalated, with government and ISIS troops, as well as other militias, turning the camp into a battlefield. According to Gunness, the refugees' "lives are threatened. They are holed up in their battered homes too terrified to move, which is why we are saying that there must be a pause [in fighting], there must be humanitarian access for groups like UNRWA."

One component of the Syrian civil war was the fight between the US and Israel versus Iran. That made Israel a player in the Syrian war, although it was not directly supporting any of the forces on the ground. Israel did intervene on its own directly, bombing Syrian targets, particularly in the non-occupied side of the Golan Heights.

The unevenness of Israel's role reflected the counterintuitive reality that for decades the Syrian regime—led by Bashar al-Assad since 2000 and by his father, Hafez al-Assad, since 1970—had served as an unacknowledged useful neighbor for Israel. Despite Syrian rhetoric about resistance and defending the Palestinians, both Assads were ultimately quite helpful to Israel, most especially by keeping the Israeli-occupied Golan Heights quiet, with its population under tight control to prevent serious uprisings or resistance.

Israel had long relied on Syria's backing of Hamas, the Islamist party elected in the Gaza Strip and the West Bank in 2006, as the basis for its claim that Syria supported terrorism. It was a blow to that Israeli propaganda campaign when Hamas openly split from the Syrian government, based on its repression of the popular uprising. Some commentators attempted to equate Hamas's militancy and past use of armed resistance to Israeli occupation with the brutal extremism of ISIS. But that claimed linkage could not hold. The popularly elected Hamas, still governing the occupied Gaza Strip, maintained ties with the outlawed Muslim Brotherhood in Egypt and the government of Qatar, not the extremists of ISIS or al-Qaeda.

As the US war on terror rose across the region, in much of the Arab world the issue of double standards also erupted powerfully in the different responses to the Syrian civil war and the rise of ISIS, versus Israel's oppression of the Palestinians, particularly in Gaza. In the summer of 2014, when President Obama talked about the urgent need to protect the Yazidis on Mount Sinjar in Iraq, he described them as "innocent people facing violence on a massive scale." That was certainly true. And across the region, many people also recognized the 1.8 million people of Gaza—where Israel had just carried out a fifty-day military onslaught that left almost 2,200 people dead—as "innocent people facing violence on a massive scale." Many wondered why the US wasn't sending an airlift to overcome Israel's siege of Gaza, to force open Gaza's sealed border crossings and allow the people to escape their crowded, desperate enclave.

What was the importance of the 2011–2015 Palestinian campaigns for membership in the United Nations, UNESCO, and the International Criminal Court?

In 2011, after twenty years of failure of the US-controlled "peace process," the Palestinians brought their quest for statehood directly to the United Nations. Palestine applied to the Security Council to join the global body as a full Member State. The Palestine Liberation Organization had been accepted as a nonmember Observer Entity of the UN since the mid-1970s; the 2011 initiative aimed to transform that status to full membership for a legally recognized State of Palestine.

The US made clear it would use its veto to scuttle the membership effort. The irony was that the US was threatening to veto a resolution aimed at achieving exactly what Washington claimed it supported—a Palestinian state [truncated, still occupied, noncontiguous, not sovereign, only nominally independent] side by side with Israel—because the US didn't want to give up control of the Middle East diplomacy and allow decisions to made by a venue like the UN, where Israeli privileges could not be guaranteed. Republican pressure in Congress demanded ever-harsher US moves against any UN recognition of Palestine, and the Obama administration capitulated to the pressures of the powerful pro-Israel lobbies in Washington.

But rising global frustration with the failure of the US-dominated peace process, increasing isolation of Israel for its consistent violations of human rights and international law, and most especially the regional shifts set in motion by the Arab Spring, all set the stage for an unusual diplomatic push-back from governments, including US allies, newly open to supporting Palestinian rights at the UN. It meant the US was isolated, and the conflict between US strategic interest in supporting Palestinian statehood, and the demands of domestic political interests requiring visible support for Israel, especially just ahead of the 2012 presidential election, was open and visible.

From the vantage point of international law and human rights, Palestinians could win at least two significant gains from the UN statehood initiative. The most important was the possibility of a break from the US-controlled "peace process" in favor of a UN-centered diplomatic initiative based on international law. Second, UN recognition would allow the State of Palestine to participate in other global engagements, most importantly to sign on to the International Criminal Court, enabling Palestine to call for the International Criminal Court to prosecute Israeli war crimes committed in what would by then be the territory of a member state of the court. There would be no guarantee; ICC prosecution, like UN membership, is a thoroughly political process. Still, the presence of the State of Palestine within the ICC could transform the potential for international accountability.

But there were dangers too. Even though the Oslo-created Palestinian Authority actually held sway in most international diplomacy, Palestinians were officially represented at the UN by the PLO, still deemed the "sole legitimate representative of the Palestinian people" by the UN itself. Unlike the limited PA, the PLO historically embodied the interests of all three sectors of the Palestinian people: those living under occupation in the West Bank, Gaza, and East Jerusalem; those living as second-class citizens inside Israel; and those millions of Palestinian refugees whose internationally recognized right to return to their homes remained unfulfilled. Many Palestinians were afraid that replacing the PLO at the UN with an inchoate "state" of Palestine could lead to the further disenfranchisement of all Palestinians outside of that "state," all those outside the 1967 occupied territory. The second danger was the potential loss of advocacy for the refugees' right of return, guaranteed by UN Resolution 194 but long denied by Israel. The fear was that a government of Palestine would not have the political will to fight for recognition and implementation of that right, given its focus on realizing the new state.

In September 2011, Palestinians brought their bid to become a member state of the UN to the membership committee of the Security Council. US pressure on council members was fierce, resulting in the Palestinians failing to obtain the minimum nine council votes in support of their application. Without that, the US did not have to use its veto, and the membership process stalled. Soon after, the UN's cultural, educational, and scientific organization UNESCO took a much more direct decision, voting overwhelmingly on October 31, 2011, to welcome Palestine as the organization's newest member. Within hours, the US announced it was cutting all funding of UNESCO, including withholding $60 million of the $70 million dues Washington owed the organization.

UNESCO's work, beyond identifying and protecting World Heritage Sites, includes protection of indigenous languages at risk of extinction, creating a new warning system that helped save the lives of countless Japanese coastal residents during the 2011 earthquake and tsunami, and providing nurturing education and cultural opportunities to some of the world's most dispossessed children without access to primary school—street children, former child soldiers, and child refugees. And yet US politics determined that defunding the organization, risking expulsion from UNESCO and global, especially Arab, opprobrium, was worth the price to reassert Washington's rejection of Palestinian statehood on any terms other than its own.

Shortly after joining UNESCO, Palestinian officials announced they would not apply for membership in any other UN agencies until the stalled Security Council process was resolved.

But that commitment didn't last. The November 2012 Israeli assault on Gaza changed conditions again. UN Secretary-General Ban ki-Moon went to the region to help build support for a ceasefire, and once it was in place, UN attention shifted to a vote on Palestinian statehood in the General Assembly. The assembly alone could not grant Palestine full membership in the United Nations. But the vote, passed overwhelmingly on November 29—the International Day of Solidarity with the

Palestinian People—by the far larger and more democratic assembly, reflected international support to recognize Palestine as a nonmember or observer state.

The new status changed little at the UN itself; Palestine was still not a member, could not vote, and still had to rely on the Arab Group to introduce resolutions in the assembly or the Security Council. But recognition from the UN that Palestine was indeed a state helped set the stage for joining other international organizations and signing treaties.

After a 2013 Israeli refusal to implement a prisoner exchange, the Palestinians announced they were signing on to fifteen international agreements and that they intended, finally, to apply for membership in the International Criminal Court. They didn't actually sign the ICC's Rome Treaty at that time, but did sign treaties including human rights instruments committing the Palestinians to protect the rights of children, women, and the disabled, as well as the Geneva Conventions and UN covenants against genocide, torture, apartheid, racism, and corruption. The US response came from UN Ambassador Samantha Power, who told Congress the next day, "The United States will stand with Israel, we will defend it ... Let me also add, given reports yesterday of new Palestinian actions [signing the treaties] that both of you have referenced, that this solemn commitment also extends to our firm opposition to any and all unilateral actions in the international arena."

By the end of 2014, following the fifty-day Israeli attack on Gaza that summer, Jordan introduced a Security Council resolution urging creation of a Palestinian state in three years. When the US again pressured council members to vote against it and the measure failed, the Palestinian leadership responded by submitting the documents to join the International Criminal Court, making clear it would seek prosecution of Israeli officials for war crimes in the territory now recognized by the UN General Assembly as the State of Palestine. Israel responded immediately with the cut-off of more than $127 million in tax payments Tel Aviv owed to the Palestinians, funds badly needed to pay Palestinian civil servants' salaries and public services. The State Department denounced the Palestinian move to join the ICC by calling it "entirely counterproductive." On November 21, 2024, the ICC issued arrest warrants for Prime Minister Benjamin Netanyahu and former defense minister Yoav Gallant. (A warrant was also issued for Hamas leader Mohammed Deif, although Israel claimed to have killed him in July.) The Israeli leaders were charged with the war crimes of starvation and directing attacks against civilians, and the crimes against humanity of murder, persecution, and (referring to the extreme pain inflicted on wounded people, especially children, facing amputation without anesthetics) inhumane acts.

For the Palestinians, gaining UN recognition as a state, joining international institutions including the International Criminal Court, and signing important human rights treaties all represented part of a major effort to undermine the legitimacy of the US-controlled diplomatic process that had failed for more than twenty-four years to bring an end to Israeli occupation. It pushed a number of European and other countries to at least consider rejecting the idea that Washington gets to call the shots in the United Nations on the question of Palestine, that the rest of the world is somehow not going to be able to play an international role, and that only the US gets to determine the legitimacy of any move by the Palestinians to obtain their freedom and independence.

Throughout this period and beyond, for many Palestinians and for much of the growing global solidarity movement, the primary issue had turned from statehood to rights-based demands for human rights, international law, and equality for all. The prospect of a real two-state solution was already deteriorating as Israeli settlement expansion and land confiscation escalated, leaving the notion of a contiguous, viable, and truly sovereign Palestinian state increasingly out of reach.

How did US policy toward Israel-Palestine change under President Barack Obama?

Early in Barack Obama's 2007–2008 campaign, he made the notable remark that "no one has suffered as much as the Palestinians." He quickly retreated from that position, however, and most of his campaign rhetoric on Israel-Palestine did not significantly diverge from a boilerplate pro-Israeli stance, including his expected visit to the American-Israel Public Affairs Committee, or AIPAC, the influential pro-Israel lobby.

After his election, Obama provided mixed messages. He remained mute during the deadly Israeli assault on Gaza that ended just hours before his inauguration on January 20, 2009. Soon after taking office, Obama announced his intention to implement George W. Bush's commitment to provide $30 billion in military aid to Israel over the next ten years. (In fact, when he actually negotiated the new agreement in 2016, the amount shot up to $38 billion over ten years, a 27 percent increase.)

His statements, however, sounded different. Obama assessed the Israel-Palestine conflict within its own regional context, removing it from Bush's "global war on terror" framework. He chose the independent-minded former senator George Mitchell as his special envoy, rather than any of the pro-Israeli "usual suspects." In his powerful speech in Cairo in June 2009, Obama said the US "does not accept" the legitimacy of continued Israeli settlements, and "it is time for these settlements to stop." His language equated Palestinian and Israeli suffering and national aspirations—a significant departure from every previous president.

But it soon became clear that while Obama talked the talk of Middle East peace and even justice, he failed to walk the walk. The administration appointed a coterie of old-guard Israel backers as White House and State Department advisors, led by people like Dennis Ross, who had crafted much of the failed US policies for more than two decades. And Obama's stated commitment to a new US diplomatic initiative was quickly abandoned.

Such a commitment would have required holding Israel accountable for its continuing violations of US and international law, using such means as withholding billions of dollars of military aid, ending the long practice of protecting Israel in the UN, and making real the often-claimed US opposition to Israeli settlements. If Obama had chosen such a trajectory, Prime Minister Benjamin Netanyahu, a right-wing militarist holding power with an even more extremist right-wing cabinet, might have made the job much easier: Netanyahu's arrogant and racist put-downs of the US president infuriated even many supporters of Washington's pro-Israel policies.

In mid-2010, a very public spat erupted between the Obama administration and Netanyahu over Israel's escalating settlement expansion in the occupied West Bank and East Jerusalem. The apparent divide became vividly public when Netanyahu visited Washington and lectured Obama as if the president was an errant schoolboy. Tensions continued to rise when Israel announced new settlement projects during visits by Vice President Biden and other top officials.

There was outrage in the media and in Congress, accusing President Obama of pressuring Israel. But the reality was that despite the public spat, the US never exerted or even threatened real pressure. The US would occasionally request that Israel stop settlement expansion, but each statement began with the reminder that the US remained committed to maintaining Israel's qualitative military edge, and never even hinted at reducing military or political support.

As the 2010 midterm election campaigns began, Republicans attacked Obama for being too tough on Israel. In response, the chairman of the House Foreign Affairs Committee, Representative Howard Berman, distributed talking points to his fellow Democrats. They included: "President Obama and Democrats in Congress have provided Israel with every single penny of foreign assistance appropriations that Israel has asked for ... Under President Obama, Israel's Qualitative Military Edge is being reestablished ... Later this year, the Pentagon is likely to sell Israel an initial batch of 25 F-35 Joint Strike Fighters, the most advanced aircraft in the US arsenal, and other sensitive technology ..."

And on the diplomatic front, the Obama administration was so eager to prove its pro-Israel credentials that it vetoed a Security Council resolution criticizing Israeli settlements that was so cautiously drafted that even Obama's UN ambassador, Susan Rice, claimed the US actually agreed with the resolution, and urged that Washington's "opposition to the resolution should not be misunderstood."

At the height of the unemployment crisis in 2011, the Obama administration requested that the all-too-willing Congress allocate an additional $205 million to pay for Israel's new Iron Dome anti-rocket system. That money could have created 4,100 new jobs at home, but the White House chose a path consistent with earlier administrations, privileging military aid to Israel over domestic economic needs.

Despite occasional reassurances to an increasingly skeptical US public that "the parties were talking," it remained obvious that resolving the Israel-Palestine conflict, initially one of President Obama's major goals, was no longer on his agenda. As the 2012 presidential election campaign took shape, it became increasingly clear that the vast transformation of public discourse, and significant shift in media coverage of the issue had not reached the White House—and that nothing would be done prior to the election out of fear of jeopardizing Obama's chances for reelection. The only campaign issue regarding the Middle East would be to determine which candidate was the most pro-Israel.

In August 2013, the Obama administration announced a new round of peace talks, to be led by Secretary of State John Kerry. The timing appeared to be rooted primarily in the escalating regional conflicts in Syria, Libya, Iraq, and beyond; the lack of a US strategy to end those conflicts made the possibility of new Israel-Palestine talks more politically important.

But that new round of talks, based on the same premises that had failed since 1991 (and led by Martin Indyk, yet another of the US officials responsible for most of the earlier failed talks), failed as well. They might have been called the "Einstein Round," reflecting the quote often attributed to the great scientist's definition of insanity—doing the same thing over and over again and expecting different results. Kerry's stated goal for the talks made clear why it wasn't going to work: he said the goal was "ending the conflict, ending the claims." Missing from his goals were ending the occupation, ending the siege of Gaza, ending the decades of dispossession and exile of Palestinian refugees, creating a diplomatic process based on human rights and international law.

Israel responded to Kerry's visits by announcing the construction of almost 1,500 new settlement units, along with 1,200 announced just before the talks began, and demanding the Palestinians recognize Israel as a "Jewish state," thus legitimizing the second-class citizenship of the 20 percent of Israeli citizens who were Palestinians. As the April 29 deadline approached, Israel refused to free the last of the 104 Palestinian prisoners it had promised to release, demanding an extension of the talks. Soon after, the Palestinians announced plans for a unity government between Hamas in Gaza and the Fatah-led Palestinian Authority in the West Bank. They also announced plans to sign fifteen international treaties—not including the International Criminal Court, which would allow them to bring charges against Israel for its violations, but treaties holding the Palestinian authorities themselves accountable for protecting the rights of the disabled, of women, of children, etc.

The talks failed, and the Obama administration pulled back from direct engagement, but maintained military aid and UN protection.

Beyond Israel-Palestine, much of Obama's second-term foreign policy centered on the Iran nuclear deal. The negotiations were complicated by Netanyahu's public and vitriolic attacks on Obama for daring to talk to Iran at all, by the White House's belief that it had to appease powerful anti-Iran positions in both Israel and key Arab states, and by the difficulty of winning congressional support.

Ultimately Obama succeeded in finalizing the agreement in 2015, despite Netanyahu's Republican-orchestrated speech to a joint session of Congress, designed to persuade members to vote against Obama's proposed deal and instead to support Israel's anti-Iran mobilization. Recognizing the unlikely possibility of congressional support, Obama crafted the deal as a bilateral agreement between Iran and the US, opening the way for Donald Trump to abandon the deal in 2018.

Why did Israeli Prime Minister Netanyahu come to address Congress in March 2015?

Within hours of President Obama's January 2015 State of the Union address, Speaker of the House John Boehner invited Netanyahu to address the US Congress. The invitation was a deliberate partisan snub of President Obama by the Republican speaker, who issued the invitation without any consultation with the White House or State Department, violating all normal protocol. It was also designed to improve Netanyahu's chances in the Israeli elections scheduled for just two weeks after the planned visit.

The shared goal of the speech went beyond partisan politics. Boehner and his Republicans, along with many Democrats, shared Netanyahu's strong opposition to the nuclear negotiations then underway with Iran. Opponents in both parties of Congress kept up a steady campaign designed to undermine the chances for a negotiated solution, demanding instead that more sanctions be added to the severe sanctions already wreaking havoc on the Iranian economy, and that the threat of military force—"all options are on the table"—be a constant part of the diplomatic litany. Congressional Republicans sent an open letter to Iran's leaders warning them that the US would not be bound by any agreement, seriously threatening the talks. Netanyahu had for years opposed any negotiations with Iran, at various times threatening an Israeli military strike, at other times demanding that the US back an Israeli strike against Iran or carry out one of its own.

Netanyahu's speech to Congress ultimately threatened war. The political situation had shifted, and he appeared to realize he did not have the clout to actually stop the negotiations, so Netanyahu's backup demand was, if not "no deal," then at least a "better deal." But his vision of a "better deal" was based on Iranian surrender. And since that was not a viable option, he was essentially calling for an end to negotiations and a return to the threat of war. He warned that "even if Israel stands alone, the Jewish people will not remain passive." The prime minister relied on the claim—denied by not only US intelligence agencies and the UN nuclear watchdog IAEA, but top Israeli intelligence officials as well—that Iran possessed a nuclear weapons program, and that it somehow represented an existential threat to Israel. He did not, of course, mention Israel's unacknowledged and uninspected nuclear weapons arsenal that continued to destabilize the region.

But the speech had another, potentially more significant result. Widespread anger rose in Congress at Netanyahu's blatant partisanship and his racist disrespect towards President Obama. It was particularly strong among Democrats and most especially in the Congressional Black Caucus. That anger, strengthened by a powerful civil society pressure campaign, led to sixty members of Congress publicly skipping the speech. The standing ovations Netanyahu received during his speech could not hide the facts that he was far more popular in Congress than with the American people (including American Jews), and that many members of Congress were missing. It was unprecedented—the most serious breach of the longstanding congressional acquiescence to Israeli influence.

Although resolutions to protect Israeli interests continued to find easy passage in Congress, the success of the 2015 "Skip the Speech" campaign set the stage for potential new challenges to the House and Senate's once-unassailable support for Israel. And the US and Iran, along with five other countries, still managed to negotiate the JCPOA.

How have Israeli politics and elections shifted to the right?

Most notable since about 2005, the political climate inside Israel had long been shifting significantly to the right. In November of that year, the right-wing Likud leader, Ariel Sharon, long known as the "Butcher of Beirut" for the role he played in the 1982 Sabra-Shatila massacre of Palestinians (for which Israel's own Kahan Commission found him "personally liable" in negligently ignoring the clear danger to civilians), joined with some Labor Party leaders to create the new Kadima party in Israel. Sharon, while supporting a shift from traditional settlement-based colonialism in Gaza to a state of siege in which settlers would be removed and troops would remain redeployed outside Gaza's borders while retaining full control, had never changed his hawkish anti-Palestinian views. And yet Kadima was immediately dubbed a "centrist" party, because in the Israeli political context, Sharon and his right-wing colleagues now faced serious political challengers to their right.

Support for the Israeli assaults on Gaza—particularly the wars of 2008–09, 2012, 2014, and beyond—were not limited to the right wing. In each case, public support rose higher than it had been previously. By the fifty-day war of summer 2014, Israeli Jewish support was above 95 percent. And these wars were accompanied by a rising, increasingly explicit level of racism across Israeli society, led in many cases by top government officials. Chants of "Death to Arabs, death to leftists!" became commonplace.

That was mainstream; the politicians affiliated with Israel's far right wing went much further. During the 2014 war in Gaza, Knesset member Ayelet Shaked, from the extreme right Israel Home party in Netanyahu's government, issued on Facebook what amounted to a call to commit genocide. "The entire Palestinian people is the enemy," she posted. "In wars, the enemy is usually an entire people, including its elderly and its women, its cities and its villages, its property and its infrastructure."

Her post went on to say that the mothers of Palestinians killed should follow their dead sons to Hell: "They should go, as should the physical homes in which they raised the snakes. Otherwise, more little snakes will be raised there."

Her language was reminiscent of that of US Col. John Chivington, a military leader during the US Indian wars. It was November 29, 1864, when Chivington, a Methodist minister and commander of a Colorado militia, ordered his troops to attack a peaceful encampment of Cheyenne families on the shores of Sand Creek. Some soldiers resisted, saying that it would violate the military's promise of protection to the peaceful village. Chivington was having none of it. "I have come to kill Indians, and believe it is right and honorable to use any means under God's heaven to kill Indians," he said. "Kill and scalp all, big and little; nits make lice." Nearly 200 Cheyenne, most of them women and children, were killed in the Sand Creek Massacre.

By the time of the Israeli election in March 2015, racist fearmongering was in full swing. On the election morning, Prime Minister Netanyahu, running for reelection, was urging his followers to get out and vote. The right-wing government's reelection was in danger, he said, because, in his words, "Arab voters are coming out in droves to the polls." When the votes were counted, Netanyahu put together a coalition of the right, the far right, and the extreme right with barely enough votes to pass— and immediately appointed Shaked Ayelet, the thirty-nine-year-old champion of the farthest right, as minister of justice.

That period of right- and far-right consolidation in Israel also saw the increasing partisanship in the US-Israeli relationship, as Netanyahu moved deliberately to court Republican support while publicly disrespecting President Obama. And the partisanship continued; according to Pew polls, from 2001 the percentage of Republicans sympathizing more with Israel than with the Palestinians rose twenty-nine points, while the share of Democrats saying that declined eleven points. By 2018 that meant 79 percent of Republicans sided with Israel, while only 27 percent of Democrats did.

In Israel, Netanyahu's sequential governments moved further and further to the right, with increasing influence of the secular settler movement and the ultra-orthodox religious Zionists. Public opinion largely went along with the far right in power.

But when Netanyahu was elected again, for a sixth term as prime minister in December 2022, the coalition he cobbled together moved further than any before. To avoid going to prison (he was facing four sets of serious corruption trials), Netanyahu created a government with the most extremist elements in the Knesset—including Itamar Ben-Gvir as minister of national security, in charge of Israel's Border Police in the West Bank, and Bezalel Smotrich, as the minister of finance and also as a minister in the Defense Ministry.

Ben-Gvir, a settler in the ultra-radically racist Kiryat Arba settlement, had been convicted of incitement to racism and supporting a terror organization; his party, Jewish Power, had long been prohibited even from running for a parliamentary seat, let alone controlling a government ministry, but by merging his party with that of Smotrich's National Union, he was allowed to run and the bloc won seats for both of them. Netanyahu put Smotrich, who defined himself as a "fascist homophobe," in charge of the newly created Settlements Agency with power to authorize settlements built without government approval, to approve housing construction in the settlements and deny it in Palestinian towns and villages, with a civilian force to carry out those plans, replacing the Civil Administration of the military, which since 1967 had controlled the West Bank. Such a move amounted to de facto (and perhaps de jure) annexation, since it meant the transfer of authority over Palestinians from military to civilian officials.

In return, they both agreed to continue supporting him as prime minister, thus keeping Netanyahu out of jail.

In that context, Netanyahu's own right-wing politics positioned him as about the farthest left within his right/far-right/fascist-right coalition government.

But when the coalition called for a set of broad judicial reforms, challenging the independence of the judiciary and threatening women's and LGBTQ rights important to a wide range of Jewish Israelis, protesters poured into the streets. From early 2023, frequent demonstrations of up to 400,000 people mobilized to demand that Netanyahu step down. Protest organizers were all too aware that including any reference to ending occupation in their list of demands would result in protests of perhaps 4,000 rather than 400,000, so the demonstrations carefully made no reference to Palestinian rights.

The protests lasted until the attack on southern Israel of October 7, when they came to an abrupt halt as Jewish Israeli public opinion unified in support of the full-scale war launched against the entire population of Gaza. While Netanyahu remained very unpopular, among other things blamed for the intelligence and response failures that helped cause the high number of civilian casualties in the October 7 attack, he managed to stay in office and keep his right-wing government in place. Smotrich and Ben-Gvir threatened to abandon his coalition if he accepted a permanent ceasefire in Gaza rather than continuing to fight until the "complete destruction" of Hamas."

Throughout late 2023 and 2024, as Israel's war in Gaza escalated and Palestinian civilians, disproportionately children and women, were killed by the tens of thousands, Israeli military and political officials, academics, Knesset members and government ministers publicly advocated for mass killing of Palestinians and the use of nuclear weapons against Gaza, and called Palestinians "human animals." The language was so extreme that when South Africa sued Israel in the International Court of Justice, alleging violations of the Genocide Convention, the necessary requirement of showing intent to commit genocide was easily available in a host of public utterances. None of the officials making such statements lost their job.

How was Palestine-Israel dealt with in the 2016 presidential election?

The 2016 Democratic and Republican party platforms that passed before the presidential election did not reflect any significant change towards a position on Israel-Palestine grounded in international law, human rights, and equality for all—or even a position closer to neutrality between the two sides. In fact, the 2016 Democratic platform was arguably more overtly pro-Israel than its 2012 predecessor. But it was clear during that election that support for Israel was losing its bipartisan consensus and becoming a partisan Republican issue.

During the final Democratic platform committee meeting in early

July 2016, several mild amendments to the language on the issue were tabled. One such amendment used the word "occupation" (otherwise missing from the draft) and tepidly criticized Israeli settlements. Another urged the United States to provide humanitarian assistance to Gaza, without mentioning Israeli violations of human rights or the US-provided weapons used illegally against civilian targets, and without holding anyone accountable. But these amendments were smacked down by candidate Hillary Clinton's supporters and party insiders without even a hint of a substantive response.

However, throughout the debates of the Democratic campaign season, the strategic value of US support for Israel, the Israeli occupation, settlements, the siege of Gaza, and more, were debated and discussed as legitimate campaign issues for almost the first time in a presidential election.

Part of the shift came from the initially unanticipated rise of socialist Independent Senator Bernie Sanders's campaign for president, which pushed a critique of Israeli policy and a challenge to unconditional US support for Tel Aviv to center stage. And those positions, at the center of a powerful mainstream party for the first time, reflected the degree to which media and public, and now even political/policy discourse on Israel-Palestine in the United States, had been transformed in the preceding ten to fifteen years. The consequences included the loosening—at least a little bit—of political strictures that were sometimes self-imposed. For the first time, a serious candidate for president from one of the two major parties recognized and acted on the reality that criticism of Israel, breaking the longstanding pro-Israel consensus in Washington, was no longer an act of political suicide.

And the shift in discourse was becoming far more partisan. While support for Israel was historically strongest among liberals and supporters of the Democratic Party, by 2010 that was changing. Especially for younger progressives, escalating Israeli violence against Palestinians was increasingly visible on social media. Israel's 2008–09 Operation Cast Lead assault on Gaza in particular, and Netanyahu's subsequent return to office within a far-right government, made it harder and harder to accept Israeli actions that traditional US liberals—mostly Democrats—had once been willing to ignore or even defend. Thus, the epicenter of uncritical support for Israel, which included funding, arming, and enabling occupation, apartheid, and colonization, rapidly shifted toward the Republicans.

By 2010, in the words of noted pollster John Zogby:

"The differences in opinion between Democrats and Republicans are stunning. Seventy-one percent of Republicans want President Barack Obama to lean the US pursuit of Mideast peace in Israel's favor. Among Democrats, 73% want a middle course, and the percentages who want either a pro-Israel or pro-Palestinian policy are nearly equal at just under 10%. Here are more examples: 92% of Republicans have a favorable attitude toward Israel, compared to 42% of Democrats ... and 72% of Democrats say the US should get tough with Israel, compared to 14% of Republicans."

That Republican shift, underway for several years already, took very real form during the GOP's platform discussions in July 2016. The Republican platform's language certainly went beyond that of the Democrats in support for Israel—it even went beyond the words of Prime Minister Netanyahu. In a section titled "Our Unequivocal Support for Israel and Jerusalem," the platform used language that linked Israel to the United States in its origins ("aspiration for freedom") and exceptionalism ("standing out among the nations as a beacon of democracy and humanity"). The conclusion was that "support for Israel is an expression of Americanism, and it is the responsibility of our government to advance policies that reflect Americans' strong desire for a relationship with no daylight between America and Israel."

Republican rhetoric aside, in substance the two platforms were almost identical. The GOP recognized Jerusalem as "the eternal and indivisible capital of the Jewish state," while the Democrats called it "the capital of Israel, an undivided city." Both supported maintaining Israel's "qualitative military edge." And both condemned the Boycott, Divestment, and Sanctions movement, although the Republicans went further, claiming that BDS is "anti-Semitic in nature and seeks to destroy Israel."

The insurgent Sanders campaign for the Democratic Party nomination played an unexpected role in the discourse shift. Surprising many, Sanders chose the issue as the centerpiece of his most important foreign policy speech.

By the standards of anyone whose analysis of the Palestine-Israel conflict is rooted in international law, human rights, and equality for all, the speech was very good. But by the standards of US electoral politics, especially for a serious Democratic Party presidential contender, it was breathtaking. And it provided clear evidence of the degree to which mainstream political discourse had shifted—and was continuing to shift—away from the longstanding Zionist assumptions of inside-the-Beltway party politics.

He called Israeli actions in the 2014 Gaza war "disproportionate" and referenced international humanitarian law in relation to Israel—unprecedented actions in mainstream party politics. While most politicians still did not recognize it, the work of social movements fighting for Palestinian rights over decades had already shifted the public debate. Sanders was able to take advantage of that shift, including in his selection of platform committee representatives as well as in his own speech. And precisely because the discourse had already so profoundly changed, Sanders went further in his own criticism of Israel than any other presidential candidate in modern history, with the exception of Rev. Jesse Jackson's Rainbow Campaigns in 1984 and 1988.

What was Trump's Middle East policy, and how was it different from earlier US policy toward Israel and the Palestinians?

During the 2016 presidential campaign, it was very clear that many of Donald Trump's positions were outside the norm of mainstream politics—including his foreign policy. There was a visible streak of isolationist rhetoric, a claimed opposition to "nation-building" as an excuse for military intervention, and at one point even an assertion that his intention was to be "sort of a neutral guy" between Israel and the Palestinians. But that was the only reference anyone heard about neutrality. Regarding the Middle East, Trump's consistent campaign theme reflected uncritical support for Israel and for its right-wing government. And from the moment he took office, his personnel appointments and policies reflected that as well.

Donald Trump's nativist, xenophobic, racist, and Islamophobic campaign had little to say about foreign policy that was coherent. His theme was "America First," but with an overlay of isolationism— appropriating, knowingly or unknowingly, the slogan of those who two generations earlier had advocated that the United States appease Hitler and Mussolini and stay out of World War II. In his campaign's one official foreign policy speech, in April 2016, Trump identified five problems with what he called the "complete disaster" of US foreign policy. The supposed problems included the claims that allies can't depend on the United States, and that enemies don't believe Washington is a threat.

To prove his point, Trump claimed that "Israel, our great friend and the one true democracy in the Middle East has been snubbed and criticized by an administration that lacks moral clarity. Just a few days ago, Vice President Biden again criticized Israel—a force for justice and peace—for acting as an impediment to peace in the region. President Obama has not been a friend to Israel. He has treated Iran with tender love and care and made it a great power in the Middle East—all at the expense of Israel, our other allies in the region and, critically, the United States."

Despite his penchant for complete reversals of positions, Trump remained consistent on supporting Israel. In March 2016, eight months before he was elected president, Trump spoke to the annual conference of AIPAC, the main Jewish pro-Israel lobby group in the US. "When I become president," he told them, "the days of treating Israel like a second-class citizen will end on day one. ...I will meet with Prime Minister Netanyahu immediately." Trump promised, "We will move the American embassy to the eternal capital of the Jewish people, Jerusalem. And we will send a clear signal that there is no daylight between America and our most reliable ally, the state of Israel." He went on, "An agreement imposed by the United Nations would be a total and complete disaster," and added, "when I'm president, believe me, I will veto any attempt by the UN to impose its will on the Jewish state. It will be vetoed 100 percent."

Soon Trump would completely disavow the long-held bipartisan US support for a two-state solution. It wasn't because he recognized that that longstanding international consensus position had been rendered moot by the expansion of Israeli settlements and resulting loss of Palestinian land sufficient for anything resembling a viable sovereign state. Trump's rejection came from his goal of supporting Israeli power and privilege, and Palestinian weakness and dispossession, as the permanent status quo to be maintained in any peace deal.

While his rhetoric was certainly provocative, it was not immediately clear how much he would actually differ from earlier presidents. Trump campaigned on the notion that Obama had sold out Israeli interests. In fact, while Obama's relationship with Prime Minister Netanyahu was certainly tense, multibillion dollar US military aid to Israel had actually risen significantly during the Obama years, culminating in the 2016 agreement to send Israel $38 billion over ten years—$8 billion more than the last aid package. The US had provided full diplomatic and military support for Israel throughout its 2008–09, 2012, and 2014 assaults on Gaza, and US opposition to settlements had largely remained at the level of rhetoric. But President Obama had issued waivers to avoid implementing the law requiring the US embassy to be moved to Jerusalem (as had every previous president since the law passed). Settlements were routinely criticized as an obstacle to peace, and by December 2016 at the end of his second term, Obama had taken the rare step of allowing a UN Security Council resolution criticizing settlements to pass 14 to 0 with the US abstaining.

Trump would turn out to be very different. One of his first appointments—made just hours after his inauguration—was the nomination of David Friedman as the new ambassador to Israel. Friedman, who was Trump's bankruptcy lawyer, had no diplomatic training or experience. A longtime settlement backer, he called the idea of a two-state solution a "damaging anachronism" and "an illusory solution in search of a non-existent problem." He claimed that Palestinian refugees were never forced to leave Israel, and served as president of American Friends of Bet El Yeshiva, a fundraising organization that in 2014 alone raised almost $2.3 million to support the illegal Bet El settlement. During his first year as ambassador, Friedman referred to Israel's control of the 1967 Palestinian territories as "an alleged occupation."

Even before his inauguration Trump announced his intention to create a new Middle East peace plan, the "ultimate deal" of his deal-making career—and placed his son-in-law, Jared Kushner, along with twenty-year Trump family lawyer, Jason Greenblatt, in charge. Kushner, the scion of a wealthy real estate family in New York, had no training or experience in diplomacy, but he had long supported illegal Israeli settlements, including by orchestrating donations of tens of thousands of dollars to West Bank settlements from his family foundation. According to *Newsweek* magazine, "the foundation donated at least $38,000 between 2011 and 2013 to a fundraising group building a Jewish seminary in a West Bank settlement known as Beit El. During that period, Kushner's foundation also donated an additional $20,000 to Jewish and educational institutions in settlements throughout the region, the Associated Press reported."

He did not disclose those donations while working on Trump's behalf during the last months of the Obama administration. And somehow the Trump son-in-law forgot to mention those transactions when he filed financial reports later required for his top-level security clearance. But the donations to illegal settlement projects fit a pattern. In late 2016, while Obama was still president, Kushner ordered Michael Flynn, then the Trump campaign's top foreign policy adviser, to persuade Russia to delay an imminent UN Security Council vote criticizing Israeli settlements. President Obama had decided to abstain and allow the resolution to pass; Trump wanted the Russians to delay the vote so the new administration could veto it. Moscow refused to play along, but not for lack of Kushner's efforts.

Special Envoy Jason Greenblatt had studied in a West Bank yeshiva, and also had a long history supporting Israeli settlements. Trump defended his selection of Greenblatt, stating, "He's a person who truly loves Israel. I like to get advice from people that know Israel, but from people that truly love Israel."

One of the key goals for Trump's May 2017 Israel trip was to reinforce his claimed commitment to a new iteration of an Israeli–Palestinian plan. Days after he returned home, he signed another six-month waiver, as earlier presidents had done, once again delaying any plan to move the embassy. In December of that year Trump issued his provocative announcement that he was recognizing Jerusalem as Israel's capital and beginning the process of moving the embassy, along with a set of additional moves called for by the most far-right settler movements and their supporters in Netanyahu's government.

What was Trump's goal in trying to bring Israel and Saudi Arabia together?

Trump embarked on his first trip to the Middle East just a few months into his presidency. He began in Riyadh, where he convened a set of mostly Sunni Gulf Arab monarchs, as well as leaders of some other Muslim-majority countries, to build what he called a mobilization against terrorism. While keeping the focus on engaging Arab leaders ever deeper in US anti-terrorism efforts in the region, Trump was clear that Iran was the designated target. But Trump barely mentioned the longstanding Saudi, UAE, and other Sunni monarchies' support for extremist organizations, from al-Qaeda to ISIS with many more in between, instead keeping the overall focus on Iran.

Trump then traveled on to Israel, leading the *Washington Post* to note that "shared hatred for Iran's Shi'a revolutionary government, perhaps even more than terrorism by Sunni Muslim groups such as the Islamic State, is an issue that unites Trump and both of his hosts on the trip so far." Transforming that "shared hatred" into a powerful Sunni Arab-dominated coalition against Iran was a key goal of Trump's Middle East trip, but with a twist.

One of the rarely mentioned objectives was to consolidate an Israeli role at the center of the mainly Arab anti-Iran coalition. This seemed counterintuitive—for decades Saudi and other Arab leaders had condemned Israel and voiced support for Palestinians. But in fact, both Israeli and Saudi leaders were quietly eager to move toward normalization of relations. By the time of Trump's 2017 visit, they had worked behind the scenes for years to construct unacknowledged commercial, diplomatic, and even strategic/military ties with each other. Both looked forward to Trump's support for such alliance.

The problem the Israeli and Arab leaders faced was not their own disagreements—the Arab monarchies had paid lip service to Palestinian issues but had done little over the years to help end Israeli oppression of Palestinians. The problem was that Arab public opinion *did* support Palestinian rights, and was historically outraged at the prospect of Arab-Israeli collusion. One part of the strategic response to that situation was the close alliance that quickly emerged between Jared

Kushner—Trump's son-in-law and Middle East advisor—and the newly appointed heir to the Saudi throne, Mohammed bin Salman, known as MBS, who together helped organize Trump's visit.

Prince Mohammed was responsible for a range of power-grabbing economic reforms that had made him a favorite of US political and media elites across party and political lines. But MBS was also responsible for initiating Saudi Arabia's lethal assault on Yemen in 2015. The Saudi military assault had killed more than 11,000 civilians by mid-2018, and the Saudi-imposed blockade had created a humanitarian crisis that at that time the United Nations deemed the worst in the world. The Saudi-led coalition, including the UAE and several other Arab countries, was backed directly by the United States. Washington sold them billions of dollars' worth of warplanes, bombs, and other weapons, and the Pentagon participated directly by sending US Air Force pilots in US Air Force planes to provide in-air refueling for the Saudi and UAE bombers so they could attack Yemen more efficiently.

In March 2018, following Trump's visit to Saudi Arabia, Prince Mohammed spent several weeks on a high-visibility PR tour across the United States, meeting with top leaders of major political, corporate, media, and educational institutions. He was reported to be meeting with leaders of a wide range of pro-Israel organizations including the major lobby group AIPAC, the Jewish Federations of North America (JFNA), the Council of Presidents of Major Jewish Organizations, the Anti-Defamation League (ADL). Some of them, including AIPAC and ADL, are among the organizations that had for years mobilized opposition to the BDS movement that calls for nonviolent economic and social pressure on Israel to end its violations of international law and human rights. Others, including JFNA, were longstanding supporters of Israeli settlements in the occupied West Bank and Arab East Jerusalem.

The tour built on the close ties forged between Prince Mohammed and Jared Kushner in setting up Trump's visit to the region. Those ties, along with MBS's rock star welcome by pundits and politicians across the US, all helped to further Riyadh's ambitious regional plans. Those plans included a US-backed Saudi resurgence in the region, including moves toward a Saudi-Israeli rapprochement. The Kushner-MBS partnership continued at a slow pace through mid-2018 and certainly helped deflect the outrage that rose across the United States after the murder of Saudi critic and *Washington Post* journalist Jamal Khashoggi later that year in the Saudi embassy in Istanbul. Within a month, the CIA concluded that MBS had ordered the murder. Despite that finding, close relations between MBS and both the Trump and later Biden administrations continued.

Washington's close embrace of Saudi Arabia, despite its repression at home and human rights and war crimes abroad, and Kushner's strong ties to MBS, set the stage for the Biden administration's adoption of Trump's regional plan and for a serious rise in the threat of war—with not only the United States but Israel and Saudi Arabia, plus Jordan, the UAE, Egypt, and others, openly unifying against Iran.

What were the Abraham Accords and Trump's Middle East peace plan?

The Abraham Accords were a set of bilateral agreements, orchestrated largely by the Trump administration, aimed at normalizing relations between Israel and several Arab countries that had for many years refused open diplomatic relations with Tel Aviv. They were tied to Trump's announced Middle East Peace Plan, which was designed largely to sideline Palestine and Palestinians and keep the focus on building up an Arab-Israeli coalition against Iran.

Despite some of the propaganda that accompanied the Abraham Accords, it was hardly the first time Arab governments and Israel had built ties. Egypt had signed the Camp David Agreement in 1979, normalizing relations with Israel on the basis of Israel returning the Sinai Peninsula, which it had occupied in the 1967 war, to Egyptian control. And Jordan had signed a peace agreement in 1994, in return for access to water, the return of a small piece of land Israel had illegally occupied, protection of the traditional Hashemite role as guardian of the al Aqsa mosque compound, and a range of cooperation agreements. But since 1994, no other Arab government had officially or openly broken the long-ago agreement of the Arab League not to normalize relations with Israel as long as it occupied Palestinian land.

In 2002, as George W. Bush's so-called global war on terror was consolidating in Afghanistan and across the Middle East ahead of the invasion of Iraq, the king of Saudi Arabia launched the Arab Peace Initiative, which called for full normalization with Israel on the basis of a full Israeli withdrawal from the occupied West Bank, Gaza, and East Jerusalem. It was widely welcomed in rhetoric, but on the ground it never existed.

Throughout the 2010s, various Arab regimes had quietly opened talks on economic, trade, and other ties with Israel. Most of the governments had long ago abandoned any real concern for Palestinians, cheering for the Arab Peace Initiative but doing little to make it real, and would have been delighted to move towards full normalization—except that their populations remained very committed to Palestinian rights, and in the context of the Arab Spring uprisings that began in 2011, an open embrace of Tel Aviv was deemed far too destabilizing for the absolute monarchies, military dictatorships, and beyond.

But by the time Donald Trump was elected, things were changing. Trump had opposed the Iran nuclear agreement from its beginning. When he was elected in 2016, he made clear that he would pull the US out of the deal as soon as he took office. Connected to that move was the consolidation of closer ties—economic and strategic/military—with the range of Sunni-based Arab governments, led by Saudi Arabia, which saw Shi'a-dominant Iran as its major challenger for regional power. Most of those governments had already been reaching out to Israel—and that continued. There were visits by Omani leaders to Israel and Israeli officials to Oman, and sports exchanges with the UAE in 2018. In 2019, the US orchestrated Arab participation in the Warsaw conference in Europe, which was focused on opposing Iran—and it marked the first time since the 1991 Madrid Peace Conference that Israeli and Arab diplomats participated publicly in a Middle East-based conference. In August 2019, the UAE and Israel announced an official military cooperation agreement.

Trump announced his peace plan in January 2020, in a joint press conference with Israeli Prime Minister Benjamin Netanyahu. It reflected the same extreme consolidation of Israeli domination over Palestinians that had been at the core of Trump's policies towards Israel announced in 2018 when he visited the country. That meant Jerusalem as the capital of Israel alone, Israeli annexation of about 30 percent of the West Bank including the entire Jordan Valley and major Jewish settlements, and a noncontiguous set of small enclaves for a non-state Palestinian entity. Credited primarily to Jared Kushner, the plan was mostly designed to end the conflict—in order to maximize economic access and profit to outside actors. Palestinians and Palestinian rights were largely invisible. The plan was widely dismissed as not serious.

But later that same year, the US arranged the announcements of bilateral agreements first between Israel and Bahrain, then Israel and the UAE. In September, Trump presided over an elaborate signing ceremony between the three countries and introduced the agreements as the Abraham Accords. In both cases, the UAE and Bahrain recognized Israeli sovereignty and announced full diplomatic relations.

The next set of agreements came with more specific prices, paid by the US. In October, Israel and Sudan agreed to normalize relations, and in return the US took Sudan off its list of state sponsors of terrorism and provided a $1.2 billion bridge loan to clear Sudan's World Bank debt. The agreement was signed on January 6, 2021, just as thousands of protesters were storming the White House in an effort to prevent the election of Joe Biden from being formalized. (As of October 2024, Sudan has still not ratified the agreement and has been enmeshed in a brutal civil war for many months; opposition to the deal remains very high.) In December 2020, Israel signed a normalization agreement with Morocco—the price for that one was US recognition of Morocco's occupation of Western Sahara, where the Sahrawi people have long struggled for independence from Moroccan rule. The US and Israel are the only two countries that recognize Morocco's annexation of Western Sahara.

When Biden took office in 2021, he followed the Trump initiative and made support for the Abraham Accords a major part of his Middle East policy. The biggest prize—Saudi Arabia—was the most difficult partly because of the dominant role of Saudi Arabia as not only the most powerful of the Arab Gulf states and its role as protector of Sunni Islam, but also because of the Saudi King Salman bin Abdulaziz al-Saud's Arab Peace Initiative in 2002. But despite the claim of power in the kingdom by his son, Crown Prince Mohammed bin Salman or MBS, that followed the aging king's long withdrawal from public life, it is widely assumed that as long as King Salman is alive, MBS will not make that final move.

Ties between Saudi Arabia and Israel certainly exist; Saudi Arabia had agreed in 2022 to allow planes flying to or from Israel to transit Saudi airspace. But in October 2024, when Netanyahu spoke at the UN General Assembly, he highlighted a proposal for an Israeli-Saudi alliance that does not yet exist. He called it a "boon to the security and economy of our two countries. It would boost trade and tourism across the region. It would help transform the Middle East into a global jugger-naut. ...Such a peace, I am sure, would be a true pivot of history. ...With American support and leadership, I believe this vision can materialize much sooner than people think." As he spun out his fantasy, the camera panned across the near-empty General Assembly hall to linger on the Saudi delegation's name plate—and behind it on the five empty chairs. The Saudi diplomats had joined the majority of the representatives of the world in a dramatic walkout as Netanyahu was introduced.

What was the significance of the Trump administration's decision to recognize Jerusalem as the capital of Israel and move the US embassy to Jerusalem?

Throughout his 2016 presidential campaign, Donald Trump promised to move the US embassy in Israel from Tel Aviv to Jerusalem. The promise—or threat—to move the embassy had a long history in US politics. Back in 1995, Israel supporters in Congress orchestrated a law mandating the embassy move, but giving the president a way out to avoid actually doing it—the president could waive the requirement if national security might be at stake. The waiver allowed congressional Israel-backers to blame the president for not implementing the law, and the White House could lament that security threats prevented the move. Every president since took advantage of that waiver—including Donald Trump for the first six months into his presidency.

But Trump's campaign commitment to move the embassy was more important to more influential supporters than was true of earlier presidents. Much of Trump's motivation was linked to his desire to please his key Israel-backing donors, particularly the Las Vegas casino mogul Sheldon Adelson and his wife, Miriam, as well as the influential

Christian Zionist component within his powerful right-wing evangelical base. And Trump's overall failure to win many legislative victories in Congress meant he had more incentive to make good on his White House-based Jerusalem promise.

As the second six-month deadline approached, in December 2017, Trump announced his intention to recognize Jerusalem as the capital of Israel and to move the US embassy from Tel Aviv to Jerusalem. In doing so he broke with decades of US and global precedent and violated international law. Jerusalem had been divided since 1948, with the newly declared State of Israel holding the western side, while the eastern side remained part of the Palestinian West Bank, under Jordanian control. Israel claimed Jerusalem as its capital, but virtually all foreign embassies were located in Tel Aviv.

Trump called the move a "recognition of reality," but it was long-standing US policy of providing Tel Aviv with billions of dollars of military aid, acceptance of Jews-only settlements within occupied Arab East Jerusalem, protection of Israel in the United Nations, all of which had enabled Trump's—and Israel's—claimed reality.

When the UN partitioned Palestine in 1947, it recognized not only what were supposed to become Jewish and Palestinian Arab states, but also a special status for Jerusalem. The city was to belong to neither "state," but rather be a *corpus separatum*, a separate body to remain under international control. In 1967 Israel illegally occupied the eastern half of the city, and in 1980 it announced the annexation of Arab East Jerusalem and the forcibly unified city as its capital. No country in the world recognized the annexation, and since that time, legally binding UN Security Council resolutions continue to reaffirm that East Jerusalem remains occupied Palestinian territory.

UN Security Council Resolution 478, passed in 1980 with the US abstaining, determined that the Israeli decision to annex East Jerusalem "constitutes a violation of international law" and called on all "States that have established diplomatic missions at Jerusalem to withdraw such missions from the Holy City." They did. So when Trump announced in 2017 he would move the US embassy to Jerusalem, not a single other country maintained an embassy there. The decision to recognize Jerusalem was in direct violation of the Security Council resolution.

Four days after Trump's announcement, on December 21, 2017, the UN General Assembly responded. Despite US Ambassador Nikki Haley's dire threats to governments that might consider voting against the United States, a huge majority of countries voted to condemn Trump's recognition of Jerusalem as the capital of Israel—128 countries voted to condemn, only nine opposed, and thirty-five abstained.

Those celebrating at the embassy opening, along with Israeli officials, were Trump's daughter and son-in-law, Ivanka Trump and Jared Kushner. Also included were the evangelical Christian Zionist pastors John Hagee and Robert Jeffress, known for their fulsome support for Israel, Islamophobia, and racist hatred towards Palestinians, as well as the belief that the second coming of Christ required all Jews to be gathered in Israel, where they would then either convert or die. Just sixty miles away, it was Nakba Day in the Gaza Strip, the commemoration of the 1948 dispossession and a day ahead of what was planned to be the culmination of the Great March of Return. At exactly the same time, Israeli sharpshooters were firing live ammunition over the fences into Gaza, where Palestinians, commemorating the Nakba on their own land, were shot by the thousands. At least sixty Palestinians were killed and almost 3,000 injured on that day, most by Israeli sniper fire as the new US embassy in Jerusalem opened its doors.

Months later, Trump addressed the Republican Jewish Coalition, and bragged about moving the embassy. Addressing his two biggest funders, longtime supporters of Israeli settlements he said, "We got you something that you wanted, I can tell you, Sheldon and Miriam."

What was Gaza's "Great March of Return" that began in spring 2018? How did Israel respond?

By early 2018 Gaza had been under a suffocating Israeli-imposed and Egyptian-supported blockade for almost a dozen years. With the crossings closed, almost two million Palestinians, 80 percent of them refugees and half under the age of eighteen, were imprisoned in the walled-off, crowded, impoverished Strip.

Back in 2012, the United Nations had assessed that Gaza would be "unlivable" by 2020, because of insufficient water, lack of medicine, limited electricity, and other factors. Conditions continued to worsen, and by July 2017 the UN humanitarian coordinator in the occupied Palestinian territory acknowledged that, "Sadly, as we check in on those same trends again in this 2017 report, the deterioration has accelerated."

That deterioration meant a whole generation of children was growing up never knowing anything close to a normal life. In response, led by the noted Palestinian poet Ahmad Abu Artema, a group of civil society activists in Gaza called for a series of protests aimed at reminding Israel, and especially the world, that Palestinians were still there, that "We Are Not Numbers," as one group called itself, that they were people with human rights. Among these was the internationally guaranteed right to return to their homes, lost when they were driven out of their land in the 1947–48 Nakba. The demands focused on both the right of return and an end to the crippling blockade of Gaza.

The plan was for protests every Friday, each time heading closer to the Israeli-built fences completely walling in the Gaza Strip (although there is no actual border—Israel is the only country in the world that has never declared its own borders). While the organizers came from a variety of civil society groups across Gaza, the protests were quickly endorsed by all Palestinian political factions.

Months before the protests began, Israeli authorities announced their intention to send sharpshooters to the boundary area with orders to shoot anyone who even approached the fence. This decision appeared to be based on the view that if a planned violation of international humanitarian law, a war crime, was announced ahead of time, it would somehow become legal. In fact, of course, a previously announced crime remains a crime—and international law prohibits using lethal force against civilians, particularly against a protected population such as one living under occupation, except in an urgent situation when a specific person's life is at risk.

The protests began on March 30, commemorated by Palestinians as Land Day in remembrance of a 1976 demonstration inside Israel, in which six Palestinian citizens of Israel were killed by Israeli police while protesting the expropriation of their land. That first 2018 protest brought about 30,000 Palestinians, many of them families who participated in cultural and children's events, staying in tents set up at half a dozen sites hundreds of meters away from the Gaza wall.

As was the case during the first Palestinian intifada, in 1987–91, the protests were overwhelmingly nonviolent. And also like the first intifada, some teenagers and young people threw stones at Israeli tanks hundreds of yards away on the other side of two sets of fences; no Israeli soldiers were seriously injured or killed. But as promised, from the first demonstration, Israeli soldiers hiding behind berms built up on the Israeli side of the wall used massive amounts of tear gas, then quickly shifted to sharpshooters who fired live ammunition at the protesters. The snipers killed fifteen Palestinians that day, with dozens more injured. As the protests went on, by May 11, the numbers killed had spiked to fifty, with thousands injured, many of them by live fire. Many of the injured faced catastrophic, life-altering disabilities, as Gaza's overwhelmed doctors in underequipped hospitals lacking sufficient drugs, equipment, and even electricity to light the operating rooms, were forced to amputate limbs they could not save.

The Monday of the following week, May 14, was Nakba Day, commemorating the Palestinian dispossession of seventy years before. The crowd of protesters was bigger, and the snipers moved in early. The first Palestinian they killed was standing on his own land inside Gaza, in the morning, before the main protests had even begun.

The news quickly streamed across televisions, computer screens, and smartphones around the world. Teenagers splayed across makeshift stretchers carried by other teenagers to waiting ambulances, tear gas so thick it was impossible to see through it even on a television or computer screen. Sharpshooters firing, with casualty counts unable to keep up. By the end of that day, at least sixty Palestinians had been killed and more than 2,400 seriously injured. Military officials stated that every target was approved by IDF commanders.

At the same moment, sixty miles away in occupied East Jerusalem, top Israeli and US officials were celebrating the opening of the new US embassy. Trump's son-in-law and top Middle East advisor Jared Kushner used the moment to assert that the Palestinian protesters, whom he defined as "those who provoke violence," were "part of the problem, not part of the solution."

The sixty Palestinians killed and the thousands injured that day included seven children. Israeli Brigadier General Zvika Fogel defended the actions of his troops. In a radio interview two days earlier, he was asked specifically about the killing of unarmed children who bear no threat to soldiers. He answered, "Anyone *who could be a future threat* to the border of the State of Israel and its residents, should bear a price for that violation." (Emphasis added). The interviewer responded, "Then his punishment is death?" And the general answered immediately, "His punishment is death."

Numerous governments and the United Nations condemned the Israeli actions in Gaza, with the UN High Commissioner for Human Rights Zeid Ra'ad al-Hussein stating, "Those responsible for outrageous human rights violations must be held to account." South Africa and Turkey withdrew their ambassadors from Israel. The United States called the deaths "tragic" and placed all responsibility on Hamas, claiming that Israel had the right to "defend its borders."

The weekly protests continued until the end of 2019. During that time, more than 220 Palestinians were killed, 46 of them children, and over 36,000 including 8,800 children were injured. Of the 7,000 injured by live fire, 120 including 20 children had had limbs amputated during the first year. The UN estimated that 1,700 more injured people, almost all of them young, would face amputation in the coming two years because the siege of Gaza meant its blockaded hospitals did not have the capacity for the delicate surgery necessary to save their arms and legs.

On October 27, 2023, just three weeks into Israel's war on Gaza, an Israeli air strike seriously injured the poet Ahmad Abu Artema, and killed five members of his family, including his twelve-year-old son.

What is the significance of the 2018 Basic Law making Israel the nation-state of the Jewish people?

On July 19, 2018, the Israeli Knesset passed a Basic Law (equivalent to a constitutional amendment) declaring Israel as "the nation-state of the Jewish people." While most of the substance reflected realities already existing on the ground, the new law made Israel's existing apartheid system official and legal.

Israel's declaration of independence called for "complete equality of social and political rights to all its inhabitants irrespective of religion, race or sex." But that was never implemented. From the beginning, Israel was established as a Jewish state designed to privilege its Jewish citizens, and key state institutions have always operated on behalf of what was defined as the Jewish nation. Citizenship rights—the right to vote and run for office—were available to all citizens, Jewish or not, but unlike in most countries, not all legal rights in Israel were determined by citizenship. Nationality rights, including land ownership, residency rights, access to bank loans and education, and more, were and are apportioned differently to Israel's different "nationalities"—which are defined on the basis of religion (see pages 7-9) So despite the official claim of "complete equality," Jewish Israelis have always had far more legal rights and privileges than Palestinian Muslim or Christian Israelis—and laws and state practice were created to maintain Jewish domination.

But while neither the notion of a Jewish state nor Jewish nation are new, the 20018 Basic Law was significant in further legalizing Jewish supremacy and negating the rights of Palestinian Arabs and other non-Jews in Israel. Provisions in the law elevated both legal and de facto Jewish supremacy in Palestine to a new level.

The new law established Hebrew as the only official language, removing Arabic from that designation. It officially encouraged Jewish-only settlements and communities as a goal of the state, legalizing exclusion and discrimination against the 20 percent of Israelis who are Palestinian. And crucially, it declared that "the right to exercise national self-determination in the State of Israel is unique to the Jewish people," legally denying the right of Palestinians to self-determination or equality.

Some provisions of the law simply reiterate things long established, such as the official name and flag of Israel, but other elements reasserted old measures in a new context—and therefore with new consequences. The law proclaimed that "Jerusalem, complete and united, is the capital of Israel." The Knesset had already proclaimed this with its annexation of occupied East Jerusalem in 1980, but it had never been recognized internationally. The 2018 declaration in the Basic Law came just a few months after President Trump broke with international law, UN resolutions, and the precedents of US policy to move the US embassy from Tel Aviv to Jerusalem and recognize Jerusalem as the capital of Israel.

As an Israeli Jewish philosopher described the new law in the *New York Times*, "Israel's policy of promoting Jewish settlements has created de facto apartheid in the occupied territories .... The nation-state law now formally endorses the use of similar apartheid methods within Israel's recognized borders."

What was the significance of the election of "the Squad" in 2018?

Partly in response to the rise of extremist right-wing white supremacist and related movements that emerged with and followed the 2016 election of Donald Trump, and partly because of the rise of Black Lives Matter and other anti-racist and broad progressive movements that were growing and strengthening even before Trump's election, progressive and left-wing activists and movements escalated their direct engagement with electoral campaigns.

In the 2018 midterms, four progressive young women of color were elected to Congress as Democrats. Together they were African-American and Puerto Rican, Muslim and immigrant, Palestinian and Somali, and collectively they became known as the Squad. They positioned themselves pointedly to the left of the vast majority of Democrats in Congress, and not coincidentally they all openly supported Palestinian rights.

Before that time, the only member of Congress known for consistent and legislative support for Palestinian rights was Rep. Betty McCollum of St. Paul, Minnesota. While not a member of the Progressive Caucus, McCollum remained a consistent supporter of human rights, and in that context, starting in 2017, quietly built coalitions to support various versions of a bill aimed at protecting Palestinian children and families. The 2023 version prohibited the use of US taxpayer dollars for the military detention or other abuse of Palestinian children, the seizure and destruction of Palestinian homes and property in violation of international law, or support for Israel's annexation of Palestinian land in violation of international humanitarian law. As of 2024 none of the bills had won enough support to pass, but each year the number of sponsors grew.

The Squad played a different role, more overtly critical of Israeli violations and supportive of Palestinian rights, and from the time they were elected they were immediately singled out for major attacks both by Republicans and by centrist and corporate-backed Democrats—all of whom were supporters of US military aid to and protection of Israel. Some of the attacks claimed to be responding to specific statements by one or more of the Squad, statements often taken out of context or completely misquoted. But virtually all of the attacks reflected racist, Islamophobic, sexist, and xenophobic views towards the four Squad members. False accusations of antisemitism, particularly against Rep. Rashida Tlaib, the first Palestinian Muslim woman elected to Congress, and Rep. Ilhan Omar, a Black Muslim immigrant from Somalia, were rampant.

In 2019, Rep. Omar was condemned for antisemitism for noting that the pro-Israel lobbies function the same way as the gun lobby, pharmaceutical lobby, big oil, and other powerful industries. Speaking at a public event in Washington, DC, Omar said, "I want to talk about the political influence in this country that says it is OK for people to push for allegiance to a foreign country. I want to ask why is it OK for me to talk about the influence of the NRA (National Rifle Association), of fossil fuel industries or Big Pharma, and not talk about a powerful lobbying group that is influencing policies?" There was no question she was describing the pro-Israel lobby, which of course includes powerful Christian sectors as well as Jewish-based groups, and was not talking about Jews, yet she was attacked for antisemitism, with critics falsely claiming she had referenced antisemitic tropes about Jews holding "dual loyalty." Until a campaign emerged that corrected what she actually said, leading Democrats had joined with Republicans to threaten a congressional resolution that would have condemned the congresswoman for something she never said. Once the clarification became public, the planned resolution was abandoned, replaced with an anodyne statement of opposition to racism, Islamophobia, antisemitism, and other forms of prejudice—without any reference to Rep. Omar. (Ironically, the actual reference to Jews' alleged dual loyalty was reflected just a month later. In April 2019, President Trump told the leadership of the Republican Jewish Coalition that he had "stood with your prime minister" when he announced the change in US policy to recognize Israel's illegal annexation of the Syrian Golan Heights—as if those American Jews were somehow accountable to Israeli Prime Minister Netanyahu.)

Later that year, both Rep. Tlaib and Rep. Omar were denied entry to Israel to visit Rep. Tlaib's family in the occupied West Bank. Reports surfaced that Trump had asked the Israeli government not to allow the congresswomen to enter. And in 2023, Rep. Tlaib was censured by the House of Representatives for her statements in response to US providing military support to Israel for its lethal assault on Gaza that began that October.

In the 2020 election, the Squad gained new members. In what the *New York Times* called a "stunning victory," African-American middle school teacher and principal Jamaal Bowman defeated Eliot Engel, a sixteen-term incumbent Democrat and one of the most powerful supporters of Israel in Congress. Bowman was joined by Rep. Cori Bush, a Black Lives Matter activist from St. Louis, who had become politically active following the police killing of Michael Brown in Ferguson, Missouri, in 2014. Both broadened the scope of the Squad's areas of work: Bowman around education and Bush particularly in housing rights and anti-poverty work. And both immediately took strong positions supporting Palestinian rights.

All six of the Squad were reelected in the 2022 midterms and were joined by three more representatives—Summer Lee from Pennsylvania, Greg Casar of Texas, and Delia Ramirez of Illinois. Support for Palestinian rights remained a hallmark of the group, and a major part of the reason for AIPAC's expanded efforts to defeat any of them deemed potentially vulnerable.

In the 2024 primary elections, AIPAC announced it would spend $100 million—an unprecedented amount in a single congressional election cycle—to defeat progressives in the Democratic primaries. Members of the Squad were among its key targets. Its support led to the defeat of Bowman and Bush, both leaders in supporting Palestinian rights, though it was notable that the AIPAC strategy was to downplay any overt focus on Israel. The vast majority of their ads and campaign strategies never mentioned Israel or US support for Israel at all. And it cost AIPAC more than $15 million to defeat Jamaal Bowman, and over $9 million to defeat Cori Bush.

That itself was a statement of the significant shift underway in Congress. The fact that it eventually took more than $20 million to defeat a very progressive African-American in a New York district that had been stripped of much of its working-class base in redistricting, and more than $9 million to defeat an African-American anti-racist and housing activist from St. Louis, both of them outspoken supporters of Palestinian rights, was testament to how the political discourse was shifting. AIPAC money could still create outsize influence and lead to defeating candidates, but a much higher price would have to be paid for it to work.

Throughout their years in Congress, members of the squad played a significant role in transforming the political discourse on the issue of Palestinian rights and especially aid to Israel. While they were not able get legislation passed, they did initiate letters to the White House, and various resolutions and statements that helped transform congressional debate. For the first time during those years, military aid to Israel was routinely and openly discussed, challenged, criticized—even if it was not yet conditioned on human rights or cut altogether.

The work of the Squad, and that of other members of Congress willing to consider Palestinian rights as part of US policy, was made more difficult because of the wide gap between the rapidly shifting position of the Democratic Party base and that of the largely stalled position of the party's elected officials. It was not surprising that a 2024 fact sheet from the Jewish Democratic Council of America trumpeted, "The record shows that Democratic support for Israel in Congress remains strong"— but made no mention of the rising Democratic criticism of Israel and support for Palestinian rights *outside* of Congress. Despite the growing divide between members of Congress and their base, those who were elected seemed stuck in the view that criticism of Israel amounted to political suicide—a position that hadn't been true for years.

That divide between the party leadership and its base surfaced powerfully—and to the detriment of the Democrats' election strategy—in the campaign for president in 2024. The rise of the Uncommitted movement led to over 750,000 voters in the Democratic primaries refusing to vote for the Democratic candidate because of the Biden administration's military support for Israel during the 2023–24 genocidal war on Gaza. The refusal of the Democratic leadership to allow even a brief symbolic statement from a single Palestinian speaker, excluding even those who were elected Democratic officials, during the August 2024 Democratic convention solidified that divide within the party even further.

But the intense involvement of Palestinian rights activists within the Democratic Party processes during the campaign, including the mobilizations demanding a ceasefire, was certainly strengthened by the presence of the Squad within Congress. The group's presence had set the stage for much more active engagement between social movements working on Palestinian rights and those who championed the issue in Congress. While that relationship often remained uneven, with the different roles required of activists, movements, and elected officials sometimes confused or blurred, the presence of the Squad in Congress made possible significant steps towards a real shift in operative policy decisions.

What was the Biden administration's policy on Israel-Palestine?

Joe Biden entered national politics as a senator in 1973—the same year he had his famous encounter with Prime Minister Golda Meir of Israel. She reportedly told him not to worry about Israel, because its secret weapon was the fact that Israelis "have no place else to go." There's no indication that Biden asked the prime minister whether Palestinians, much of whose land was expropriated by war to create the self-defined Jewish state, had some place else to go.

According to Reuters, "during his 36 years in the Senate, Biden was the chamber's biggest recipient in history of donations from pro-Israeli groups, taking in $4.2 million." And a 2024 fact sheet from the Jewish Democratic Council of America bragged, "No candidate for president in either party has ever run with as long and as strong of a pro-Israel record as Joe Biden. As Vice President, Joe Biden played key roles in ensuring

Israel's security, including through his support of unprecedented levels of security assistance to Israel. Biden opposes the global BDS movement and opposes cutting or conditioning military aid to Israel."

Throughout Biden's 2020 campaign and as he moved into the White House, he claimed human rights would be the centerpiece of his presidency. But the frequent retelling of his Golda Meir story and his proud statement that "I am a Zionist" made clear his embrace of the Israel exception that characterizes so much of US foreign policy. The Middle East positions Biden supported and initiated throughout his tenure reflected those positions—for reasons both geopolitical and sentimental—far more than they reflected human rights.

In 2017 Donald Trump's first trip abroad as president had been to the Middle East—just months into his presidency. He went first to Saudi Arabia, where he signed a $110 billion arms deal. In Israel he met with Netanyahu, announced a new "peace plan" being crafted by his son-in-law and designed to sideline Palestinians to favor normalization between Israel and several Arab states against Iran. A year later Trump withdrew the US from the Obama-Biden Iran nuclear deal—in order to strengthen a military Saudi- and Israeli-led anti-Iran coalition. He then announced a set of new US policies towards Israel, including recogniz-ing Jerusalem as the capital of Israel and moving the US embassy there, declaring the Jews-only settlements across the West Bank and occupied East Jerusalem to be legal, diplomatic recognition of Israel's annexation of Syria's Golan Heights, and shutting the East Jerusalem consulate that had long served as the US representative to the Palestinians.

During the first two years of Biden's presidency and well into 2023, US foreign policy was still focused more on the broad issue of competi-tion with China and the immediate crisis of the war in Ukraine than on the Middle East. Biden's first trip to the Middle East, in July 2022, had a lot to do with consolidating US power and countering Chinese and Russian influence there—particularly in strengthening the Israeli- and Saudi-led anti-Iran coalition under US leadership and increasing arms sales. The timing had a lot to do with the recently launched Russian war in Ukraine—and the price of oil at home, with global shortages and price hikes linked to war-driven sanctions against Russian crude.

Biden publicly reaffirmed Washington's strategic ties with both

Saudi Arabia and Israel, and he made clear that human rights concerns, even if mentioned in passing, would have no impact on actual relations—specifically, no impact on billions of dollars in US military aid to Israel and arms sales to both countries. He reiterated the pride of place Israel and Saudi Arabia held in US Middle East policy, both with their bilateral ties with Washington and their increasing ties with each other, at the center of US plans to remain the dominant global power in the region.

During the 2020 campaign, Biden had called Saudi Arabia a pariah and, reflecting US intelligence agencies' findings, called out the Saudi leader for the brutal murder of Jamal Khashoggi, a well-known Saudi critic and *Washington Post* journalist, in the Saudi consulate in Istanbul in 2018. Biden also made clear he didn't agree with Trump's extreme positions on Israel. So on day one in the White House, Biden could have reversed those positions to bring his policy into line with his expressed commitment to human rights. But right up to the 2024 election, Biden refused to reverse Trump's policies towards Israel or Saudi Arabia, with the partial exception of a statement from Biden's secretary of state, Antony Blinken, that new settlements were counterproductive and inconsistent with international law. (Blinken made no mention of existing settlements, and no mention of any actual consequence for that finding.)

As a result of his failure to explicitly reject Trump's policies, those extremist positions became Biden's own. So when Biden headed to the region in 2022 and greeted MBS, whom he ostensibly held responsible for the murder of Khashoggi, with a friendly fist bump, and in 2023 embraced Netanyahu in an emotional bear hug, it was consistency with his predecessor's positions, not a reversal of them, that the world was seeing. During the Saudi trip, Biden said that he had told MBS that he believed the prince was responsible for Khashoggi's murder—and that MBS had denied he was involved. "I indicated I thought he was," Biden went on. And that was the end of it—Biden then went on with negotiating with the prince to increase oil production, normalize relations with Israel, and build opposition to Iran (which justified virtually unlimited US arms sales to Saudi Arabia). Biden also made very clear, in his joint 2022 appearance with Palestinian President Mahmoud Abbas, that Washington's supposed support for a two-state solution did not mean a commitment to any action that might actually help make it happen—telling the Palestinians instead that "the ground is not ripe at this moment to restart negotiations."

Despite public assertions about the centrality of human rights to his foreign policy, Biden did not announce or make any moves to hold either Israel or Saudi Arabia to account for their violations. Like all his predecessors, he did not move to make US military aid to Israel conditional on ending any of its specific human rights violations. He did not announce plans to cut that military assistance, despite the Leahy Law's prohibition on aid to any military unit that "has committed a gross violation of human rights," even though the US had admitted the Israeli military was, among other things, "likely responsible" for killing Palestinian journalist Shireen Abu Akleh, who was a US citizen.

US support for Israel as the center of the anti-Iran coalition remained at the top of every statement. The "Jerusalem Declaration of the US-Israel Strategic Partnership" was the symbolic centerpiece of Biden's 2022 trip. It said nothing about returning to the Iran nuclear deal but included the reaffirmation of Washington's "commitment never to allow Iran to acquire a nuclear weapon." It included a specific threat "to use all elements of its national power" to prevent an Iranian nuclear weapon—a direct reference to military force. The declaration also celebrated the "unshakeable US commitment to Israel's security." It included Washington's guarantee of Israel's "qualitative military edge," a pledge "to preserve and strengthen Israel's capability ... to defend itself by itself against any threat or combination of threats," and a promise for even more military aid, beyond the 2016–2026 starting level of $3.8 billion every year.

Biden and his Israeli counterparts also signed off on an attack on the nonviolent Boycott, Divestment, and Sanctions (BDS) movement, promising to "combat all efforts to boycott or de-legitimize Israel" and to protect Israel at the United Nations and the International Criminal Court. Biden agreed to allow all Israelis to enter the United States under the supposedly reciprocal visa waiver program, despite Israel's refusal to allow all US citizens the same privilege in entering Israel. The State Department's own advisory continued to warn that "US citizens of Arab or Muslim heritage (including Palestinian-Americans) have experienced significant difficulties and unequal and occasionally hostile treatment at Israel's borders and checkpoints."

Violence against Palestinians in the West Bank and Gaza committed by military personnel and settlers (often working together) continued to rise through 2022 and 2023. The events of October 7, 2023, when Hamas-led militants broke through the walls surrounding Gaza and attacked military and civilian targets in southern Israel, and of October 8, when Israel responded with full-scale war against the 2.3 million Palestinians living in the besieged Gaza Strip, led to the Biden administration being forced to put Israel and Palestine—specifically Gaza—on top of its agenda.

Why was Israel's killing of journalist Shireen Abu Akleh in 2022 so important?

Preventing media coverage of actions that violate international law, human rights, and UN resolutions has long been a goal of the Israeli government. That has meant refusing visas and significant levels of military censorship of foreign journalists, denial of access to all journalists, and repression including arrests, detention, and deliberate, sometimes lethal attacks on Palestinian journalists.

In May 2022, Israeli troops launched a series of raids in Jenin, a city in the northern West Bank, and the adjoining refugee camp. Early on the morning of May 11, a group of journalists gathered to cover the attack on a family inside the camp. One of them was Shireen Abu Akleh, an experienced and well-known al-Jazeera correspondent who had worked in and around the occupied Palestinian territories for more than 25 years. A Palestinian as well as a US citizen, Shireen was known and beloved by Palestinians around the world for her consistent on-the-ground narration of Palestinians and Palestine.

All the journalists wore helmets and blue protective vests marked "PRESS" in big letters. While standing in a group on a quiet street just outside the camp, where no clashes or gunfire were underway, Abu Akleh was shot and killed. Another Palestinian journalist was shot and injured, and a third who tried to help Abu Akleh as she lay face-down and unmoving after being shot, was fired on as well. Shireen was declared dead at the hospital. Two days later, Israeli soldiers violently attacked her funeral procession as it headed into the Jerusalem church, throwing Palestinian flags to the ground and beating the mourners, including those carrying Shireen's coffin, almost forcing them to drop it.

It was hardly surprising. At that time, according to the Palestinian Journalists Syndicate, Shireen Abu Akleh was the 86th journalist to be killed while covering Israeli military and police actions in the West Bank, Gaza and East Jerusalem since they were occupied in 1967. Just sixteen months later, that number had grown to 202 journalists killed. Of those, 116 were killed in Israel's war in Gaza from October 2023 until September 2024.

Initially, Israeli officials tried to claim that the bullet that killed Abu Akleh was fired by a Palestinian gunman. But that was quickly exposed as false by the journalists who had been present when she was killed, as well as through a full examination by B'tselem, a globally respected Israeli human rights organization. Demands rose for a full and independent investigation; within a few days Israel announced the Military Police Criminal Investigation Division would not investigate—because questioning Israeli soldiers who might be suspects "would provoke opposition and controversy within the IDF and in Israeli society in general." In December 2022, al Jazeera asked the International Criminal Court to investigate the killing of their journalist. In response, Yair Lapid, then the prime minister of Israel, stated "No one will investigate IDF soldiers and no one will preach to us about morals in warfare, certainly not al-Jazeera."

In September 2023, the United Nations' independent International Commission of Inquiry issued a report on Israel's use of force in the occupied territories. Based on their earlier finding that the Israeli occupation of the West Bank, Gaza and East Jerusalem was itself "unlawful under international law, owing to its permanence and to actions undertaken by Israel to annex parts of the land de facto and de jure," the second report included an investigation into the killing of Shireen Abu Akleh.

The commission concluded that "the Israeli security forces used lethal force without justification under international human rights law and intentionally or recklessly violated the right to life of Shireen Abu Akleh." It went on to find that, "During law enforcement operations, lethal force is only permissible in self-defense or to protect the lives of others. In the case of Abu Akleh, the Commission concludes without doubt that Abu Akleh and the other journalists did not pose an imminent threat of death or serious injury to anyone and that there was no gunfire originating from Abu Akleh's location or from near her. In an occupation, the willful killing of a protected person constitutes a grave breach of article 147 of the Fourth Geneva Convention and is a war crime. Abu Akleh and other journalists, who were clearly identifiable as journalists, were protected persons."

The commission also determined the specific unit—the Duvdevan Unit—of the Israeli security forces who were involved in the Jenin operation and were likely to have been in the vehicle from which the shot that killed Abu Akleh was fired. That information should be critical under US law, where the Leahy Law states that "no assistance shall be furnished to any unit of the security forces of a foreign country if the Secretary of State has credible information that such unit has committed a gross violation of human rights." But more than two years after the killing, the US had still refused to act. Israeli officials announced Israel would not cooperate with an FBI investigation into the killing, but the Biden administration would not even acknowledge such an investigation had been launched.

The killing of Shireen Abu Akleh was part of the longstanding pattern of Israel's attacks on journalists. One year after her death, a report from the Committee to Protect Journalists documented Israeli military killings of at least twenty journalists. "Despite numerous IDF probes," the CPJ said, "no one has ever been charged or held responsible for these deaths. The impunity in these cases has severely undermined the freedom of the press, leaving the rights of journalists in precarity."

Israel's goal is to suppress coverage of Israel's violence and collective punishment of all Palestinians, and to avoid any threat to the impunity that US protection provides. But not only have Israeli actions against journalists failed to hide those realities (particularly in the era of ubiquitous social media and the rise of Palestinian journalists working in their own communities), but they serve to demonstrate ever more clearly the structural nature of Israeli racism and violence against Palestinians. As Amnesty International described it in its analysis of Israeli apartheid, Israel's "regular violations of Palestinians' rights are not accidental repetitions of offenses, but part of an institutionalized regime of systematic oppression and domination." And that started years before Israel's 2023 assault against Gaza began, in which just in its first months, more journalists would be killed in the tiny Gaza Strip than were killed in all of World War II.

PART III:
THE ASSESSMENTS—
Where Are We Now?

What has changed in the US discourse regarding Israel and Palestine?

US policy towards Palestine and Israel—grounded since 1967 in unchallenged military, economic, political, and diplomatic support for Israel—did not significantly change until 2017, when Donald Trump became president. His election set the stage for a significant move toward an even stronger level of political support for the farthest right-wing forces within Israel than had been the case through decades of largely unchallenged pro-Israel policies.

But while overall policy remained largely the same, changes in public perception had been underway for a long time. Years before Trump's election, public and media discourse on the issue had already begun a qualitative shift. A Palestinian rights movement had been growing since before the turn of the twenty-first century. Built on the legacy of earlier movements, made up largely of Palestinian students and academics during the 1970s and the left-created Palestine solidarity movement of the 1980s and into the '90s, much of the movement from 2000 or so was shaped around a primary focus on changing US policy—and that meant a major emphasis on education and changing the public debate and public narrative.

While public opinion in the US does not automatically lead to government policy changes, there is no question that winning public support is a necessary first step in successful campaigns to change what that policy is. It is for this reason that many supporters of Palestinian rights in the United States have focused their work on campaigns of public education and advocacy. And after years of activism, such efforts, along with the deteriorating situation in Palestine and Washington's on-going relationship to it, were having a growing impact.

In 2006, former US president Jimmy Carter published *Palestine: Peace Not Apartheid*. The book was not mainly about Israel-Palestine; it was essentially a recap of Carter's own experience negotiating the Israeli-Egyptian Camp David Agreement, with a few ideas of how Israeli–Palestinian peace might take shape. But the then-startling title and the cover photograph of Israel's Apartheid Wall made it enormously important in exposing millions of Americans, many for the first time, to the idea that Israel was part of the problem, not the solution, in achieving

Middle East peace. It also reflected the expanding understanding of many in the US—particularly many African Americans—who had come to understand Israeli policy towards Palestinians in the familiar framework of Jim Crow segregation in the American South—and for some, that of South African apartheid.

A year later, two well-known mainstream academics from Harvard and the University of Chicago published *The Israel Lobby*. While many criticized aspects of their analysis, including their definitions of the lobby and their assertions regarding Israel's role in the run-up to the Iraq war, the book broke a longstanding academic taboo against acknowledging the power and influence of AIPAC and other components of the pro-Israel lobby. Publication of the two books both exemplified and expanded the shift in discourse. The changing political climate made the books less threatening for publishers, and their publication moved public opinion even further.

Changing assumptions in Israel-Palestine coverage in the most influential media, print media in particular, became more visible around 2006—and played a huge role in changing mainstream public opinion. That was particularly evident in the coverage of Israel's wars—the Gaza-Lebanon war of 2006, then Operation Cast Lead in December 2008–January 2009, the assault on Gaza in December 2012, the lethal fifty-day war against Gaza in summer 2014, and the attack of 2021, all leading to the extraordinary public response to the assault on Gaza that began in 2023 following the Hamas-led attack of October (see pages 257–264).

In all those cases, part of Israel's strategy was to exclude the international press from Gaza, to prevent documentation and publication of the shocking effects of Israel's mostly US-supplied weapons, particularly on children and other vulnerable civilians. The strategy failed, partly because key mainstream outlets had Gazan reporters already on the ground on a permanent basis, and partly because of the rise of social media. While the IDF's attack on the generating plants meant that electricity was scarce throughout the wars, Gazans immediately grabbed any brief chance access to electricity to charge their cell phones and computers to quickly send photographs, video, and sound across the globe. For many people, especially in the United States, it was the first time they were seeing the reality of Israeli war crimes and the reality of what occupation looked like in real time—and the effect on public opinion was dramatic.

Access to the mainstream press for Palestinian voices and analysis highlighting Palestinian victims of Israeli human rights violations increased over the years as well. Looking, for example, at just a few weeks in January and February 2014, the *New York Times* published an analysis by British-Israeli scholar Avi Schlaim, "Israel Needs to Learn Some Manners," exposing Secretary of State John Kerry's latest peace process proposal as a "clever American device for wasting time." The *Times* also ran an op-ed by BDS founder Omar Barghouti titled "Why Israel Fears the Boycott." The same week the *Washington Post* published BDS supporter Vijay Prashad's op-ed "A Caution to Israel," explaining the significance of the American Studies Association's decision to boycott Israeli academic institutions. And a few days later, the *Post* acknowledged in a major news piece that "talk about a boycott of Israel is in the mainstream." Organizations like the Institute for Middle East Understanding were seeing astonishing levels of success in placing Palestinian voices in the mainstream media.

Three years earlier, the online magazine Salon.com titled a major article "The Media Consensus on Israel Is Collapsing." It described how "slowly but unmistakably, space is opening up among the commentariat for new, critical ideas about Israel and its relationship to the United States. Freedom of this sort was visible in the pages of the *New York Times* last week. Thomas Friedman, the paper's foreign affairs columnist, wrote that American leaders were betraying the country by outsourcing their foreign policy to Israel. A standing ovation given to the Israeli prime minister by the US Congress this year was "bought and paid for by the Israel lobby," he wrote.

Mainstream religious denominations—including the Presbyterians and the Methodists—endorsed strong boycott resolutions, with votes also for divestment from some corporations profiting from Israeli occupation and violations of international law.

Perhaps the most vivid example of the shifting discourse among the US public was seen during summer 2010, when the rhetorical feud between President Obama and Prime Minister Netanyahu reached a fever pitch. The issue was largely over settlements, with the Israeli prime minister deliberately announcing new settlement expansions during high-level official US visits to Israel, and treating President Obama with visible racist disdain. Tensions ran high. In fact, there was never any indication that the Obama administration ever actually intended to change US policies toward Israel, no threats to even consider cutting military aid or reducing the full-throated defense of Israel in the United Nations, for instance, but political relations were tumultuous and antagonistic. News coverage focused on exaggerated claims that the US was essentially abandoning Israel.

During the height of that tension, a Zogby poll asked US voters to choose which of two sentences best described their view of Israeli settlements. The first choice said that Israelis built settlements for self-defense and they should be allowed to build wherever they chose. The second choice said that settlements were built on "expropriated" land and that they should all be torn down and the land returned to its original owners. Despite the deliberately provocative language, 63 percent of Democrats chose the second sentence.

With the creation of the Black Lives Matter movement, and especially during the summer of 2020 following the police murder of George Floyd, massive protests against racism and police violence brought young people out into the streets. The "justice generation" was visible in a whole new way. Palestinian rights became integrally connected to the anti-racist Black freedom movement, and ties between Palestinian and Black activists grew exponentially. The normalization of Palestinian rights as a component within the broader progressive movement became increasingly visible. Links between Palestine and the immigrant rights, climate justice, LGBTQ+ rights, the women's movements, and others became more common.

Changes within the Jewish community have been perhaps the most visible and dramatic. While in the past, staunchly pro-Israel organizations such as AIPAC and the Council of Presidents of Major Jewish Organizations faced little challenge to their claim to represent Jewish voters across the country, quite suddenly that was no longer the case. Those organizations remained powerful and were still backed by some of the wealthiest sectors of the Jewish community, but a massive shift was underway in Jewish identity and connection to Israel.

It was partly generational—young Jews were moving rapidly away from the kind of embrace of Israel that shaped many of their parents' and grandparents' political and cultural assumptions. Instead, many chose a Jewish identity rooted in a much broader vision of social justice. A 2013 Pew poll found that 25 percent of Jews between eighteen and twenty-nine agreed with the statement "Israel isn't making a sincere attempt to make peace." Only 5 percent of Jews over fifty agreed. In 2021, in a Jewish Electorate Institute poll, 25 percent of American Jews said that Israel was an apartheid state; 38 percent of young Jews took that position.

Jewish organizations reflected the shift. Roughly a decade after its founding, Jewish Voice for Peace was emerging as one of the most important components of the progressive movement and the movement for Palestinian rights, while providing a home for the rising numbers of Jewish activists breaking with Zionism. JVP's appeal was in its stance supporting Palestinian rights based on equality for all, international law, and human rights, as well as its endorsement of the global call for BDS. When the national leadership of Hillel, the mainstream Jewish student organization, banned discussions of BDS and limited speakers critical of Israel, outraged members created a new and vibrant organization called Open Hillel to encourage free discussion of all opinions. Numerous participants in Birthright Israel, which provided subsidized trips to Israel for any young Jew, ended up condemning its overt pro-Israel propaganda campaigns and created their own Birthright Unplugged as an alternative.

By 2014, AIPAC and its supporters became so worried about losing the young generation that they began to include the demand to continue the multibillion-dollar annual US military aid grant to Israel in their package of legislative "asks" for their members lobbying Congress—despite the fact that no one in Congress was even considering cutting aid to Israel. It also led to an increase in AIPAC and other lobby organizations targeting campus campaigns for Palestinian rights. Wealthy pro-Israel organizations coordinated continuing infusions of funds and support to pro-Israel groups on campuses that were designed to undermine the growing support for BDS and the rising criticism of Israeli occupation and apartheid by students and academics. Faculty members lost jobs, student organizations came under new pressures, and Jewish students made claims of a "hostile environment" on campus to try to weaken Palestinian rights campaigns.

After a 2009 Israeli call for using legislation to counter BDS, efforts began in the US to pass laws, first at the state level and in 2017 at the federal level, that effectively criminalized BDS. Students remained a particular target. While the increasingly successful BDS campaigns in mainstream Protestant churches arguably had greater economic impact with their multimillion or even billion-dollar retirement-fund investments at stake, losing the minds and hearts of young Jews and other Israel supporters was deemed more dangerous. So the focus on students, who are of course more vulnerable to political pressure, continued to rise.

But it didn't work. Even before the Gaza war and genocide crisis that began in 2023 and saw the rise of the student encampment movement that galvanized so much US and global attention, Students for Justice in Palestine had grown from a few scattered local groups to a coordinated national movement.

The BDS movement, begun in 2005, had become a consistent component of student, faith-based, and many quite mainstream organizations and movements.

Despite these signs of progress in changing public opinion, key aspects of actual US–Israeli relations changed mainly for the worse. In 2016, the Obama administration signed off on an increase in direct military aid to Israel from $3.1 billion to $3.8 billion per year that would take effect in 2019. Protection of Israel in the United Nations continued—though a lame-duck President Obama did agree to one abstention in December 2016, allowing the UN Security Council to pass an otherwise unanimous 14-0 resolution condemning Israeli settlements. Trump and Biden both relied on Security Council vetoes to prevent Israel from being held accountable, and to prevent ceasefires until Israel decided it was ready.

The longstanding collaboration in police training—in which local and state US law enforcement officials traveled to Tel Aviv for joint training in Israeli methods of "crowd control," counterterrorism, intelligence gathering, and more—continued. But the anti-racist and anti-police-violence Black Lives Matter movement across the United

States, along with JVP and other allies, made challenging that collaboration a regular feature of local progressive coalitions. The group worked to stop the Pentagon program that provided combat equipment—including tanks, armored personnel carriers, and anti-tank weapons brought home from Washington's Iraq and Afghanistan wars—to local police forces across the country.

Changes in congressional and other policy discussions, while still dominated by pro-Israel positions, also increased, if more slowly than the public and media shifts. In 2015 the "skip the speech" movement saw sixty members of Congress refuse to attend Netanyahu's anti-Obama speech aimed at defeating the Iran nuclear deal. Three years later, Rep. Betty McCollum introduced a bill to protect Palestinian children from the horrors of Israel's military juvenile court system. In 2018, four women of color soon nicknamed the Squad, were elected to Congress for the first time. Rashida Tlaib, the one Palestinian-American member of Congress, was part of it, along with Ilhan Omar, a Somali immigrant Muslim woman who wore her hijab proudly in the halls of Congress, African-American Ayanna Pressley, and Puerto Rican activist Alexandria Ocasio-Cortez. They brought genuine support for Palestinian rights directly into the halls of Congress, and in 2020 and 2022 elections they were joined by more new members, and the Squad grew.

Small steps. The unfulfilled challenge remains how to broaden and deepen this remarkable shift in public discourse and transform it into a real shift in US policy.

What did the movement for Palestinian rights look like and what was its impact during the Trump and Biden administrations?

The Palestinian rights movement in the US has been around for decades. Since 2000 or 2001, the traditionally Palestinian-led movement began to expand its traditional base in the Palestinian and Arab-American communities, and much of it consolidated its work around the goal of ending US support for Israeli occupation and oppression of Palestinians. That meant an increased focus on congressional pressure, and soon, particularly among students and some of the faith-based sectors, campaigns for boycotting and divesting from various companies who were profiting from or in some ways enabling Israel's actions. When Palestinian civil society launched the call for the global Boycott, Divestment, and Sanctions initiative, in 2005, much of the US movement, coordinated largely by what was then the large coalition known as the US Campaign to End the Israeli Occupation, endorsed BDS as a key component of its work.

Palestinian rights was still marginalized to a large degree when the US Campaign was launched in 2001. But by 2004, work to integrate Palestine into the broad anti-war movement that had been built to prevent and ultimately to try to end the US war in Iraq was well underway. By 2007, the US Campaign co-sponsored the first national march in Washington against US support for Israeli occupation with the even broader Iraq war-focused United for Peace and Justice coalition. Through the 2010s, work to influence public opinion and US media coverage became key, even as congressional pressure and BDS campaigns continued. Work within the Democratic Party led to some shifts in language of the party platform, but the longstanding US policy of massive military aid, as well as political and diplomatic protection of Israel, did not qualitatively change.

During that period, Palestinian rights activists also expanded ties with other components of the progressive movement, most notably the anti-racist and Black freedom movements that were rising in response to police murders of Black women and men. That relationship grew and was consolidated following the brutal police murder of Michael Brown in Ferguson, Missouri, in 2014. Protests erupted and Palestinians in the occupied territories, watching the televised coverage of the police assaults on demonstrators, sent messages of solidarity along with advice on how to deal with US-made tear gas, something they had learned over the years of being attacked by Israeli soldiers with the same US-made gas. Ferguson campaigners traveled to the occupied territories, and Black activists across the country took up Palestinian rights as part of their own mobilizations.

When Donald Trump took office, bringing his embrace of the most extreme elements of Israeli policy against Palestinians, the movement grew in response. During that same period, recognition of apartheid as the most accurate and appropriate description of Israel's treatment of Palestinians expanded. Even before the 2021–22 period of US, Israeli, and international human rights organizations documenting Israeli violations of the International Covenant for the Suppression and Punishment of the Crime of Apartheid, Palestinian rights activists were pushing members of Congress, faith leaders, and others to adopt that language. In 2018, at the national convention of the US Campaign (by then known as the US Campaign for Palestinian Rights), the two keynote speakers demonstrated that shift underway from movement to media to leaders. Rep. Betty McCollum, who had introduced the first bill aimed at protecting Palestinian children by preventing the use of US aid funds for a number of repressive Israeli practices, described the just-passed Israeli "nation-state" bill that had codified longstanding discrimination against Palestinians into law. "The world has a name for the form of government that is codified in the Nation-State Law," she said. "It is called apartheid." She was followed by Rev. William J. Barber II, co-chair of the Poor People's Campaign and one of the leading Black ministers in the country. He thundered, "Apartheid is apartheid is apartheid," and went on to define the intersectional links between the movements for Palestinian rights and those defending civil rights and economic justice. "The same corporate interests that used white nationalism to put Trump in the White House, and leaned into Zionist extremism to move the US embassy to Tel Aviv," he said, "also want to cut taxes for corporations, deregulate, ignore climate science, take away health care, deny living wages, cut the social safety net, and give more and more money to the US military."

The movement's success at winning changes in the discourse reflected—and simultaneously pushed further—the new political moment facing the Trump presidency, in which Palestinian rights found center stage in a widening range of organizations and move-ments. Palestinian rights organizations across the country endorsed the 2016 Policy Platform of the Movement for Black Lives, and as their work with Black community organizations expanded, they became part of new alliances focusing on ending police violence. That included the Deadly Exchange campaign initiated by Jewish Voice for Peace, which worked to prevent local law enforcement agencies from sending their agents for training with the Israeli military and national police. It was visible in the Palestine contingent of the huge immigrant rights march in August 2018 that protested Trump's separation of children from their families at the southern border. The signs read "From Palestine to Mexico, All the Walls Have Got to Go!" The work of media-focused organizations like the Institute for Middle East Understanding (IMEU) achieved consistently escalating levels of success in getting Palestinian voices and pro-Palestinian analysis into mainstream media outlets.

While the pace of public discourse shift was rising to unprecedented levels, the movement faced continued challenges. It was never easy to consolidate relationships with the most progressive sectors organizing in communities of color and movements fighting for immigrants, environmental justice, women, and LGBTQ rights, against racism, for Native justice, and other causes—all while trying to build ties with more mainstream organizations.

While the Palestinian rights movement was not defined on political partisan lines, a major partisan divide continued throughout the Obama, Trump, and Biden years, with key Democratic constituencies, including people of color, young Democrats, and crucially, young Jews, turned away from Israel in larger numbers. Poll after poll showed support for Israel rising among Republicans and rapidly falling among Democrats, who increasingly were taking positions more explicitly favoring Palestinian rights. In April 2023, a Brookings poll found that 44 percent of Democrats expressing any opinion described Israel as "like apartheid." Respondents had been offered three other descriptions, including "a vibrant democracy," "a flawed democracy," or "a state with restricted minority rights." And yet the largest plurality of Democrats linked Israel to apartheid.

The movement in the United States was grounded in the understanding that US support for Israel—military, economic, diplomatic, and beyond—was by far the most important enabler of Israeli oppression of Palestinians. So changing US policy remained the primary goal for most of the influential components of the movement. At the same time, movement activists had long built international ties, with Palestinian civil society activists and organizations in Palestine, including the occupied territories and inside Israel, as well as with counterparts in South Africa, Europe, parts of Asia and Latin America, and with a few governments and international civil servants at the UN and other intergovernmental organizations. Those ties grew over years and led to increased coordination on protest plans, sharing of resources, collaboration on campaigns, and beyond.

The Palestinian rights movement itself remained relatively small but continued to grow, both in size and—more importantly—in influence. Its decades-long work to transform public and media narrative was bearing significant fruit, and even some of the political and policy discourse was showing signs of change. The challenge to move from public and media discourse shift to actual policy change remained, even as small-scale modifications in the policy debate took shape. Unknowingly, the movement was setting the stage for the much more challenging work that lay ahead, in the aftermath of October 7, 2023.

The 2023 Gaza war also resulted in an unprecedented rise in levels of public participation in protests and demands for a ceasefire and integration of the Palestinian rights movement into broader progressive coalitions involved with both international solidarity and a wide range of domestic issues. It also brought the Palestinian rights movement into close proximity with power for the first time (see pages 257–264).

Why do so many people refer to Israel's policies toward the Palestinians as "apartheid"?

In 2021 and 2022, a number of influential international and Israeli human rights organizations issued major reports documenting the evidence that Israel was an apartheid state. They included the UN Commission on West Asia, Amnesty International, Human Rights Watch, B'tselem, Yesh Din and more. It should be noted that they were not the first—In 2014, Archbishop Desmond Tutu said, "I know first-hand that Israel has created an apartheid reality within its borders and through its occupation. The parallels to my own beloved South Africa are painfully stark indeed." And for many years before that, Palestinian and South African activists, analysts, and historians had long made the link. But the shift in language by influential, Western-oriented human rights organizations reflected the long years of work, especially in the United States and parts of Europe, to change the public, media, and political discourse on Palestine-Israel, making the apartheid reference not only acceptable but increasingly necessary.

The word "apartheid" is the Afrikaans word for "apartness" or "separation." The term came into use in the 1930s, and in 1948 became the official policy of the white South African government, referring to a system of segregation institutionalized to maintain the supremacy of white settlers over the indigenous Black population. Since that time, the term was most often used to describe white-dominated governments in South Africa and the former Southwest Africa (now Namibia).

But "apartheid" refers to a system, not limited to the specific examples in southern Africa. In 1973, the United Nations General Assembly passed the International Convention on the Suppression and Punishment of the Crime of Apartheid. The convention defined the "crime of apartheid" as a crime against humanity, one that was not specific to southern Africa. The crime of apartheid is based on segregation and discrimination, and includes a list of "inhuman acts" that, if committed for the purpose of establishing and maintaining domination of one racial group over another racial group, would result in systematic oppression and be identified as "apartheid."

These "inhuman" acts include murder of the subordinate group's members; denying its members "the right to life and liberty"; inflicting "serious bodily or mental harm, by the infringement of their freedom or dignity, or by subjecting them to torture or to cruel, inhuman or degrading treatment or punishment"; "arbitrary arrest and illegal imprisonment"; imposing on the group's members' "living conditions calculated to cause its or their physical destruction in whole or in part."

Other "inhuman acts" identified in the convention that could constitute the crime of apartheid include actions that bar the subordinate group's participation in the "political, social, economic and cultural life of the country, and the deliberate creation of conditions preventing the full development of such a group or groups, in particular by denying to members ... basic human rights and freedoms, including the right to work, the right to form recognized trade unions, the right to education, the right to leave and to return to their country, the right to a nationality, the right to freedom of movement and residence, the right to freedom of opinion and expression, and the right to freedom of peaceful assembly and association." Other such acts include measures "designed to divide the population ... by the creation of separate reserves and ghettos for the members of a racial group or groups, the prohibition of mixed marriages ... the expropriation of landed property," and finally, measures that deprive people and organizations of their "fundamental rights and freedoms because they oppose apartheid."

Israel practices many of those actions against Palestinians—those in the occupied territories, those inside pre-1967 Israel, and those in the diaspora. And the history of those actions go back to the very creation of the state of Israel. As Amnesty International noted in their report, "Since its establishment in 1948, Israel has pursued an explicit policy of establishing and maintaining a Jewish demographic hegemony and maximizing its control over land to benefit Jewish Israelis while minimizing the number of Palestinians and restricting their rights and obstructing their ability to challenge this dispossession." This meant that the "demography of the newly created state was to be changed to the benefit of Jewish Israelis, while Palestinians—whether inside Israel or, later on, in the OPT—were perceived as a threat to establishing and maintaining a Jewish majority, and as a result were to be expelled, fragmented, segregated, controlled, dispossessed of their land and property and deprived of their economic and social rights." Amnesty's conclusion was that "the racial discrimination against and segregation of Palestinians is the result of deliberate government policy. The regular violations of Palestinians' rights are not accidental repetitions of offenses, but part of an institutionalized regime of systematic oppression and domination."

Certainly there are significant historical and political differences between the well-known practices of South African apartheid and the system of discrimination against Palestinians that Israel practices. In South Africa the discrimination was based on race, while in Israel the parallel categories are Jew and non-Jew, and there are differences regarding citizenship, labor and other issues. But there are significant similarities as well, both in the settler-colonial histories of South Africa and Israel, the centrality of the apartheid systems to that settler-colonial history, and in the practices themselves. These similarities include laws that divide families, prevent Black South Africans or non-Jewish Israelis from owning land, discriminate in access to education, employment, social services, and more. Further, there is analogous, though clearly not identical, history of earlier pre-state persecution of the dominant group (Afrikaners and Jews), and the history of both Afrikaner and Zionist settlers themselves turning against their British colonial overlords.

One of the most important parallels, though, is the fact that South African apartheid and Israeli apartheid both were and are fundamentally about control of land for the domination of one group over another. The ideologies of racial, national, and religious discrimination were created and imposed to justify the consolidation of power over land and labor. In South Africa, the apartheid government controlled all the land by keeping the non-white labor force under control in urban townships and distant bantustans. In Palestine, the Zionist goal of controlling as much land as possible with as few Palestinians as possible led to the large-scale expulsions and ethnic cleansing of 1947–1948 and 1967, and later to the creation of truncated, non-contiguous, bantustan-like cantons in the West Bank that enabled Israeli control of the land through settlements, a matrix of Jews-only roads and bridges, and annexation of huge swathes of territory.

Some argue that because the term "apartheid" is so fraught with history, so persuasive in evoking injustice, that it should not under any circumstances be used against Israel, because Jews were themselves victims of such a great historical injustice in the Holocaust. But criticism of Israel is not the same as criticism of Jews. Israel may define itself as a "Jewish state" or the "state of all the Jews in the world," but Israel is a powerful, wealthy, nuclear-armed modern nation-state, which must, like any other country, be held accountable both for its accomplishments and for its violations of international law. Many Jews, in Israel, in South Africa, in the US, and elsewhere around the world, reject the claim that Israel speaks for them. They believe that precisely because the term "apartheid" so powerfully describes the impact of Israeli policies on Palestinians, it should become the term of necessity to describe the systematic Israeli occupation of Palestinian land and denial of Palestinians' equal rights.

Does Israel have the right to use military force as self-defense against Hamas in Gaza, as well as against Hezbollah in Lebanon?

Every country has the right to defend itself and its residents against a military attack by another country. Article 51 of the UN Charter describes that right of self-defense, and goes on to clarify that any such "measures taken by Members in the exercise of this right of self-defense shall be immediately reported to the Security Council." Those measures, the charter says, "shall not in any way affect the authority and responsibility of the Security Council ... to take at any time such action as it deems necessary in order to maintain or restore international peace and security." The charter also makes clear that the right of self-defense exists only "until the Security Council has taken measures necessary to maintain international peace and security," thus giving the council the power to impose a ceasefire or otherwise act to end any military acts even if they are claimed by the perpetrator government to be self-defense. But even that carefully limited international law-determined right of military self-defense does not apply to Israel in Gaza or the West Bank.

In 2004, the International Court of Justice, at the request of the UN General Assembly, responded to a question regarding Israel's separation or apartheid wall built in and around the West Bank. In its response, it reaffirmed that the charter's recognition of the right of self-defense applies only "in the case of armed attack by one State against another State." The court made clear that a country occupying another people's land does *not* have the right to use military force to attack or invade that already-occupied territory—specifically including the territory Israel had occupied in 1967. It concluded that Article 51 of the charter—the right of self-defense—had "no relevance" regarding Israeli actions in the Occupied Palestinian Territory.

Israel, backed by its international supporters, most vociferously in the United States, has consistently claimed precisely that "right" of self-defense—which does not apply to an occupying power. What Israel had, in the situation of an attack from the occupied territory such as that led by Hamas and other militants from Gaza on October 7, 2023, was the right to arrest and put on trial anyone it believed had attacked people or property within its borders—and to use only the minimal level of force needed to carry out those needed police actions. That did not include the right to wage full-scale war against a population of 2.3 million people, half of them children, to kill tens of thousands and injure more than 100,000, or to destroy the vast majority of the infrastructure of an entire territory that was already under full military occupation and siege—all actions that Israel began in Gaza on October 8, 2023.

Separately, even in a war that might otherwise be legal under international law, no country has the right to violate international humanitarian law—the laws of war—against others in the name of self-defense. The laws governing warfare, such as the Fourth Geneva Convention, prohibit collective punishment, demand a complete distinction be made between military and civilian targets, and require that the impact on civilians of all weapons used and attacks waged cannot be disproportionate to the specific military goal sought.

The genocidal war that Israel launched in October 2023 following the Hamas-led attack of October 7 was not the first time it went to war against Gaza falsely claiming the right of "self-defense." In 2006 Israel claimed that its right of self-defense included the "right" to attack much of Gaza's infrastructure and to kill scores of Gaza civilians, because Hamas had captured an Israeli soldier at the crossing from Israel into Gaza. But according to international law, there was no justification for Israel's assault in Gaza.

The war that Israel launched against Gaza in June 2006, and expanded against Lebanon weeks later, began when Israel chose to escalate border skirmishes to full-scale wars against civilian populations. Hamas had attacked an Israeli military post just over the Gaza border—an act of resistance to military occupation considered legal under international law since it was against a military, not civilian target.

As Human Rights Watch described it, "the targeting and capture of enemy soldiers is allowed under international humanitarian law." Israel responded first with cross-border raids of their own to try to get its captured soldier back, also legal under international law. But Israel then took the step of escalating from a small-scale border skirmish into full-scale war—by launching major attacks against civilian targets. Israel destroyed the only power plant in Gaza, plunging the 1.4 million

Gaza residents (more than half of whom were children) into months of hot, thirsty darkness at the height of the desert summer.

Explanations about the legalities of Israel wars against Gaza—both in 2006 and in 2023—differed because media outlets and analysts began their chronologies at different points—and because they mostly ignored international law. In the US, most mainstream outlets and commentators claimed the summer 2006 war began when Hamas captured an Israeli soldier, ignoring that under international law, resistance, including armed resistance against a military occupation, is a legal act. The chronologies also mostly ignored the act that provided the immediate spark of resistance—Israel's artillery attack on a Gaza beach a week earlier, which had killed seven members of one family, four of them children and babies under five years old. Israel said it "regretted" the deaths. And the killings led to the armed wing of Hamas calling off its sixteen-month-long unilateral ceasefire.

Israelis rarely refer to actual international law in claiming what they say is their "right of self-defense," almost never mentioning the UN Charter or Article 51. (Just two weeks into Israel's October 2023 war on Gaza, the US tried—and failed—to persuade the Security Council to vote for a resolution that did claim Israel could rely on Article 51.) Instead, as Gideon Levy wrote in the Israeli newspaper *Ha'aretz* in 2006, Israelis and most Americans tend to start with the assumption that the Palestinians started it. "'They started' will be the routine response to anyone who tries to argue, for example, that a few hours before the first Qassam [rocket] fell on the school in Ashkelon [a city inside Israel], causing no damage, Israel sowed destruction at the Islamic University in Gaza. Israel is causing electricity blackouts, laying sieges, bombing and shelling, assassinating and imprisoning, killing and wounding civilians, including children and babies, in horrifying numbers, but 'they started.'"

The impact of Israel's attacks on the besieged Gaza Strip, whether in 2006 or 2023 or in between, built on the existing humanitarian crisis underway in Gaza that became particularly dangerous for people when US-backed and Israeli-orchestrated sanctions were imposed against the Palestinians following the January 2006 election of the Hamas-led parliament. That collective punishment represented a clear violation of the Fourth Geneva Convention, which deals with the protection of occupied populations. Article 33 states, "No protected person may be punished for an offense he or she has not personally committed. Collective penalties and likewise all measures of intimidation or of terrorism are prohibited." Article 36 makes clear that for the occupying power the "taking of hostages is prohibited." That meant the Israeli arrests of about one-third of the elected Palestinian Legislative Assembly and about one-half òf the Palestinian Authority's cabinet ministers, whom Israel kidnapped largely to serve as bargaining chips, were illegal.

Seventeen years later, Israel was still illegally occupying and besieging Gaza, and the war that began in 2023 quickly turned into ethnic cleansing—trying to make real what its slogan falsely claimed: that Palestine was a land without a people. Palestinian violence, even those actions that might violate international law such as attacks on civilian targets, occur in response to that occupation. While there should be accountability for those individuals responsible for resistance acts that violate international law, such as attacking civilians, Israel does not have the right, under international law or United Nations resolutions, to continue its occupation, let alone to use tools of war to enforce it. Israel, like other UN member states and parties to numerous treaties and conventions of international law (many of which Israel has chosen not to sign) all have a myriad of ways to seek accountability for any individual or organizations they believe committed war crimes. And while Israel has chosen not to join the International Criminal Court, it could certainly reverse its position at any time and become a party.

Instead, since the attacks of 9/11, Israeli politicians ratcheted up their rhetoric equating the US "war on terrorism," in Afghanistan and later Iraq, with Israeli assaults in the occupied Palestinian territories, apparently on the assumption that such a comparison would make their actions more acceptable. Immediately after the September 11, 2001, attacks, Benjamin Netanyahu blurted out, "It's very good." Then, editing his words, he added, "Well, not very good, but it will generate immediate sympathy." That comparison continued through decades of escalating Israeli assaults, to the full-scale genocidal war that began October 8, 2023. Few commentators pointed out that, sympathetic or not, the US decision to respond to the huge terrorist crime committed on 9/11 with an act of full-scale war against an entire population was, just like Israel's attacks on Gaza in 2006, 2008-09, 20014, or 2023, completely illegal.

What is Zionism? Do all Jews support Zionism?

Zionism is a political movement that calls for the creation of a specifically Jewish state. When the movement began in the late 1880s, antisemitism was a powerful and growing force in Russia and Europe. Most Jews at that time believed that the best way to stop antisemitism was either through some kind of assimilation, or through alliances with other political movements. But a small number of Jews believed that antisemitism was a permanent feature of national and world politics, and that the only way for Jews to be safe would be for them to leave their home countries and establish a Jewish state elsewhere.

Early Zionist leaders believed that a Jewish state could be established anywhere (Uganda, Argentina, and Turkey were all considered at different times); it was a thoroughly secular movement. But the founder of the modern Zionist movement, Theodore Herzl, recognized that linking Zionism to Palestine would gain wider support for the movement among Jews, including more religious elements in the Jewish community who had not been early supporters. Herzl, who is known as the founder of political Zionism, also believed that a Jewish state could only be created with the support of a colonial sponsor, and he traveled the imperial capitals of the world seeking a patron.

Many Jews opposed Zionism. Most of the ultra-orthodox Jews in Palestine believed that only God could deliver a state to the Jewish people, and that a human-based effort was against God's will. Many Jews facing anti-Semitic attacks, especially in Russia and eastern Europe, rejected Zionism's call for them to leave their homelands, seeing that position as reflecting the demand of the anti-Semites themselves, to "get out of our country."

The Zionist movement won strong support from the British when the League of Nations gave London control of Palestine after the defeat of the Ottoman Empire in 1922. Earlier, in 1917, the Balfour Declaration stated that "His Majesty's Government views with favour the establishment in Palestine of a national home for the Jewish people, ...it being clearly understood that nothing shall be done which may prejudice the civil and religious rights of existing non-Jewish communities in Palestine." In the stroke of a pen, the vast majority of the population of Palestine was reduced to the "non-Jewish communities."

Zionism gradually gained more adherents, though slowly. It was only in the 1930s and '40s, as German, Polish, and other European Jews frantically sought to escape Hitler and their first-choice countries of refuge, the US and Britain, denied them entry, that Zionism and the call to create a Jewish state in Palestine became a more popular view among Jews. After World War II, with desperate Holocaust survivors filling displaced persons camps across Europe, Zionism became the majority position.

The Zionist slogan claimed that Palestine was "a land without a people for a people without a land." Certainly the second part was true—the European Jews who had escaped or survived the Holocaust had lost everything—their homes, their families, their countries, their land. Turned away from the US because of a combination of antisemitism and anti-communism, and encouraged to go to Palestine instead, it was not surprising that thousands flocked to join Jewish communities there. But the first part of the slogan hid the reality—for Palestine was not a land without a people. Its indigenous people had been there all along.

The fundamental nature of the Zionist movement was perhaps most clearly defined in the diary of Theodore Herzl, known as the father of modern Zionism. While he was more famously the author of "The Jewish State," outlining his defense of the idea of a separate Jewish-dominated state as the only way to challenge antisemitism, his diaries included some of the most important of his beliefs. One such component of Herzl's Zionism was included in the text of a letter he wrote to Cecil Rhodes, the infamous British colonialist for whom Zimbabwe was once named Rhodesia, asking for Rhodes's help in getting the British crown to support the creation of a Jewish state in Palestine. In the letter Herzl noted that he knew that Rhodes's interest was in Africa, not the Arab world, that his concern was for Englishmen, not Jews, and then asked rhetorically why he would ask Rhodes for such help. "How, then, do I happen to turn to you since this is an out-of-the-way matter for you? How indeed?" he asked. Herzl then answered his own question, telling Rhodes he should support Herzl's vision of Zionism "because it is something colonial."

The nature of that vision of colonialism in Palestine was very specific: it was not simply seizing land to gain control of resources to be sent back to the home country; it required settling the land with a new population, with European Jews replacing the indigenous people, Palestinians who were not considered in Herzl's plan. Settler colonialism—to treat the land as if it were an empty "land without a people" before nineteenth- and twentieth-century European Jewish settlement became a reality.

With the creation of the State of Israel, the mobilizing organizations of the Zionist movement such as the Jewish Agency became adjuncts of the state apparatus, focusing on recruiting and settling Jews from all over the world in Israel.

Jewish opposition to Zionism continued to exist, even throughout the periods of World War II, the Holocaust, and after, when Jews faced horrific repression and the lack of refuge in much of the world. Anti-Zionist Jews of that period included Albert Einstein, Hannah Arendt, Primo Levy, and Marek Edelman (the last surviving leader of the Warsaw Ghetto Uprising). But throughout the post-World War II decades of the twentieth century, support for Israel and Zionism became a powerful majority view in the Jewish community, and Jewish identity, especially in the United States but also in Europe, South Africa, and elsewhere, was thoroughly bound up with that support.

By the beginning of the twenty-first-century, Jewish identity, particularly in the United States and Europe, began shifting away from automatic support for Israel. Jewish organizations supporting Palestinian rights had been around since at least the 1970s in the US, and they increased and started to gain significant influence within the progressive movements in the context of the broad anti-war mobilizations against the Iraq war.

The shift in public discourse was at least partly generational. Young US Jews had, for some time, been growing away from the pro-Israel assumptions of their parents' and grandparents' generations. During the summer of 2020, when the country was wracked with protests over the police killing of George Floyd, young Jews were heavily represented in the "Justice Generation" that emerged. For many, their Jewish identity was now bound up with a broad social justice agenda, not with support for Israel—and it was that broad social justice agenda that shaped their activism. In a 2021 poll, the Jewish Electorate Institute found that 25 percent of US Jews said that Israel was an apartheid state—and 38 percent of young Jews said the same thing. And by the time of the 2024 movement of encampments on college campuses calling for a ceasefire in Gaza and demanding their universities divest from Israel bonds and from corporations profiting from occupation, Jewish students were a visible and vocal component of those multi-racial, multi-faith, and generally Palestinian-led mobilizations.

Groups like Jewish Voice for Peace (JVP), organized specifically around Palestinian rights, was founded in 1996, and by 2024 had over 750,000 members and supporters, dozens of members of its Rabbinical Council, and chapters in seventy cities and thirty-eight college campuses. When the Israeli assault on Gaza began after the October 7, 2023 Hamas-led attack on southern Israel, JVP, the newly created Rabbis for Ceasefire, If Not Now, and other organizations of Jewish critics of Israeli occupation and apartheid were among the most visible parts of the dramatically broad coalition calling for an immediate and permanent ceasefire, the resumption of support for UNRWA, massive humanitarian aid to Gaza, and conditioning and ending US military support for Israel.

Positions on political solutions varied, and increasing numbers of organizations and activists—Jewish and otherwise—who supported Palestinian rights, largely turned away from debates over two-state vs. one-state solutions, to focus instead on the struggle for human rights and equality, regardless of how many states might ultimately exist. During the Israeli assault on Gaza that began in October 2023 and that so many viewed as genocide, the percentage of Jews openly criticizing and indeed breaking with Israel skyrocketed. It was not only the organizations that had been supporting Palestinian rights before, but now even larger percentages of Jews who were outraged by Israel's war against the entire population of Gaza with its horrific human consequences.

For many, it was also a critique of Jewish supremacy in Israel—clearly distinct from rejecting the presence of a Jewish population. That meant opposing how apartheid—the forced separation of racial, religious, or ethnic groups in order to ensure the domination of one over the other—had shaped Israeli relations with the Palestinians from the very origins of the state.

What role do the Israel lobby organizations play in setting US policy?

There is no question that pro-Israel lobbies have played a major role in determining US policy towards Israel and the Palestinians. And from the beginning, the lobbies have maintained both levels of power and influence, and a consistent level of limitation on that power. This was true for decades even before the creation of the state of Israel, and shifted again after the 1967 war with the Pentagon's recognition of the young state's strategic value. By the end of the twentieth century, the lobby—with its range of constituent organizations, mainly Jewish and Christian—held more influence in US policymaking than ever before.

With the rise of political Zionism at the end of the nineteenth century, supporters of the movement in the US, almost all of them Jewish, pressed sequential US governments to support the concept of creating a Jewish state in what was then Ottoman-controlled Palestine. They had relatively little influence, not least because Zionism still held a significantly minority position in the Jewish community. While that increased a bit following the new post-World War I colonial arrangements in the Middle East, notably the League of Nations' assignment of the "Palestine Mandate" to Great Britain, the minority status of Zionism among Jews continued. That began to shift during World War II, particularly as news of the Holocaust emerged, and many European Jewish survivors ended up in displaced persons' camps scattered across Europe. US laws rooted in antisemitism and anti-communism were instituted that prevented large percentages of Jewish escapees and survivors of the

Holocaust, most of whom wanted to come to the United States where many had families and there were established Jewish communities, from entering the US. The British government, which had issued contradictory positions following World War 1—issuing the Balfour Declaration in 1917 promising support for a "Jewish homeland" in Palestine, and in 1918 the Anglo-French Declaration promising independence to former Ottoman colonies including Palestine—similarly rejected large-scale Jewish immigration. London's commitment to Arab independence was largely ignored, and instead the British government, still in control of Palestine, enabled many European Jewish refugees to settle there. With the US and Britain out of reach, Palestine was, for many Jewish refugees, their only potential safe haven.

Not surprisingly, given their own government's harsh limitation of Jewish immigration, more US Jews turned to support the idea of creating a Jewish state in Palestine, and support for the Zionist settlement project moved closer to becoming a majority opinion. When Israel declared itself a Jewish state in 1948, at the height of the Nakba, or Palestinian catastrophe of expulsion and dispossession, most Jewish organizations in the US took on support for the new state.

Members of Congress who criticized Israeli violations or voted evenhandedly on legislation concerning the Middle East have been regularly punished by the increasingly powerful pro-Israel lobby. Congressman Paul Findley and Senator Charles Percy, who advocated for a more even-handed Middle East policy, lost their seats during the 1980s. In 2002 two African-American representatives, Cynthia McKinney and Earl Hilliard, both from the south, lost their seats in the Democratic primaries after lobby-funded campaigns were launched on behalf of their challengers.

The power of the pro-Israel lobby grew exponentially from the 1990s on, as right-wing Christian evangelical organizations supporting what was known as "Christian Zionism" grew in numbers, financing, and political clout. While the traditional, largely Jewish lobby groups such as the American-Israel Political Affairs Committee (AIPAC) and the Council of Presidents of Major Jewish Organizations remained powerful in the Democratic Party and especially influential in Congress, where coordinated fundraising campaigns increased their power, the newer Christian Zionist groups gained strength in the Republican Party, and from 2001 became increasingly prominent in the White House of George W. Bush.

Within the first decade of the twenty-first century, the lobby was moving unmistakably to the right, and a few years later was shifting explicitly away from its historic commitment to bipartisanship to reflect a much more direct alliance with the Republicans. By the time of the post-October 7 Israeli assault on Gaza, and soon in Lebanon as well, those shifts were also taking place in a political moment of unparalleled influence of a movement for Palestinian rights that was broader, more influential, and operating closer to power than ever before.

The main organization of an identifiable pro-Israel lobby took place in 1954. Some of the urgency of that move reflects an effort to repair a potentially serious rupture in US support for the new state, resulting from US public outrage over reports of an Israeli massacre in the West Bank village of Qibya, then part of Jordan, in 1953. According to *Time* magazine, "Israeli artillery, previously zeroed onto target, opened up, and a 600-man battalion of uniformed Israeli regulars swept across the border to encircle the village. For the next two hours the town shuddered under shell bursts and small-arms fire; villagers, screaming and milling, rushed out to the surrounding fields and olive groves. Then the guardsmen's ammo (25 rounds per man) gave out, and the Israelis moved into Qibya with rifle and Sten guns. They shot every man, woman and child they could find, then turned their fire on the cattle. After that, they dynamited 42 houses, a school and a mosque. The cries of the dying could be heard amid the explosions. The villagers huddled in the grass could see Israeli soldiers slouching in the doorways of their homes, smoking and joking, their young faces illuminated by the flames. By 3 a.m., the Israelis' work was done, and they leisurely withdrew. ...Sixty-six died that night; eleven from one family, ten of another. It was the bloodiest night of border warfare since the 1949 armistice—the armistice that won Dr. Ralph Bunche the Nobel Peace Prize, but brought no peace."

In response to the public and official government outrage, key US Jewish leaders gathered and announced the founding of the American Zionist Committee for Public Affairs (later called the American-Israel

Public Affairs Committee) and the Conference of Presidents of Major American Jewish Organizations. The move was significant for uniting explicitly Zionist and non-Zionist Jewish groups around support for the Israeli state, as well as for the influence and direct involvement of Israeli leaders in creating the new organizations. The new lobby focused on maintaining both political support and especially financial backing for Israel from the US government.

The next major shift happened in 1967, when the Six-Day War resulted in the Israeli seizure and occupation of the Palestinian West Bank and East Jerusalem from Jordan and the Gaza Strip from Egypt, along with seizing Egypt's enormous Sinai Peninsula and the Syrian Golan Heights. The lobbies mobilized the Jewish community to engage in very direct ways to raise funds, influence cultural and educational production, and exert political pressure to back Israel's new occupation of Palestinian and other Arab lands. The result was a successful campaign that helped move public opinion towards widespread national support for Israel, a narrative that remained dominant for decades.

At the same time, in the midst of and in the immediate aftermath of the war, the Pentagon recognized the potential strategic value of a close relationship with this new power in the Middle East—this was in the middle of the Cold War, after all. And as Israel's star rose in official Washington's lineup of close allies against Soviet influence, the pro-Israel lobby began to appear significantly more influential—less because it actually did wield more influence than before than because its longstanding goal of building a tight supportive relationship between Washington and Tel Aviv now matched Israel's regional military/strategic value to the Pentagon. The lobby's work also strengthened the new relationship between US military corporations and Israel's nascent but increasingly strong military production system.

Since that time, the intersection of strategic (regional power projection and military production—led by the Pentagon and the State Department) and political (led by the lobbies) interests shaped the relationship between the US and Israel. Global, regional, and US national events meant that at times the US-Israel relationship was shaped by the strategic value, at other times by its domestic political importance—but always leading to a close embrace.

From 1967 through the end of the Cold War, Israel's value was mainly strategic. Along with its direct engagement in the Middle East region, Israel was a reliable ally in challenging Soviet interests around the world. When horror at the actions of the Guatemalan military government's attacks on indigenous communities there led to the US cutting off arms sales, Israel stepped in and the Galil rifle replaced the US-made M-16 as the rifle of choice for the Guatemalan military. The US-backed military junta that overthrew the democratically elected government of Chile in 1973 bought Israeli helmets for their army. So the lobby, while still influential, was less important to US policy determinations than the governmental interests of the State Department and especially the Pentagon.

By 1991, with the fall of the Soviet Union and the US decision to attack Iraq (ostensibly in response to Iraq's illegal occupation of Kuwait, but largely to show the world it remained the global hegemon in what was now a unipolar world), Israel lost much of its strategic value, particularly in the region. Washington needed a visible Arab coalition to back its attack on Iraq, and the willingness of Syria, Egypt, Saudi Arabia, the UAE, and other Arab countries to join the US air assault on Iraq was contingent on Israel staying out of view. Washington ordered Israel not to respond militarily when a few Iraqi scuds landed in Israeli territory, and Tel Aviv complied. (Casualties were low; Human Rights Watch reported that while official reports varied, between one and four Israelis were killed by the missile attacks.) The Arab coalition played a major role in Washington's quick victory in not only reversing Iraq's occupation of Kuwait but also devastating much of Baghdad, other cities, and much of the electricity, water treatment, health care, and other civilian infrastructure across the country. Operation Desert Storm was billed as a huge military and strategic success, while the pro-Israel lobbies, which were certainly actively cheerleading for the invasion and occupation, were much less influential in setting the policy.

That period lasted about a decade, known briefly as the "post-Cold War era," in which the US operated largely as an uncontested global superpower. The US orchestrated a soon-to-fail set of Arab-Israeli negotiations, launched in a high-visibility global conference in Madrid in 1991, and Iraqis continued to struggle for survival under crippling sanctions. The power of the first intifada in the occupied territories began to wane as the Oslo process took hold in 1993 and 1994. By the end of the decade Oslo's failure was becoming visible and the second intifada began, characterized by a significant rise of armed actions on the Palestinian side and a dramatic escalation of military assault by the IDF. Throughout those years, while Israel's strategic value to the US had significantly diminished, the lobby's role appeared much more influential in ensuring that the US-Israeli relationship continued.

The reassertion of Washington's strategic reliance on Israel took hold with the terrorist attacks of September 11, 2001. The likelihood of that process emerged within hours of the attack on the Twin Towers in New York, when Prime Minister Benjamin Netanyahu was asked for his response. "It's good," he said, making clear his real opinion before going on to explain he meant it would create more sympathy for Israel.

As George W. Bush's so-called global war on terror took hold, leading to the massive expansion of militarization, base creation, and power projection all centered in the Middle East, Israel returned to its position as one of Washington's closest strategic allies. In August 2002, just as the White House campaign to build support for war against Iraq was taking shape, then-Prime Minister Ariel Sharon described how intelligence coordination between the US and Israel had reached "unprecedented dimensions." But again, the relationship of the day was strategic, not lobby-driven, despite the effort of some parts of the Israel lobby later to claim that they were responsible for the close ties.

That reality—a strategic, rather than lobby-driven relationship between the US and Israel—continued through the Obama presidency. That included the shift in the nature of the US war in Iraq from massive troop deployments to a reliance on escalating air strikes, drone attacks, and small groups of special forces operatives, the withdrawal of almost all the troops in 2011, and the return of troops and launching of a major air war in Syria and Iraq against ISIS in 2014. Israel remained an important asset in providing intelligence across the region. By 2017, ISIS had lost all the territory it had seized in Iraq and almost all in Syria. In November 2020 Trump ordered a draw-down of troops, leaving about 2,500 troops remaining in Iraq.

During the Trump presidency, the lobby focused much more on direct US relations with Israel. The traditional Jewish and Christian lobby organizations—AIPAC, the Council of Presidents, CUFI and others—were less visible than the wealthiest individual supporters of Israel, such as Republican financiers and casino billionaires Sheldon and Miriam Adelson, who were personally among the strongest backers of Trump's campaign. The close ties between Netanyahu and his extremist Knesset allies, with Trump and members of his family and close circle, led to a near-complete embrace of Israel's farthest right-wing forces. Trump's 2018 policy pronouncements—recognizing Jerusalem as the undivided capital only of Israel, moving the embassy to Jerusalem, pronouncing the West Bank and East Jerusalem settlements as legal, recognizing Israeli sovereignty over the occupied Syrian Golan Heights, and more—reflected the views of those close Trump advisors, allies, and funders.

By the end of Trump's term in 2021, the Jewish component of the pro-Israel lobby had lost a great deal of its public influence. While it still maintained significant amounts of money and used it skillfully to influence elections—funding challengers to any potentially vulnerable member of Congress who was thought to be insufficiently pro-Israeli in their voting record—it was rapidly losing influence and the ability to persuade Jewish voters. Much of that shift was generational—young Jews were moving away from an automatic embrace of Israel as part of their Jewish identity, and many were instead defining themselves in the context of social justice and anti-racism in general, and support for Palestinian rights in particular.

Those shifts were not passively accepted by Israel's supporters, particularly by the powerful lobbies, both the traditional largely Jewish organizations such as AIPAC, the Anti-Defamation League, and many others, and the newer but very influential Christian Zionist/Christian nationalist organizations such as Christians United for Israel (CUFI). They pushed back, using political donations, junkets to visit Israel, and most powerfully, false claims that support for Palestinian rights and challenging Israel policies amounted to antisemitism. The result, over a decade or so, was the rise in state-based campaigns to prohibit and even criminalize as "hate speech" support for Palestinian rights.

Support for Israel was also becoming an overwhelmingly partisan issue—polls were showing a consistent pattern of Republican support for Israel rapidly rising, while Democratic support was quickly diminishing in favor of rising rates of support for Palestinian rights. In the context of losing young Jews, and increasingly losing support among progressives and in communities of color, over the last several years lobby priorities have shifted. Instead of focusing on convincing newer, younger elected officials or potential candidates, as well as trying to win over students with a pro-Israel message, the lobbies have shifted significantly to repression rather than persuasion.

AIPAC, ADL, and other parts of the Jewish pro-Israel lobby, sometimes backed by CUFI and other components of the Christian pro-Israel lobby organizations, have been focusing on social media venues, suppressing speech that supports Palestinian rights and/or exposes and criticizes Israeli actions. By 2024, despite longstanding US laws guaranteeing the right to boycott as part of First Amendment-protected free speech, thirty-eight states had passed bills or issued executive orders punishing (by denying contracts, for instance) or even criminalizing support for BDS campaigns aimed at pressuring Israel to end its violations of human rights and international law.

Much of the lobby's role, also taken up by other political actors, has relied on the weaponization of antisemitism—creating false claims that any criticism of Israel amounted to antisemitic language and therefore should be prohibited as "hate speech" or making some students "uncomfortable." This led to campaigns requiring universities, city councils, federal government departments, state governments and other official agencies to officially endorse a definition of antisemitism posited by the International Holocaust Remembrance Association. The longstanding expert on antisemitism who originally drafted the IHRA language in 2004, Kenneth Stern, has repeatedly stressed that the working definition "was not drafted, and was never intended, as a tool to target or chill speech on a college campus."

The short text of Stern's definition stated, "Antisemitism is a certain perception of Jews, which may be expressed as hatred toward Jews. Rhetorical and physical manifestations of antisemitism are directed toward Jewish or non-Jewish individuals and/or their property, toward

Jewish community institutions and religious facilities."

The problem was not with its basic characterization of antisemitism —it was with the examples appended to the definition. Of the eleven examples, about half reference Israel—such as "denying the Jewish people their right to self-determination, e.g., by claiming that the existence of a State of Israel is a racist endeavor" or "applying double standards by requiring of it [Israel] a behavior not expected or demanded of any other democratic nation."

In 2017 Stern testified against a congressional bill that would have required the Department of Education to use the IHRA definition in determining discrimination against Jewish students in colleges. The bill didn't pass. But Trump did sign an executive order in 2019 that expanded Title VI of the 1964 Civil Rights Act's prohibition against discrimination originally based on "race, color and national origin" to include antisemitism—and that federal agencies would have to consider the IHRA definition in their enforcement of such cases.

As the 2022 midterms approached, halfway through Biden's presidency, the lobby organizations moved into high gear. Their goal was to ensure that the now-strengthened Squad—with the original four members bolstered by five or six new supporters—would emerge from the election weaker than before. Their strategy, as before, was to raise sufficient funds to ensure that the targeted incumbent members, in this case Rep. Jamaal Bowman from outside of New York City, and Rep. Cori Bush from St Louis, Missouri, would face challengers so well-financed that the two young, Black representatives, progressive and outspokenly supportive of Palestinian rights, would go down to certain defeat. Their challengers did achieve that goal—but not without an unprecedented level of spending in a midterm congressional race to accomplish it. AIPAC's super PAC alone spent $14.5 million just in one month leading up to the election to defeat Bowman, more than any PAC had ever spent on a single congressional race in an off-year. The group spent more than eight million dollars to replace Bush. As the *New York Times* described the funding blitz, "AIPAC had been lobbying American politicians of both parties for decades, enjoying close ties to presidents and legislative leaders. It only formed its own super PAC around the 2022 midterms. It spent $26 million that cycle, mostly targeting progressive Democrats who in recent years had begun to pull their party toward a more critical view of Israel."

Efforts to suppress pro-Palestinian speech on campuses continued to escalate, and in many areas, local supporters of AIPAC, ADL, and other parts of the pro-Israel lobbies led or supported publicity campaigns and pro-Israel student activists challenging the Palestinian voices. At times, lobby-linked op-eds or television commentators encouraged shutting down protests and pro-Palestinian speech on the grounds that it made some Jewish students uncomfortable. There was little effort to distinguish between being made to feel uncomfortable by language and ideas that challenge closely held beliefs, and actually being threatened by such talk or ideas.

Students, and sometimes academics who were deemed vulnerable, were targeted particularly harshly. Campus speakers, protests, even academic discussions challenging pro-Israeli assumptions or presenting Palestinian voices reflecting a Palestinian narrative were shut down with growing frequency. Student organizations were increasingly de-funded or even prohibited from operating. Student activists were threatened with campus sanctions, suspension, or even expulsion, which for foreign students could lead to deportation.

Legal support organizations such as Palestine Legal and the Center for Constitutional Rights were mobilized to provide support across the country for student groups facing major attacks on their right to organize and to petition for their campuses to divest their rich endowments from companies profiting from Israeli occupation and apartheid. By the time the student protest movement—particularly the extraordinary campus encampment effort—emerged in the spring of 2024 in response to Israel's war in Gaza, university administrators had clamped down with harsher measures than US students had experienced in generations. At Columbia University, city police were called in to shut down the encampment and stop the occupation of Hamilton Hall, the same building occupied by Vietnam anti-war protesters in the 1960s and anti-apartheid activists in the '80s. But this time, massive police violence was unleashed on the students, with one student thrown down a flight of stairs and many others beaten by a notorious special unit of the NYPD known for particular violence towards protesters. At UCLA, police stood by and watched as a cohort of masked pro-Israel outsiders assaulted the students in their encampment, leading to over sixteen injuries. Students faced disciplinary charges, including suspension and expulsion from campus buildings, including their dorms. Professors, including those in the newly created Faculty for Justice in Palestine groups, faced discipline as well, and college presidents from top universities including Harvard, Columbia, the University of Pennsylvania, and Cornell were hounded out of office, some of them following Republican-led attacks when they testified in congressional hearings.

What was the significance of the ICJ's ruling on the illegality of Israeli occupation?

In July 2024, in response to a request from the UN General Assembly, the International Court of Justice issued an advisory opinion on the question of the "legal consequences arising from the ongoing violation by Israel of the right of the Palestinian people to self-determination, from its prolonged occupation, settlement and annexation of the Palestinian territory occupied since 1967." A further question asked about the legal status of Israel's occupation, and "what are the legal consequences that arise for all States and the United Nations from this status?"

While earlier UN resolutions had made reference to illegality in Israel's occupation of the West Bank, Gaza and East Jerusalem, they generally focused on specific acts—house demolitions, settlement practices, settler violence, etc.—that violated various international humanitarian laws. The assumption was that military occupation, assumed to be a temporary result of war, was not itself illegal, and that the laws of war—the Geneva Conventions, various other conventions, treaties and other laws—were in place to make sure that the occupying power treated the occupied population in a manner as humane as possible. The significance of the 2024 opinion lay precisely in the court's findings not only that certain Israeli policies and practices that continued in the occupied territory were "in breach of international law," but that Israel's occupation itself, "the continued presence of Israel in the Occupied Palestinian Territory," was explicitly illegal.

The occupation, the ICJ found, violated "the prohibition on the acquisition of territory by force and the right to self-determination of the Palestinian people. Consequently, Israel has an obligation to bring an end to its presence in the Occupied Palestinian Territory as rapidly as possible." It went on rule that "Israel is under an obligation to cease immediately all new settlement activities, and to evacuate all settlers from the Occupied Palestinian Territory." And it found that "the State of Israel has the obligation to make reparation for the damage caused to all the natural or legal persons concerned in the Occupied Palestinian Territory." It was the first time an international court had made so clear not only the judgement of illegality, but what Israel would have to do in response: end the settlements, evacuate all settlers, and pay reparations to Palestinians for their losses.

The court also found that in its discriminatory practices that violated the CERD—the International Convention on the Elimination of All Forms of Racial Discrimination—Israel was in violation of the crime of apartheid. That's because according to Article 3 of CERD, which Israel had signed and ratified, all countries party to the convention must "particularly condemn racial segregation and apartheid, and undertake to prevent, prohibit and eradicate all practices of this nature in territories under their jurisdiction."

The ICJ then went further, outlining the responsibilities of other governments and the United Nations itself in bringing an end to the illegal occupation. The court said that all states were obliged not to recognize the occupation as legal, and "not to render aid or assistance" to Israel in maintaining the occupation. International organizations including the United Nations, the court specified, were under the same obligation not to recognize the occupation as legal. And it concluded that the UN, and especially the General Assembly had the obligation to consider what action to take to end Israel's unlawful occupation "as rapidly as possible."

It was an unexpectedly powerful finding, strengthened further by the direct call on the General Assembly to determine how to implement the ruling. In response, in a clear showing of just how isolated the United States and Israel were in the world, the Assembly voted 124 in favor and only 14 opposed for a resolution calling on Israel to withdraw its military from the land, sea and airspace of the occupied territories, evacuate all settlers, and dismantle the parts of the apartheid wall inside the territory. The countries joining the US and Israel in opposition included several far-right governments—Hungary, Argentina, Paraguay—and seven small island states that are highly dependent on US economic assistance (some of which are also treaty-bound to endorse US foreign policy). Forty-three countries abstained.

The resolution called on Tel Aviv to repeal all laws that discriminate against Palestinians, to return land and property seized from Palestinians and pay reparations for losses, to allow at least some Palestinians to exercise their right of return, to abide by all provisional measures imposed by the ICJ in the genocide case, and to stop impeding Palestinians from exercising their right to self-determination including their right to an independent state.

Even more important, since Israel had made clear its intention to ignore the Assembly's call, the resolution called on member states to impose a wide range of sanctions on Israel to bring about an end to its illegal occupation and apartheid practices within twelve months. They ranged from refusing to render aid in maintaining the occupation, not to recognize any change in the physical or legal status of the territory and to distinguish between Israel and the occupied territories in diplomatic, trade or other relations, not establishing diplomatic missions in Jerusalem. And crucially, it called on all states to stop providing arms or other military equipment to Israel if there are "reasonable grounds to suspect that they may be used in the Occupied Palestinian Territory," and to work to end Israel's systemic discrimination and its violations of Article 3 of the Convention Against Racial Discrimination—the part that prohibits apartheid.

The resolution called on the secretary-general to report back to the General Assembly within three months on steps taken to implement the resolution, and to include proposals for a UN mechanism that would follow up on Israeli violations of Article 3 of the racism convention—which refers to apartheid. In an unusual move, it requested that the secretary-general consult not only with the UN's high commissioner for human rights but also with "Member States with relevant experience and expertise" in preparing those proposals—a clear reference to South

Africa and Namibia, both of which had suffered under and triumphed over apartheid systems of their own. Since both of those countries had earlier indicated support for the reopening of the UN's Committee Against Apartheid, which helped build the global anti-apartheid movement in the 1970s and 1980s, the resolution signaled widespread assembly support for the UN to play a serious role in building a renewed and strengthened anti-apartheid movement that would include opposition to Israeli apartheid in the 2020s.

The resolution remained officially unenforceable, and its linkage to the model of the similarly limited General Assembly resolutions of the South African anti-apartheid era was unmistakable. In that earlier period, Security Council resolutions condemning or trying to impose sanctions against apartheid South Africa were routinely vetoed by the United States (sometimes joined by Britain). Most of the resolutions then went to the assembly, where they passed with huge majorities. And while they were officially nonbinding, those resolutions became important tools in the hands of anti-apartheid campaigners around the world. Country after country began to implement the resolutions' calls for sanctions—corporate divestment, banking sanctions, especially cutting arms sales and other military sanctions. Eventually the global public pressure—now involving key US allied governments as well as broad social movements—was too much, and by 1986 the US Congress agreed to impose sanctions on South Africa. (The congressional action was quickly vetoed by President Ronald Reagan, but under the leadership of the Congressional Black Caucus, there were soon enough votes to overturn the veto.) The US was finally part of the overwhelming global majority supporting democracy and an end to apartheid.

The July 2024 General Assembly resolution may represent the beginning of a similar transformative trajectory for the United States regarding its relations with Israel in the twenty-first century.

PART IV:
OCTOBER 7
and its Aftermath

What happened in the attack on Israel of October 7, 2023, and how was it viewed?

On October 7, 2023, a large number of Palestinians inside Gaza broke through the militarized wall that surrounded the Strip and moved quickly into areas of southern Israel where they launched attacks against both military posts and civilian communities, including several kibbutzim (collective villages) and a music festival. At least 1,150 people were killed, of whom about 350 were soldiers and police, and about 800 were civilians, young and old, women and men, mostly Israeli but scores from other countries too. Most were killed by the Gazans, fewer by Israeli forces fighting against them. About 250 others were kidnapped and taken back into Gaza where they were held as hostages.

The breakout from Gaza was planned and led by Hamas, the Islamist organization made up of political, social, and military wings that had won the last Palestinian elections held back in 2006 and had administered the besieged Gaza Strip since 2007. Militants from other armed organizations, notably Islamic Jihad, participated as well, and they were followed by many unaffiliated young men who suddenly saw an opportunity to break out of the long-sealed-off enclave.

The first attacks were on military targets—mainly bases surrounding and close to Gaza. According to France24's investigation a year after the October 7 attack, Hamas attacked at least seven military bases, and notes that "at 10 a.m., the Israeli army acknowledged that armed Palestinians had entered at least three military sites. Fierce fighting ensued. ...At least fifty soldiers were killed in Nahal Oz, including many unarmed women [soldiers]. The Re'im military base, headquarters of the Gaza Division, was also captured. Israeli forces did not regain control of it until the end of the day."

Attacks on civilian targets began soon after, primarily small towns and collective villages in southern Israel. The attacks were brutal; people were killed in their homes, or shot trying to escape. Some families managed to get to the safe rooms Israelis are required to have in their homes, but many did not have time to react.

The single largest group of victims on October 7 were the 364 people—mostly civilians and mostly young—killed at the Supernova music festival nearby. The first Israeli police investigation report of the assault, widely disseminated in Israeli media including Ha'aretz, indicated a "growing assessment in Israel's security establishment" that Hamas fighters had not planned ahead of time to target the music festival, but learned about it by chance as they entered Israel. The earlier morning violence continued against the young concert-goers; along with the hundreds killed, 40 were forcibly taken into Gaza.

Three weeks after the attack, Israel's Ynet news reported that the IDF admitted that "casualties fell from friendly fire on October 7," although they focused only on Israeli soldiers. Released hostages themselves made clear, and investigations by Ha'aretz newspaper and the Australian ABC television network reported that some of the civilians killed at the festival were also killed by friendly fire, as military helicopters shot at vehicles heading out of the festival area towards Gaza which turned out to be carrying kidnapped Israelis. Under an initially secret 1986 Israeli policy known as the Hannibal Directive, kidnapping must be prevented by any means, even if the result causes harm to soldiers themselves. It emerged in the context of Israeli soldiers being kidnapped in Lebanon, later in the occupied territories as well, and then traded for Lebanese or Palestinian prisoners being held in Israel in exchanges that became very controversial. Israel claimed the Directive was canceled in 2016, but that remains unclear.

The attack on the music festival was also the site of the largest number of allegations of sexual assault on October 7. Sexual assault and rape, along with the killing of children, remain among the most horrific crimes in any military attack situation. And sexual assault of survivors, let alone of people who are then killed, is among the most difficult to document. It is certainly likely that some level of sexual assault occurred on or after October 7—sexual violence has been a constant partner of military attack throughout history, and remains so. And as is most often the case in war situations, little reliable evidence has been obtained. Journalists, the United Nations and other international agencies have the capacity and access to highly skilled investigators to determine what happened, but they have not been allowed to interview survivors, medical personnel or other potential witnesses. In response to efforts by the Commission of Inquiry established by the UN's

Human Rights Council, for example, one of several sets of UN experts trying to strengthen their investigations of the allegations, Israel's Kan public radio and *Times of Israel* newspaper reported that "the Justice Ministry instructed the legal department of the Health Ministry to tell Israeli doctors and others involved in the care of October 7 victims and released hostages not to speak with the committee of inquiry." So clear information remains unknown, including how many of any sexual assaults may have been carried out not by Hamas but by Palestinian civilians who followed the fighters into Israel.

What is known is that beyond the real horror of the events that day, the issue of sexual violence became part of a wide-ranging propaganda campaign based on false allegations designed to further dehumanize Palestinians and justify the soon-genocidal war Israel began against the entire population of Gaza. One of the most dramatic examples was President Biden's statement, "I never really thought that I would see and have confirmed pictures of terrorists beheading children." The White House quickly walked back the statement, admitting that he never saw any such pictures, and that despite that, he still made the statement in order to "underscore the utter depravity" of the October 7 attack. According to the Washington Post, Biden had earlier explicitly turned down staff advice to cut the line from his speech because it could not be verified. In fact, no such thing ever happened.

What was the context in which the October 7 attack occurred?

At the time of the October 7 attack, Gaza had been walled off and surrounded by Israel Defense Forces for almost seventeen years. Many of those who participated in the violence of that day, including both members of Hamas and unaffiliated young men, had never been outside the narrow confines of the Strip, where 2.3 million people, most of them refugees, lived in the tiny, congested enclave that remains one of the most densely populated areas on earth. After the 2005 withdrawal of Israeli settlers and redeployment of its soldiers from inside the Strip to surrounding it from outside, Israel had also imposed a permanent blockade against Gaza, strictly limiting what could be brought into or out of the territory. That meant that food was always limited, water always insufficient because parts to repair the water treatment plants were usually not allowed in, electricity and building supplies scarce, medicine never easily available. Things like books and computers, let alone toys or bicycles, were often out of reach. And crucially, Gazans were kept imprisoned in the Strip—almost never able to get permits to get out, to enter Israel, even to visit family or seek needed medical care in the West Bank, which required transiting through Israel.

In 2012, the United Nations issued a dire report concluding that without major changes, Gaza would be "unlivable" in just eight years—from lack of water, insufficient access to health care, and other crucial human necessities. Some of it reflected the terrible destruction wrought by Israel's 2008–09 attack on Gaza, known as Operation Cast Lead. Just a few months after the 2012 report, another assault was launched. And in 2014, Operation Protective Edge lasted for fifty days and left about 2,200 Palestinians dead, two-thirds of them, according to the UN, civilians. Some UN officials changed their warning to say Gaza would likely be unlivable by 2018—apparently the earlier warning of 2020 hadn't taken into account three major Israeli assaults before 2020.

But there were still plenty of reasons for concern—whether the tipping point would come in 2018 or 2020. Unemployment across Gaza had already gone up from 29 percent in 2012 when the UN issued their first warning, to 45 percent as 2020 dawned, with a rate of 60 percent unemployment among the youth. By 2020 less than 4 percent of water in Gaza was safe to drink—the water treatment plants could not be repaired. After examining a set of studies from 2011 to early 2023, the US National Institutes of Health determined that "one-fifth of the boys and girls were stunted by 2 years of age in the Gaza Strip." One of every five children. And it had been going on for more than twelve years.

None of those realities justify the crimes committed on October 7, 2023. The killing, injuring, attacking of civilians were war crimes. Taking hostages were war crimes. And those responsible for those crimes, whether part of Hamas or other organizations, or individuals who followed them through the holes in the fence and attacked civilians, should all be held accountable.

It's also true that not all Palestinian actions that day constituted war crimes. Gaza is a territory being held under belligerent military occupation. Under international law, an occupied population has the right to escape a siege imposed by the occupying power—in the words of the International Committee of the Red Cross (which is responsible for implementing the Geneva Conventions), "a besieging party may not force civilians to remain against their will in the besieged area." So breaking through the wall surrounding Gaza to get out of the besieged area was not a crime.

And because international law links the right of self-determination to the right to resist military occupation, UN Resolution 45/130 from 1990 "*Reaffirms* the legitimacy of the struggle of peoples for independence, territorial integrity, national unity and liberation from colonial domination, apartheid and foreign occupation by all available means, including armed struggle." Any such armed struggle is bound and restricted by the same international humanitarian law that regulates other uses of military force—including the requirement to distinguish between combatant and civilian targets. So while attacks on civilians do constitute war crimes, attacks by an occupied population on the military outposts and soldiers of the occupation forces are not illegal.

What kind of war did Israel launch following the October 7 attack and how did the US respond?

The conditions that existed in Gaza before October 7 did not justify the illegal acts that were part of the Hamas-led attack. They do, however, help explain why they happen. And to be sure that such attacks on civilians, and the wars that follow those attacks, do not happen in the future, it is crucial to understand those root causes, and to change the conditions that give rise to them.

In the case of the October 7 events, quite the opposite occurred. The massive US and global media response to the attack focused overwhelmingly on the civilian victims—largely ignoring the military installations and personnel who were the first targets. And the attack overall was widely portrayed in the US and much of Europe as something not only shocking, which it certainly was, but as astonishing and surprising—which it most certainly was not. It was placed outside of history, as if it had occurred out of thin air, denying that the attack, however brutal much of it was, occurred in response to years of imprisonment, siege, blockade, and massive air and ground military assaults against Gaza every two or three years, that killed hundreds or thousands of people but were justified in Israeli political life as "mowing the grass" to tamp down any hint of resistance.

In Israel, the popularity of the war against the entire population of Gaza in response to the crimes of October 7 mirrored, in some ways, the overwhelming US public support for George W. Bush's call for global war against the entire population of Afghanistan after the crimes of 9/11. International media coverage of the October 7 attack, particularly in the US, was nonstop, and immediately turned into cheerleading for the Israeli assault. That onslaught soon became what the International Court of Justice identified as plausibly genocidal. Reporting of the actual brutality that occurred in many of the October 7 attacks on civilians was soon bolstered with false claims of ruthless acts of violence that never happened. While alternative and eventually mainstream press investigations eventually laid bare the false claims, debunking them as complete fabrications, many political and media figures continued to repeat them for months, building greater support for the Israeli military offensive.

Throughout the first weeks of Israel's war on Gaza, some US officials supported the call for a ceasefire, but always limited and temporary, always framed around bringing home the hostages, and always beginning with statements of support for "Israel's right to self-defense." Other necessary aspects of even a temporary ceasefire—actually stopping the bombing and other means of killing, allowing in the massive levels of humanitarian aid so desperately needed in Gaza—were always secondary. The initial temporary truce, carefully not called a ceasefire, in November 2023, lasted for a week, and led to the release of 105 Israeli and international hostages and 240 Palestinian prisoners, along with bringing in briefly significant amounts of food, medicine, and other humanitarian supplies goods.

But after that, calls for a ceasefire—even use of the word—largely disappeared from the White House. It was not until the Uncommitted movement began to be seen as a potential threat to the president's re-election, that Biden began to change his language. That was the mobilization of Palestinian-, Arab- and Muslim-Americans, along with young people, African-Americans, and other progressive sectors, who voted "uncommitted" in the Democratic primaries in the spring of 2024 to protest the Biden administration's support for Israel's war. And even then, it was Vice President Kamala Harris, months before she replaced Biden as the 2024 presidential candidate in July, who first reflected the rhetorical change. It was a high-visibility moment for Harris, at the annual commemoration of Bloody Friday, the iconic moment when civil rights marchers were assaulted by Alabama state police in 1964 as they tried to cross the Edmund Pettus Bridge in Selma, when she first called directly for an immediate ceasefire. It was a limited shift—she didn't call for a permanent ceasefire, instead referencing Biden's call for a six-week "pause"—but her use of the ceasefire term at all seemed to reflect a small step away from Biden's refusal to break from his whatever-Israel-wants-Israel-gets position.

Ceasefire negotiations sputtered on and off for months. A pattern emerged that saw optimistic reports of diplomatic talks in Qatar or Cairo, then a press report of a breakthrough, that Israel had agreed to new terms or that Hamas had accepted an Israeli-initiated version, followed by a "clarification" from the Israeli prime minister's office indicating that Netanyahu had not agreed to any such thing. The White House's linguistic shift to talk about a ceasefire, to request support for a cease-fire, did not lead to an actual ceasefire, or to any willingness from Israel to even consider a ceasefire because the change in language—ceasefire vs. pause, immediate vs. permanent, request vs. urge—had nothing to do with the consistency of action: the weapons kept on flowing. The death toll continued to rise - by November 2024 more than 43,300 Gazans had been killed, and the UN confirmed that during a six-month period of that first year, seventy percent of the victims were children and women.

By October 3, 2024, almost a full year into the Israeli assault, the Biden administration was acknowledging what many observers of the failed ceasefire "efforts" had already seen: Matthew Miller, spokesman of the State Department, announced in a briefing that "we've never wanted to see a diplomatic resolution with Hamas."

Biden's fervent bear-hug greeting of Netanyahu on his arrival in Israel in October 2023 was symbolically powerful—but it was hardly the most important part of Washington's backing. Over that first year of the war the US gave Israel $12.5 billion in direct military financing, accounting for a full 40 percent of Tel Aviv's military spending. The White House signed off on sending US-made warplanes, 500- and 2,000-pound bombs, tank ammunition, and much more. (One small batch of 2,000-pound bombs was delayed in May 2024, but that was after Israel had amassed an arsenal of more than 1,400 of those bunker-busters. Several were used in September that year in Israel's assassination of Hezbollah leader Hassan Nasrallah in Beirut, an attack that killed at least six Lebanese civilians and left more than ninety seriously injured.) And the $12.5 billion didn't even include the military actions that the Pentagon undertook on behalf of Israel—which brought the total cost for aiding Israel's war in Gaza for its first year to $22 billion of US taxpayer money.

Those numbers explained a great deal about Benjamin Netanyahu's willingness to ignore President Biden's requests for a ceasefire in Gaza and his pleas for preventing escalation to a region-wide war: as long as the billions of dollars' worth of weapons continued, as long as the US continued to supply 65 percent of Israel's weapons and military equipment, it mattered not at all what language the White House used, what requests were made, what appeals were issued.

In 2024, ProPublica published leaked memos from both USAID and the State Department's own refugee agency documenting how Israel was blocking US humanitarian aid for Gaza, using "arbitrary denial, restriction and impediments." Under the Foreign Assistance Act of 1961, any country responsible for preventing US assistance from reaching people in need must be denied access to US military aid. But in Israel's case, just a month after the April 2024 memos were written, Secretary of State Blinken delivered his department's official report to Congress, saying exactly the opposite: "We do not currently assess that the Israeli government is prohibiting or otherwise restricting the transport or delivery of US humanitarian assistance." His department's own agencies' reports were discarded, and with the false claim in place that Israel was not interfering with the aid shipments, virtually unlimited military aid to Israel—bombs, warplanes, tank ammunition, and other weapons of war—continued to flow. A ceasefire remained out of reach and the Israel exception continued.

Little changed after Israeli troops killed Hamas leader Yahya Sinwar in mid-October 2024. Despite claims from Biden, Harris, and others that this should open new possibilities for a ceasefire, there was still no evidence of actual US pressure in the form of ending arms transfers and military aid. A leaked letter of October 13 from US secretaries of state and defense to Israel's ministers of defense and strategic affairs spoke with "deep concern about the deteriorating humanitarian conditions" in Gaza, calling the situation facing two million people in Gaza "increasingly dire." The letter reminded Israel of its obligations to facilitate access to humanitarian aid and noted that US law required the US government to assess that process as well. It went on to name several specific actions Israel needed to take within the next thirty days—which would end only after the US elections of November 5. The letter mentioned that the US assessment was required under the terms of the Foreign Assistance Act. But it did not provide any specific consequences if Israel failed to comply, and US officials in the days that followed stated specifically that "the letter was not meant as a threat. ...The letter was simply meant to reiterate the sense of urgency we feel and the seriousness with which we feel it." When the ostensible deadline passed on November 12, 2024, eight widely respected international aid organizations reported that "Israel not only failed to meet the US criteria," but also had taken actions "that dramatically worsened the situation on the ground, particularly in Northern Gaza. ...That situation is in an even more dire state today than a month ago." The State Department, however, announced that the Biden administration "had not assessed" Israel to be in violation of US law. And the weapons continued to flow.

What was the humanitarian impact of Israel's post-October 7th war on Gaza, and what did the UN aid agency for Palestinians—UNRWA—have to do with it?

In 2006, a senior advisor to Prime Minister Ehud Olmert had stated that Israel's policy was "to put the Palestinians on a diet, but not to make them die of hunger." Later, Israeli authorities calculated the minimum calories needed for Palestinians to avoid outright malnutrition, and for seventeen years the people of Gaza, half of them children, lived with insufficient food.

On October 9, 2023, just twenty-four hours after Israel's assault began, the defense minister, Yoav Gallant, announced, "I have ordered a complete siege on the Gaza Strip. There will be no electricity, no food, no fuel, everything is closed." His plan worked; this time, Palestinians soon began to die of hunger.

Even as air strikes and bombing began killing people across the Gaza Strip, hunger soon became obvious. On October 18, 2023, the World Food Program said that the Gaza population was at risk of starvation. Three days later, the UN's five main humanitarian assistance agencies jointly issued an urgent statement calling for support as they documented 1.6 million people in Gaza in critical need of aid: "With so much civilian infrastructure in Gaza damaged or destroyed in nearly two weeks of constant bombings ... time is running out before mortality rates could skyrocket due to disease outbreaks and lack of health-care capacity." They warned that water production was down to 5 percent of the already-insufficient "normal" level. And that food stocks "are nearly exhausted." They called for a humanitarian cease-fire and immediate unrestricted humanitarian access, at scale and sustained, throughout Gaza. They ended with an urgent call: "Gaza was a desperate humanitarian situation before the most recent hostilities. It is now catastrophic. The world must do more."

Just a few weeks later, the World Health Organization warned that the near-total collapse of the water treatment, sanitation, and health care systems meant that more people could die from disease than from bombings in Gaza.

In July 2024, a group of Special Rapporteurs of the United Nations, human rights experts in a variety of fields, issued an urgent plea. They stated that the recent deaths of more Palestinian children due to hunger and malnutrition "leaves no doubt" that famine has spread across the entire Gaza Strip.

"Fayez Ataya, who was barely six months old, died on 30 May 2024 and 13-year-old Abdulqader Al-Serhi died on 1 June 2024 at the Al-Aqsa

Hospital in Deir Al-Balah. Nine-year-old Ahmad Abu Reida died on 3 June 2024 in the tent sheltering his displaced family in Al-Mawasi, Khan Younis. All three children died from malnutrition and lack of access to adequate healthcare," the experts said.

"With the death of these children from starvation despite medical treatment in central Gaza, there is no doubt that famine has spread from northern Gaza into central and southern Gaza."

The experts said the death of a child from malnutrition and dehydration indicates that health and social structures have been attacked and are critically weakened. "When the first child dies from malnutrition and dehydration, it becomes irrefutable that famine has taken hold," the experts said.

"We declare that Israel's intentional and targeted starvation campaign against the Palestinian people is a form of genocidal violence and has resulted in famine across all of Gaza. We call upon the international community to prioritize the delivery of humanitarian aid by land by any means necessary, end Israel's siege, and establish a ceasefire."

"When a 2-month-old baby and 10-year-old Yazan Al Kafarneh died of hunger on 24 February and 4 March respectively, this confirmed that famine had struck northern Gaza. The whole world should have intervened earlier to stop Israel's genocidal starvation campaign and prevented these deaths," the experts said. "Thirty-four Palestinians have died from malnutrition since 7 October, the majority being children. Inaction is complicity."

Some people tried to do more. Groups of medical workers continued to travel to Gaza to help their Palestinian colleagues cope with the devastation underway. On October 2, 2024, a group of ninety-nine doctors, surgeons, nurses, midwives, and physicians' assistants, some of them also public health experts, sent an open letter to President Biden and Vice President Harris describing in shattering detail what they had seen and experienced over the year, working in bombed-out hospitals and clinics across the Gaza Strip. In the extensive appendix to their letter, the medical teams noted that, "The fact that Palestinians in Gaza are so hungry that many have died, or that this is the result of deliberate Israeli policy, is not in dispute. However, the scale of this starvation is not widely appreciated." They went on to document their calculation that "in total it is likely that 62,413 people have died of starvation and its compilations in Gaza from October 7, 2023, to September 30, 2024. Most of these will have been young children."

The humanitarian conditions created by deliberate Israeli military actions were highlighted in South Africa's petition to the ICJ. In their January 2024 ruling, the justices imposed provisional measures that included requiring that Israel "shall take immediate and effective measures to enable the provision of urgently needed basic services and humanitarian assistance to address the adverse conditions of life faced by Palestinians in the Gaza Strip." Israel ignored the court's order.

Indeed, just hours after the court's decision was read out in The Hague on January 29, Israel went public with an unsubstantiated allegation that twelve Gazan employees of the UN Relief and Works Agency, the primary body providing humanitarian and development support to Palestinian refugees, were supposedly connected to Hamas and might have played some role in the October 7 attack on Israel. No evidence was provided, and UNRWA had given Israel the names of all their employees for vetting earlier that year; Israel had raised no concerns. It quickly became clear that two of those named had already been killed by Israeli bombs. And despite the lack of evidence, UNRWA fired the remaining ten named employees even before UNRWA and the UN launched separate investigations.

The timing of the Israeli release of the allegations—just hours after the ICJ's ruling that Israeli actions "plausibly" constituted genocide—indicated to many that it was deliberately announced to undermine international support for the court's interim decision. The US responded exactly along those lines—announcing just a few hours later that it was cutting its entire aid allocation to UNRWA. Washington was the largest single donor to UNRWA, which played by far the most important role of all humanitarian agencies working to get desperately needed aid into Gaza. Just a few hours after the US announcement, key US allies publicly joined Washington's aid cut—within a day or two, eighteen countries had pulled or paused their funds.

The US was providing about $300 million to UNRWA; losing that money, along with the funding promised by the other countries that joined the US cuts, had a serious negative impact on UNRWA's ability to provide even the most minimal of basic humanitarian services. When early investigations turned up no basis for their punishment, virtually all of the other countries restored their funding. For the US allocation, however, things got worse. Two weeks later, Israel launched another public relations attack on UNRWA, claiming to have found a tunnel under the agency's Gaza City headquarters that Hamas had used for something—it was never clear exactly what. Again no evidence was made public. But the US Congress voted to pass a law prohibiting any humanitarian assistance funds designed to help Palestinians from going to UNRWA. US officials themselves had argued that UNRWA was "the only game in town" among humanitarian organizations trying to get help into Gaza, but Congress passed the ban anyway.

The aid cuts seriously threatened the lives of the 2.3 million Gazans, almost all of them displaced from their homes, as well as millions more Palestinian refugees in the West Bank, Jordan, Lebanon, and Syria. Some US officials suggested that UNRWA funds be sent instead to UNICEF and the World Food Program, ignoring the stark reality that those two agencies together had seventy staff members on the ground in Gaza, while UNRWA had 13,000. UNRWA workers had been providing, for more than half a century, all the services that would ordinarily be provided by a government civil service. Most of Gaza's health workers, teachers, engineers, and street sweepers were UNRWA employees. Drastic funding cuts put at risk the health, safety, and lives of tens of thousands or more civilians, especially the most vulnerable—babies, children, pregnant women, and the elderly. And Washington's role in cutting funds, thus undermining the capacity of UNRWA to provide Palestinians' access to water, food, shelter, medicine, and fuel, made it again directly complicit in Israel's genocidal attack.

Along with UNRWA's importance in providing humanitarian assistance in Gaza, the agency had another important role in the UN system. It remained the only UN agency whose mandate included protection of Palestinian refugee rights—meaning that its work went beyond providing food, medical care, and education. Its work, from its creation by the UN General Assembly in 1949, was explicitly designed to continue until Palestinian refugees achieved "a just and durable solution to their plight" on the basis of UN resolution 194 and all the human rights and refugee rights to which they are entitled. That meant that UNRWA was designed to continue its work until the refugees' right to return to their homes, as guaranteed by international law, was realized. Refugees—dispossessed in 1948 in the Nakba, from land that became southern Israel—made up about 70 percent of Gaza's population. Without UNRWA, their right of return, and the existence of Palestinians as a refugee community with guaranteed rights, would be threatened with erasure. And that would qualify as creating conditions that make the survival of all or part of a threatened group as a group impossible—part of the very definition of genocide.

In late September 2024, a group of reserve officers released what Israel soon referred to as "the Generals' Plan" for Gaza. It called for using "humanitarian aid as a strategic lever for the return of the abductees and the defeat of Hamas." Phase 1 of the plan called for "evacuation of the population from the north of the Gaza Strip" and Phase 2 was simply titled "Siege." At the same time, Israel issued a so-called evacuation order for the entire population of northern Gaza. As was always the case with orders to leave, many people were unable to follow the order—pregnant women, the disabled and elderly who couldn't walk, families simply too aware that there was nowhere safe to go. A siege was imposed, and for the first two weeks of October, Israel blocked all food and water from northern Gaza—not a single truck was allowed in. Hospitals were surrounded and attacked to force out staff and patients, schools where people were sheltering were bombed and destroyed, families fled with nothing, despite knowing there was nowhere safe for them to go. The attacks were launched with particular ferocity against the Jabaliya refugee camp, where tens of thousands of people remained, but continued across the rest of north Gaza as well.

Israel's Ceasefire Coalition—made up of four major human rights organizations, B'tselem, Gisha, Physicians for Human Rights–Israel, and Yesh Din—were soon calling Israel's actions "ethnic cleansing," designed to empty northern Gaza altogether. As *Democracy Now* described the area, "In the Jabaliya refugee camp, Israeli forces stormed at least three schools sheltering Palestinians, forcing those inside to leave at gunpoint, before setting fire to the buildings. Palestinians fleeing the shattered remains of Beit Lahia report seeing bodies in the streets and Israeli soldiers detaining and beating men. The stench of death is everywhere."

Two weeks into the siege, the human rights organizations warned the international community that any country that did not take action to stop the forcible transfer of people out of the northern Gaza Strip could be held accountable as complicit in ethnic cleansing. They said there were "alarming signs" that Israel's siege meant that "the Israeli military is beginning to quietly implement the Generals' Plan ... for complete forcible transfer of the civilians of the northern Gaza Strip through tightening the siege on the area and starving the population."

Despite the warnings, Israel's siege and bombardment continued, and weapons shipments, particularly from the United States, continued unabated. More than three weeks into the total siege, US Secretary of State Antony Blinken went to Israel, to once again meet with Prime Minister Netanyahu. According to the State Department, Blinken "emphasized" the need for more humanitarian assistance into Gaza; the Israeli report of the meeting made no mention of humanitarian aid.

In remarks to the press, Blinken lauded Israel for having achieved many of its goals in Gaza, including largely destroying Hamas as a military force and eliminating most of its leadership, including the killing of Hamas leader Yahya Sinwar, with only a passing reference to "the great cost of Palestinian civilians in Gaza" and then said, "Now is the time to turn those successes into an enduring strategic success." Pushed by journalists about why there was no consequence when Blinken had warned Israel back in April 2024, six months earlier, about the need to ensure access for humanitarian aid, he responded, "Why wasn't that warning enough once they backslid? Because we saw—we saw them take action, we saw concrete improvements and then, as we saw it abate again—"

The journalist cuts back in, "Is it an empty threat to withhold the weapons, as is congressionally mandated by law?"

"I am determined to follow the law," Blinken responded. "I will follow the law."

As if to prove its disdain for US or international law, on October 30, 2024, the Israeli Knesset voted to cut all ties with UNRWA and to prohibit the UN agency from operating in Israel or Israeli-controlled territory. Response from the United Nations was quick and clear: "Without UNRWA," the spokesperson for the UN's High Commissioner for Human Rights said, "the delivery of food, health care, education, among other things, to most of Gaza's population, would grind to a halt. Civilians have already paid the heaviest price of this conflict over the past year. Truly, this decision will only make matters worse for them, far worse." He reiterated previous concerns "about Israel's compliance with international law" with regard to its intense bombardment of Gaza and the killing of tens of thousands of civilians.

The head of the World Health Organization, Dr. Tedros Adhanom Ghebreyesus, noting that one of every four of the 13,000 UNRWA staff in Gaza were health workers, called the Knesset decision "intolerable" and said the attack on the aid agency was "threatening the lives and health" of all those who depended on UNRWA. According to the UN children's agency UNICEF, "with the children of Gaza already facing one of the gravest humanitarian crises in recent history, if fully implemented, this decision will be deadly."

And as UN Secretary General Antonio Guterres described the Israeli decision, "There is no alternative to UNRWA. The implementation of the laws could have devastating consequences for Palestine refugees in the Occupied Palestinian Territory, which is unacceptable. I call on Israel to act consistently with its obligations under the Charter of the United Nations and its other obligations under international law, including under international humanitarian law and those concerning privileges and immunities of the United Nations. National legislation cannot alter those obligations."

What was the significance of South Africa's ICJ case against Israel for violating the convention against genocide?

Soon after the assault on Gaza began on October 8, 2023, Israel's actions began to be described as "genocide." Following the Hamas-led attack on military and civilian targets in southern Israel the day before, the ferocity and level of destruction of Israel's one-sided war, along with the plethora of statements from high-ranking Israeli military and political officials as well as cultural figures calling for their forces to "kill alike men and women, infants and sucklings" (Netanyahu); "Erase Gaza; don't leave a single person there" (pop singer Eyad Golan); "We are fighting human animals" (defense minister Yoav Gallant); "Horrible, inhuman animals" (former UN ambassador Dan Gillerman) all led to a rising chorus around the world calling out Israel's war as genocide.

It had taken more than twenty years for US public opinion, mainstream media coverage, and a few brave policymakers and faith leaders to shift their narrative and recognize apartheid as the legally correct and politically appropriate term to describe Israeli policy towards the Palestinians. It took about twenty days for "genocide" to emerge in the dominant narrative of 2023.

Many people began to speak of genocide based on the popular understanding of its definition—mass killing. Certainly the rapidly rising numbers of people—including babies, children, elders—being killed by Israeli bombs made that appropriate. But the term does not only refer to massive death—in international law, genocide has a very explicit definition. According to the Convention on the Prevention and Punishment of the Crime of Genocide, the word refers to efforts to destroy all or part of a specific group—defined by race, religion, ethnicity, language, location or other social categories.

Two things are required for acts of violence to be considered genocide. First, there must be evidence of the specific intent to destroy all or part of the group. That doesn't necessarily mean killing everyone in the group; genocide refers to destruction of the group (or part of the group) *as* a group, as a collective entity, not necessarily the death of each individual. Second, along with the specific intention, genocide requires evidence of at least one of five separate acts: killing members of the group, severely injuring (physically or mentally) members of the group, deliberately inflicting conditions of life calculated to bring about the group's physical destruction, imposing measures intended to prevent births within the group, and forcibly transferring children of the group to another group.

So, if matched by the intent to destroy all or part of the group, things like mass expulsion or dispossession of a group, or creating conditions so dangerous that people in the group felt they had no choice but to leave, could qualify as genocide.

There was little question that Israeli attacks matched at least three or four of the convention's named actions. What made the case even more definitive, and thus more unusual, were the open statements of intent from top Israeli officials. In past cases, it had always been very difficult to prove a genocide, since showing the specific intent required was almost always impossible. In Israel's case, following October 7, it was easy. Key military and political officials from the whole range of political parties and opinion were proudly asserting their desire and intent to destroy the people of Gaza—it was all available in real time in mainstream and social media, public pronouncements, tweets, Facebook entries, and official speeches.

So the question that emerged was who—what country—would take the initiative to hold Israel accountable for this clear violation of the Genocide Convention. Within just a few weeks of the Israeli assault, South Africa stepped up to take that responsibility. There were political, legal, and especially moral reasons for the post-apartheid government to take it on. For both South Africa and Palestine, 1948 had been a pivotal year. Apartheid was made the law of the land in South Africa, and Zionist militias in what was then Palestine carried out the mass expulsion and dispossession of the majority of the indigenous population to create present-day Israel.

For decades, Palestinians and South Africans recognized the parallels—not exact but historically consistent—between apartheid-era South Africa and the unnamed but similarly discriminatory system designed to maintain Jewish domination over Palestinians in Israel and in what twenty years later became the occupied territory of the West Bank, Gaza Strip, and East Jerusalem. It took people in the West, especially in the US, much longer to recognize Israeli apartheid.

For decades, the horrors of the Nakba were answered with absolute impunity for Israel, granted and protected by the US, thus encouraging an ever-escalating level of Israeli state and settler violence against Palestinians. In 2018 Israel passed the Nation-State Law, equivalent to a constitutional amendment in the United States, making Jewish supremacy officially the law of the land by defining Israel not as the state of all its citizens, but as the "national home of the Jewish people" and that "the right to exercise national self-determination in the State of Israel is unique to the Jewish people." Palestinians would have no such right.

But then, for the first time, almost three-quarters of a century after the Nakba and three decades after the overthrow of apartheid in South Africa, Israel was suddenly being challenged and held accountable for its genocidal actions—and it was the post-apartheid "Rainbow Nation" that took the lead.

On December 29, 2023, South Africa became the first country to file an application to the UN's highest judicial arm, the International Court of Justice, instituting genocide proceedings against Israel for "acts threatened, adopted, condoned, taken, and being taken by the Government and military of the State of Israel against the Palestinian people."

In wrenching detail, its eighty-four pages documented a litany of Israeli actions as "genocidal in character, as they are committed with the requisite specific intent ... to destroy Palestinians in Gaza as a part of the broader Palestinian national, racial, and ethnical [sic] group." On the question of specific intent, South Africa pointed to dozens of statements by Israeli leaders, including the president, prime minister, other cabinet officials, as well as Knesset members, military commanders, and other high-ranking officials.

Accustomed to decades of US-backed impunity, those Israeli officials openly described their intent to carry out "another Nakba," to wipe out all of Gaza, to raze Gaza to the ground, to reduce it to rubble, to bury Palestinians alive, among many other similar statements—all of which, if carried out, would violate the laws of war that prohibit collective punishment, require distinguishing between combatants and civilians, and demand protection of civilians.

Their deliberately dehumanizing language included descriptions of Palestinians as animals, subhuman, Nazis, a cancer, insects, vermin—all language designed to justify wiping out all or part of the group. Prime Minister Netanyahu went so far as to invoke a Biblical verse commanding that the "entire population be wiped out, that none be spared, men, women, children, suckling babies, and livestock."

Two weeks later, on January 11, 2024, the South African legal team, led by veteran human rights lawyer and former UN Special Rapporteur on Human Rights in the Occupied Palestinian Territory John Dugard and Minister of Justice Ronald Lamola, presented a three-hour explanation of the charges outlined in their application. As they introduced the thesis of their charge, the South Africans made clear that they would not use their time showing videos whose impact was sure to raise emotional and/or angry responses. Their intention, they said, was to rely on the law and on the facts as they appeared in open sources and from witnesses on the ground. The argument was broadcast around the world, and hundreds of thousands watched it live, many getting up at 4:00 a.m. to sit glued to computer screens while hundreds of Palestinians and others rallied outside the Peace Palace in The Hague, where the ICJ meets, cheering for justice.

The Israelis argued the following day. Their defense lawyers spent significant parts of their three hours showing photographs and videos of the events of October 7, 2023. While clearly harrowing, the killing and kidnapping of Israeli and other civilians on that day inside Israel were not legally relevant to the charges of Israeli genocide against the people of Gaza. The brief had stated that South Africa "unequivocally condemns all violations of international law by all parties, including the direct targeting of Israeli civilians and other nationals and hostage-taking by Hamas and other Palestinian armed groups." It had also reminded the court that, according to international law, "No armed attack on a State's territory, no matter how serious—even an attack involving atrocity crimes—can, however, provide any possible justification for, or defense to, breaches of the [Genocide Convention] whether as a matter of law or morality."

Israel did not substantively deny that its troops had committed the specific military and other acts that were even then continuing to devastate the population of Gaza. Beyond relying on the legally immaterial evidence of the crimes against civilians committed on October 7, the Israeli team focused on trying to dismiss the vast array of statements by Israeli officials indicating genocidal intent—not claiming they did not occur, but rather that they were irrelevant. They were only joking, the lawyers said, or the statements were not meant as a guide to action by the military. But given the highly influential military and political positions held by many of those officials, and how closely their statements matched Israel's military and related actions since October 7, it was difficult to view them as somehow detached from those acts that had already caused tens of thousands of deaths, hundreds of thousands of forced displacements, destruction of huge swathes of Gazan territory and infrastructure, and countless further acts of devastation.

Another two weeks later, the court issued its preliminary ruling—finding that it was "plausible" that Israel's actions against the entire population of Gaza constituted genocide. It was not yet a full determination of the facts and the law—those issues in international legal venues take years. Yet the initial ruling still represented a hugely important step, particularly as the ICJ went beyond its finding of plausible genocide to impose six provisional measures aimed at ensuring that the rights, indeed the lives, of Palestinians must be protected from those actions. The measures imposed by the court stated that Israel "shall take all necessary measures" to prevent the commission of any of the five acts named in the Genocide Convention from being used against the Palestinians, to ensure that the Israeli military did not commit any of those acts, to punish any public incitement to those acts, to take all measures to provide humanitarian assistance, to prevent the destruction of evidence relevant to the charges of genocide, and to report to the court within one month on what Tel Aviv was doing to abide by the court's ruling.

South Africa had asked the court to order a ceasefire as a provisional measure. While the ICJ did not explicitly name a ceasefire, the first two measures it imposed (preventing the commission of, and ensuring the Israeli military did not commit, any of the five acts) included an order not to kill Palestinians—the first of the five prohibited acts. Therefore, any Israeli act that could lead to killing Palestinians—such as bombing, air strikes, withholding food, etc.—would be a violation of the court's provisional orders.

In February, South Africa returned to the court, asking for additional provisional measures to respond to the increasingly dangerous conditions facing Palestinians in Gaza, including the Israeli threat to invade the small city of Rafah, which had been identified as a "safer" area for Palestinians fleeing Israeli attacks. The court agreed that those developments, especially an attack on Rafah "would exponentially increase what is already a humanitarian nightmare with untold regional consequences," and reminded Israel that the "perilous situation demands immediate and effective implementation" of the actions it had already ordered, rather than imposing any additional provisional measures.

In March, South Africa returned again, this time requesting new measures in response to reports that starvation was rising across Gaza. The court agreed that Gaza's "catastrophic living conditions" had deteriorated, and that "Palestinians in Gaza are no longer facing only a risk of famine ... but that famine is setting in." The justices indicated that "the provisional measures indicated in the Order of January 26, 2024, do not fully address the consequences arising from the changes in the situation ... thus justifying the modification of these measures." The court then ordered Israel additionally to ensure unhindered access to "urgently needed basic services and humanitarian assistance, including food, water, electricity, fuel, shelter, clothing, hygiene and sanitation requirements, as well as medical supplies and medical care to Palestinians throughout Gaza." The justices also repeated their earlier order to make sure that the Israeli military "does not commit acts which constitute a violation" of the Genocide Convention, and ordered Israel to be sure its troops did nothing to prevent the delivery of urgently needed humanitarian assistance.

Israel remained in violation of all of the provisional orders the International Court of Justice had issued.

In Washington, in both the national domestic and global diplomatic contexts, the Court's decisions posed a huge problem for the Biden administration. Even before South Africa's original petition had been made public, White House and State Department officials staked out an unconditional position that the claim of genocide was "meritless." But with a virtually unanimous court ruling that Israel's assault on Gaza was indeed plausibly genocidal—and with the one US judge (who happened to be the presiding judge of the ICJ) standing with the majority—that dismissive attitude, and related claims that "the UN is biased against Israel" did not get much traction.

While briefly referencing the obligation of other parties to the Genocide Convention to stop or prevent a present or future genocide, South Africa's petition kept its main focus sharply on Israel's violations of the convention. It did not request provisional measures to deal specifically with the complicity of other governments, most significantly of course the United States, by funding, arming, and shielding Israel as it carried out its genocidal acts.

But the role of the United States in the Israeli onslaught, while hardly surprising given the long history of US support for Israel, did receive significant global attention in the wake of South Africa's initiative. As a state party to the Genocide Convention, the US shared the obligation of all such parties to act to prevent or stop genocide. Instead, the US not only failed in its obligation to stop what the court ruled was plausibly a genocide, but instead actively provided economic, military, intelligence, and diplomatic support to Israel that enabled its mass atrocities in Gaza.

This constituted not only US inaction in the face of genocide, but also a case of direct complicity—a distinct crime under the Genocide Convention. The Center for Constitutional Rights in New York, on behalf of Palestinian human rights organizations and individual Palestinians and Palestinian-Americans, filed a suit in US federal court in California about the same time that South Africa filed at the ICJ, charging US officials with complicity in Israel's acts of genocide. They sued President Joe Biden, Secretary of State Antony Blinken, and Secretary of Defense Lloyd Austin for failing to prevent genocide and for aiding and abetting Israel in carrying out a genocide against the Palestinian people in Gaza.

In January 2024, federal district Judge Jeffrey Wright reluctantly dismissed the charges, because of the "political question" legal doctrine that says foreign policy decisions belong only to the executive branch. But in his opinion, he made clear that the witness testimony presented, including that of a doctor who survived the siege in Gaza and that of a genocide and Holocaust expert, along with the ICJ ruling itself, had indeed demonstrated that "it is plausible that Israel's conduct amounts to genocide." He described the testimony he had heard from the Palestinian witnesses as "truly horrific, gut wrenching, no words to describe it." The judge noted that the US government did not dispute the evidence of a "genocide in progress," and in his ruling he implored the Biden administration to "examine the results of their unflagging support of the military siege against the Palestinians in Gaza."

The case was appealed to the Ninth Circuit Court of Appeals in June 2024, and was rejected in July. In September 2024 a new appeal was filed.

What was the movement that mobilized against Israel's war?

The movement for Palestinian rights is not new. And in the last quarter-century or so since, that movement has been responsible for significant shifts in the public, media, and ever-so-slowly policy discourse on Palestine and US relations with Israel. But the Israeli assault on Gaza that followed the Hamas-led attack of October 7, 2023, brought about an entirely new level of mobilization and transformation of the narrative.

Within the first few days of the war that Israel launched on October 8, a series of huge national protests took place in Washington, DC. Led separately and jointly by Muslim, Jewish, and diverse organizations already committed to Palestinian rights, they brought tens of thousands, eventually hundreds of thousands, to the streets of the capital—chanting and praying outside Congress, filling the streets across the city, conducting sit-ins inside congressional offices. Soon parallel protests burst out across the country, in the biggest cities and in small towns, bringing together students and peace campaigners, faith-based and anti-racist organizations, organizations of Palestinians and other Arabs, people of color, Jews, and unnumbered categories of human beings. It was broader than any previous mobilizations focused on Palestinian rights.

And the protests maintained an extraordinary—and, for the Palestinian rights movement of the past, unusual—level of message discipline: "Ceasefire Now!" was the cry that erupted from all the protests. There was a recognition, by virtually all the organizers and the vast majority of participants, that the core issues, the profoundly necessary demands of the self-defined movement for Palestinian rights—end the occupation, stop Israeli apartheid, equality for all—would for the moment take a back seat to the urgent immediacy of stopping the Israeli assault that was rapidly becoming genocidal. Those crucial demands remained strategically central, but the tactical shift required a new—and broader—point of unity.

The movement—now far larger and politically broader than the traditional movement for Palestinian rights—quickly settled on the demand for an immediate ceasefire. And virtually all the protests, mobilizations, banners, posters, online announcements made that their central focus. That was surprising—the longstanding movement had a history of diversity of demands and focus issues. But somehow this broader iteration of collective action, pulling in large numbers of people with no prior history of working for Palestinian rights, managed to maintain a level of message discipline previously rare.

And this new, broad (though not necessarily as deep) movement accomplished something else as well. It managed to expand the meaning of the core demand, even while deepening its meaning, what it required. Within weeks, the call for an immediate ceasefire was retooled to call for an immediate and permanent ceasefire—rejecting the premise of the November 2023 temporary ceasefire that had accepted the idea of Israel resuming its onslaught as soon as some number of its hostages was released.

Then, over the next weeks and months, the very definition of ceasefire was retooled. Now, it was understood that the ceasefire the movement demanded, the ceasefire that would be acceptable, required not only the complete cessation of bombing, tank fire, of killing. That was only step one. Step two meant ensuring access for the massive amounts of humanitarian assistance that the devastated population of Gaza now required—food, clean water, medicine, shelter, health facilities, electricity—and reopening the funding of UNRWA to be sure it got to everyone who needed it. Step three, the new understanding of ceasefire now required an end to arms transfers. The US—whatever language it used and however many times it requested a ceasefire—had to actually stop sending the weapons and military funding that enabled Israel's attack to continue. Only with all three steps would any claimed ceasefire be accepted. So the movement's call for ceasefire remained, while continuing to evolve over the months.

In the White House, language shifted as well, but it never reflected any authentic change in policy. On April 1, 2024, a deliberate sequence of Israeli drone strikes attacked a convoy of humanitarian workers from the World Central Kitchen, a global charity affiliated with progressive celebrity chef José Andrés. The strikes killed seven workers, six of whom were from the US, Britain, Poland, and Australia, and reports of the attack went viral around the world. President Biden announced he was "brokenhearted" at the news—and within a few hours, on the same day, news broke that his administration was "set to greenlight" Israel's long-sought $18 billion purchase of as many as fifty Boeing-made F-15 fighter jets, exactly the warplanes the IDF had been using since it attacked Gaza on October 8, 2023.

Following the brief temporary ceasefire in November 2023, the White House largely abandoned any discussion of a ceasefire. Biden himself virtually stopped using the word at all. Kamala Harris, months before she supplanted Biden as the Democratic candidate for president, called for an immediate—though only a temporary—ceasefire on March 3, 2024, while meeting with influential Black leaders at Selma. It was limited—she made clear she was only calling for a six-week pause—but the fact that she called for a ceasefire before Biden did gave some people hope that she might be trying to distinguish herself at least slightly from Biden's unconditional military support for Israel. Biden began to use the term—in even more limited ways—some weeks later.

The shift in language that began to come from the White House reflected the growing power of the widespread ceasefire movement. One of its most creative and almost certainly the most influential component was launched as the Uncommitted movement. Targeting the spring/ summer Democratic primaries ahead of the November 2024 presidential election, organizers began in February to build a network of voters across the country who pledged to vote "uncommitted" rather than supporting the then-candidate, incumbent President Joe Biden. From swing states like Michigan and Wisconsin, to traditional Democratic strongholds such as Hawaii, ultimately more than 750,000 voters didn't just reject a candidate, they sent a clear message to Biden that they would not vote for someone who was funding, arming, and protecting Israel's assault in Gaza. The numbers surprised even the organizers; in Hawaii, almost 30 percent of Democratic voters chose "uncommitted," while in parts of student-heavy Madison, Wisconsin, the numbers shot up to 32 percent. In at least nine states, Uncommitted delegates represented voters at the Democratic National Convention in August.

Biden's reluctant embrace of the formerly rejected call for a cease-fire, however qualified, was at least partly in response to the protest vote campaign. It wasn't sufficient—his version of a ceasefire was always conditional, always viewed as temporary, and never seriously fought for—but it did represent the first break in what had been an absolutely consistent refusal to even say the word.

By the time the Democratic National Convention opened in Chicago in August, however, Harris was the candidate for president, and hopes were diminishing that her position would represent anything more than a difference in tone. After failing to get a commitment to stop sending weapons to Israel, the Uncommitted movement reduced its demand to simply getting a brief speaking slot for a Democratic elected official, a state representative in Georgia who was Palestinian-American. They were rejected again, and a number of both the Uncommitted, now part of a broader grouping identified as ceasefire delegates, launched a daylong sit-in outside the main convention venue. Gaza did, however, remain a major issue throughout the convention.

There were also incredibly creative demonstrations. Palestinian organizers brought together some of the largest protests in the history of Washington, DC, with hundreds of thousands filling the streets of downtown. Activists with Jewish Voice for Peace organized sit-ins in the halls and offices of Congress and occupations of New York's Grand Central Station and the island site of the Statue of Liberty. Rabbis for Ceasefire, organized early in the crisis, took over the UN Security Council chamber to protest how Washington was preventing the UN from doing its job, and later met with the secretary-general to urge the global organization to stand up to US pressure. In April, they also sent a Passover delegation to Israel, where they attempted to bring half a ton of rice and flour into Gaza.

The broad national movement for ceasefire included a number of other features that were creative and new to Palestinian rights organizing. Beginning quite early in the crisis, the horror at what US military support was enabling in Gaza sparked a series of large-scale protests from public officials of the federal government—congressional staff and White House interns, 1,000 staff of USAID and hundreds more from the State Department, even staff members of Biden's reelection campaign headquarters. They made public objections sent to internal opposition venues, published statements in the press, gathered on the steps of government buildings to read collective statements of outrage. Eventually protest resignations began, of political appointees and civil servants, high-ranking officials, and young staffers risking careers ahead of them, Palestinian and Jewish Americans, from US departments of education, interior, state, defense, and beyond, all unwilling to remain part of an administration that they viewed as complicit in a global atrocity.

The recognition of Israeli behavior as something more than just ordinary, even one-sided warfare, but as genocide, soon took hold. It had taken close to twenty years for public opinion in the United States to begin to acknowledge what Palestinians and South Africans had long known—that Israeli treatment of Palestinians was, and should be named, apartheid. It took less than twenty days for the word "genocide" to become inextricably linked to Israeli actions—along with the US money and weapons that enabled them.

And that increasingly widespread acknowledgment emerged because experts immediately made clear their own recognition that genocide in Gaza was imminent or already underway. Less than two weeks after the Israeli assault began on October 8, 2023, a group of over 800 scholars of international law and genocide issued a report warning of "the possibility of the crime of genocide being perpetrated by Israeli forces against Palestinians in the Gaza Strip. Ten days later, one of the top human rights officials of the United Nations, Craig Mokhiber, who had for many years been in charge of the UN Office of the High Commissioner for Human Rights in New York, resigned. In his final letter, he excoriated the UN and its most powerful member states for not responding sufficiently to what he called a "text-book case of genocide." On November 2, a group of UN human rights experts issued a joint statement warning that "Palestinian people are at grave risk of genocide. The time for action is now. Israel's allies also bear responsibility and must act now to prevent its disastrous course of action." And on December 29, South Africa filed its application to the International Court of Justice, charging Israel with the violation of the Genocide Convention.

Use of the term genocide helped to shock people into recognizing just how serious the crisis in Gaza really was. And it was young people who responded with the most energy, the most people, the most creativity. For the young African-Americans outraged by the police murder of George Floyd in 2020, who had grown up with the protests flooding the streets in response, the young Palestinians mourning and raging the killing of their families back home, the young Jews who had redefined their identity in the context of social justice and anti-racism rather than support for Israel, the young students of every race, religion, ethnicity, gender, language, immigration, and economic status, came together to challenge Israel's occupation, apartheid, genocide. This was indeed what some had begun calling the "Justice Generation."

The most powerful expression of this young energy erupted on college campuses across the country, from small community colleges to huge public universities and the most elite private institutions. Student organizing had been going on for years, but the horror of the Israeli assault, with live video magnified and replicated on screens around the clock, pushed the mobilizing to a whole new level. The most visible reflection was in the creation of student encampments, with tents pitched on campuses to symbolize the Nakba, when the grandparents and great-grandparents of the current generation of young Palestinians were dispossessed of their land and forced to live for many years in tents provided by aid agencies.

The encampments soon became symbols of resistance to the Israeli assault on Gaza. On campuses across the country—eventually more than 175—groups of student activists often led by Students for Justice in Palestine, student branches of Jewish Voice for Peace, Black and other people of color-led student organizations pitched tents and for days used the area for round-the-clock teach-ins, for history lessons, in April for student-run Passover seder dinners. They issued demands, usually beginning with the broad demand for an immediate permanent cease-fire—they definitely saw themselves as part of the broader Ceasefire Now movement—and moving on to specific demands to university administrations. Most often those included calls for university divestment from companies profiting from Israeli occupation and apartheid, or producing weapons or other military goods being used against Gaza.

Many of the encampments faced harsh campus penalties, including bringing in city police (as in New York, at Columbia University and the City University of New York) who responded with extraordinary levels of violence aimed at shutting them down, or allowed campus and/or city police to stand by while non-student pro-Israel groups violently attacked the encampments, as occurred at UCLA. But the visual power of the encampments went viral on social media, and the phenomenon soon spread to campuses around the world. And the historic links of these protests to earlier student movements—mostly notably the Vietnam-era anti-war occupations of campus buildings in the 1960s and '70s and the encampments constructed on campuses to resemble shantytowns during the anti-apartheid movement of the 1980s—provided a powerful resonance for the twenty-first-century students.

For many of the activists, whose ranks included students and many newly involved participants—the next step in the ceasefire movement may also be based on a South Africa model. With the International Court of Justice issuing a July 2024 ruling that Israel's occupation violated numerous international laws—including the prohibition against apartheid included in Article 3 of the Convention on the Elimination of Racial Discrimination—the UN General Assembly passed a key resolution in September, aimed at implementing the ICJ's decision. Among a long list of economic and political sanctions that member states were urged to carry out, was the call for all states to cease "the provision or transfer of arms, munitions and related equipment to Israel, the occupying Power, in all cases where there are reasonable grounds to suspect that they may be used in the Occupied Palestinian Territory." As was the case at the UN in the 1970s and '80s, when General Assembly resolutions called for sanctions and arms embargos against apartheid South Africa, GA resolutions are considered nonbinding. But the resolutions turned out to be powerful weapons in the hands of anti-apartheid movements around the world, which used the UN positions to pressure their own governments to stop trading, arming, or otherwise engaging with the apartheid regime in Pretoria. The activists of the 2023–24 movement for Ceasefire Now can use the language of the General Assembly resolution the same way: to pressure their governments to stop sending arms, buying from settlements, or otherwise engaging with Israel's military or economy. If enough countries follow the demands of their own mobilized civil society, it is possible the United States, as it finally did, however grudgingly, in the 1980s, will finally impose its own sanctions—starting with an end to arms transfers—on Israel.

What was the impact of the Gaza crisis in the West Bank, Lebanon, and beyond?

The crisis underway in Gaza did not remain in Gaza. In its first year, while the Israeli assault and harsh siege that led to famine and near-famine conditions roared across the Gaza Strip, major Israeli escalations of repression and war erupted across the occupied West Bank and Lebanon, while dangers grew of direct conflict between Israel and Iran, and regional attacks between Israel and Yemen, Syria, and Iraq, continued to raise the threat of all-out regional war.

Within days of the Israeli launching of war on Gaza following the October 7 Hamas-led attack on Israel, both Hezbollah in Lebanon and the Houthi movement in Yemen announced they would act in solidarity with Hamas and with the Palestinians of Gaza. Their goal aimed at making Israel operate militarily in diverse arenas and therefore with less focus on the fighting in Gaza.

In Lebanon, tit-for-tat rocket fire across the border was a longstanding story, certainly since the end of the 2006 Israel-Lebanon war. The UN-brokered ceasefire had required Israel to end its occupation of southern Lebanon, and Hezbollah to pull back from the border, but cross-border rocket and other attacks continued on a small scale. After October 8, Hezbollah launched several rockets into Israel, and the attacks continued through the year. Israel expanded its attacks on Lebanon to hit much more of the country, including Beirut, and carried out a set of targeted assassinations of Hezbollah leaders.

On September 17, 2024, Israel launched a major escalation in Lebanon, planting explosives in over 3,000 pagers and simultaneously detonating them. The following day, a similar attack was launched against walkie-talkies. Together the attacks led to at least 42 people killed, including children, and more than 3,200 injured. Many of the injuries were very serious, including but not limited to the loss of eyes, hands, and arms. The devices were used by Hezbollah operatives, some of them militants but many of them health care workers, teachers, mechanics, and others connected with Hezbollah's vast array of social welfare agencies in Lebanon. Many of the exploding devices killed and injured people nearby, including children.

According to Amnesty International, "The mass explosions across Lebanon and Syria in recent days bear the hallmarks of a sinister dystopian nightmare. Using hidden explosive devices concealed within everyday telecommunications devices to wage deadly attacks on such a scale is unprecedented. Even if the attacks intended to target military objectives, detonating thousands of devices simultaneously without being able to determine their exact location or whose possession they were in at the time of the attack demonstrates a flagrant disregard for the right to life and for the laws of armed conflict. International humanitarian law prohibits indiscriminate attacks—meaning attacks that fail to distinguish between civilians and military targets. It also prohibits the use of the type of booby-traps that appear to have been used in these attacks. The UN Security Council should take all the measures at its disposal to ensure protection of civilians and avoid more needless suffering. An international investigation must urgently be set up to establish the facts and bring the perpetrators to justice."

In the next several days, Israel carried out a targeted assassination of another Hezbollah leader, then ordered an evacuation of whole stretches of south Lebanon and began air strikes. By September 23, Israeli bombing had killed 492 people in southern Lebanon, thirty-five of them children, and injured 1,645 more. Four days later, Israel carried out its most high-profile assassination, that of the widely revered longtime Hezbollah leader Hasan Nasrallah, in Beirut. Israeli ground troops began their invasion of south Lebanon on October 1.

According to the United Nations, by October 13, 2,229 Lebanese people had been killed and 10,380 injured by Israeli attacks across Lebanon. As of October 16, nearly 60 people had been killed in Israel, half of them soldiers. By mid-August in northern Israel 96,000 people had been displaced since the beginning of the war; during that same period 110,099 Lebanese had been displaced. One month into Israel's September escalation, 1.2 million people across Lebanon had been forced from their homes. And by October 22, the World Health Organization reported that 100 out of 207 health centers across Lebanon had been attacked had been damaged badly enough to be forced to close. Conditions in Lebanon were dire enough that thousands of the refugees, who had sought safety in Lebanon from the brutality of the Syrian civil war for over a decade, were trying to return to Syria where despite the war still continuing they believed they could keep their families safer.

On October 2, Israel announced that UN Secretary General Antonio Guterres would be considered persona non grata because his condemnation of Iran's retaliatory missile strike was deemed not strong enough. Throughout October 2024, Israeli troops in south Lebanon continued to fire on facilities of UNIFIL, the multinational UN peacekeeping force charged with maintaining some level of stability in the area—mainly by implementing Resolution 1701's requirement that the only armed forces that could be present between the border and the Litani River would be the Lebanese national army and UNIFIL itself. Israel told the UN that the best way to prevent casualties among the peacekeepers would be for them to withdraw. The UN refused to pull them out.

The expansion of Israel's war against Gaza was not only in Lebanon. Houthi rebels in Yemen had indicated a commitment similar to that of Hezbollah to challenge Israel in what they saw as solidarity with Hamas and the people of Gaza. Yemeni forces had occasionally attacked commercial shipping in the Red Sea that was seen as having some tie to Israel—and those attacks continued. Shortly after the Israeli war against Gaza began in October 2023, the Houthis also launched a number of missiles and armed drones towards Israel. In July, one man was killed in one of those attacks. In response, Israel attacked Yemen's major port city, Hodeidah, claiming the port was used to store weapons. The impoverished country relied on the port for desperately needed access to food, medicine and other necessities. The strikes damaged an oil refinery and fuel storage facilities, a power generating station, and port cranes. At the end of September, Israel attacked Yemen again, this time sending dozens of US-made fighter jets targeting power plants and two different ports. The air strikes killed at least four people and wounded twenty-nine, and caused power outages across Hodeidah.

In mid-October, Washington joined the Israeli action with a massive air strike, including B-2 stealth bombers for the first time, to attack Yemeni sites that the US claimed were being used to store munitions. Secretary of Defense Lloyd Austin made clear that the strike and especially the inclusion of the powerful B-2 bombers had a political goal beyond the Yemeni target. "This was a unique demonstration," Austin said, "of the United States' ability to target facilities that our adversaries seek to keep out of reach, no matter how deeply buried underground, hardened, or fortified. The employment of US Air Force B-2 Spirit long-range stealth bombers demonstrate US global strike capabilities to take action against these targets when necessary, anytime, anywhere." That demonstration was not aimed at Yemen, or even at the Houthis specifically; it was aimed at Iran.

Hamas, Hezbollah, the Houthis, and some Iraqi and Syrian militias all have ties of various kinds with Iran—some quite close, particularly Hezbollah, and others, including Hamas, getting some support from Iran while operating very much independently. The Israeli and US talk of Iran's alleged control of the various militias of the so-called Axis of Resistance has almost always been exaggerated. Israel had waged a kind of shadow war against Iran for many years, characterized by assassinations of Iranian nuclear scientists and others, frequently enough to become almost routine.

During the Gaza war, on April 1, 2024, Israel carried out an attack on the Iranian consulate, a protected diplomatic mission, in Damascus. Sixteen people were killed, including a top commander of Iran's Islamic Revolutionary Guard Corps, as well as other militants and two civilians: a Syrian woman and her child. Iran made clear it did not want to escalate to full-scale war, instead responding with a carefully calibrated strike against Israel that allowed notice and plenty of time for Israel, with direct support from the US, Britain, Jordan, and France, to mobilize all necessary anti-missile defenses. One Israeli Bedouin child was injured. The US claimed it was responding to Israel's right of self-defense, ignoring the role of the Israeli attack on the consulate that had sparked the confrontation.

On July 31, Hamas leader Ismail Haniyeh was assassinated in the heart of Tehran, in a strike widely understood to have been carried out by Israel. Haniyeh was visiting the Iranian capital to celebrate the inauguration of the new Iranian president, Masoud Pezeshkian, and was killed in a government guest house just hours after the ceremonies ended. Because of the location, the assassination served as an attack not only on Hamas but on the Iranian government as well. Less than two months later, Israel assassinated the Hezbollah leader Hassan Nasrallah.

The assassination of Nasrallah as well as other key Hezbollah and Hamas leaders formed the main justification for Iran's direct response against Israel on October 1 with a large-scale missile attack. The missiles were aimed at military targets, and it appears most fell at or near two air bases, one of which houses the headquarters of Israel's top intelligence service, the Mossad. Military bases reported no casualties; the only person known to have been killed in the attack was a Palestinian from Gaza who had been sheltering in Jericho, in the occupied West Bank, since the beginning of the Gaza war.

Israeli leaders quickly issued calls for revenge. Naftali Bennett, the former prime minister, said, "We must act now to destroy Iran's nuclear program, its central energy facilities, and to fatally cripple this terrorist regime." National Security Minister Itamar Ben-Gvir said, "What we did to Lebanon must also be done to Iran ... no political arrangements, no diplomacy—crush, crush, crush." Knesset member and former foreign minister Avigdor Lieberman called for an immediate attack to "bomb all the oil, gas, and nuclear facilities, and destroy the refineries and dams."

Netanyahu had long showed signs of wanting to pull the United States into directly backing and participating in an Israeli war against Iran. The Biden administration pushed back, supporting Israel's ostensible right of self-defense but urging Tel Aviv to attack only military targets and avoid hitting any of Iran's nuclear power installations or its oil facilities. Despite President Biden's longstanding claim of wanting to get back into negotiations with Iran to reestablish the nuclear deal, he did not use the opportunity to remind Netanyahu or the Israeli population or indeed the people of the United States that there is only one nuclear weapons arsenal in the region, and it belongs to Israel, not to Iran.

EPILOGUE: WHAT HAPPENED IN THE US PRESIDENTIAL ELECTION OF 2024?

The November 2024 election that sent Donald Trump back to the White House for his second term provided a powerful example of the longtime principle that support for Israel—including massive military support—is an issue of bipartisan consensus. And it provided another example: of how profoundly distant the political leadership of at least one of the two US political parties is from its base.

In this case, the consensus came down to leadership. Polls indicated that much of Trump's Republican base agreed with his anti-Palestinian and unalterably pro-Israel positions—despite what they might have felt about his documented misogyny, Islamophobia, racism, antisemitism, xenophobia and criminality. On the other hand, much of the Democratic base had moved away from the party's longstanding pro-Israel positions, leaving the leadership behind. That process had been underway for most of a decade, but during the first year of Israel's brutal war in Gaza, the shift among Democrats away from automatic support for Israel had grown to unprecedented levels.

Vice President Kamala Harris, the Democratic candidate for president after incumbent Joe Biden stepped down from the campaign, took on Biden's political priorities and policies and held on to them as her own. Despite a popular campaign theme that she was from a younger generation and it was time to "turn the page" to new leadership, she made clear that she would not diverge from Biden's approach, particularly on continuing military support to Israel's war. At various points Harris seemed to want to signal a slight difference from Biden, showing more empathy towards Palestinians and calling for a (limited, temporary) ceasefire before Biden did. But she began every reference to Gaza with an unequivocal "our support for Israel is iron-clad" and rejected any possible shift in actual policy.

The Uncommitted movement emerged in the spring of 2024 and worked tirelessly to pressure, persuade, and demand that the Biden-Harris administration make good on its claimed interest in ending the war—specifically by cutting US arms transfers to Tel Aviv, widely understood as necessary for a ceasefire to take hold. During the primaries, more than 700,000 people in numerous states voted "uncommitted" instead of for the otherwise unopposed candidate Joe Biden. *The Guardian* reported the overall protest vote against Biden was 13 percent.

But by the summer, the primaries were over, Biden rescinded his candidacy after a disastrous televised debate against Donald Trump, and as the Democratic National Convention convened in Chicago, the Democratic Party leadership under then-candidate Harris rejected every request from the Uncommitted movement for recognition of their influence in the party. Their initial request reflected the position of large Democratic majorities: a commitment to ending arms transfers to Israel. When that was rejected, things that should have been easy were requested, such as a face-to-face meeting with the candidate. Those were refused as well. Finally the Uncommitted leaders, themselves Democratic activists working within party structures to try to change it from within, appealed simply for a vetted, two-minute convention speech by a Democratic elected official, a state assemblywoman from Georgia, who was a Palestinian-American. That too was rejected (see pages 259–261). Post-DNC entreaties similarly fell on deaf ears, and fury and desolation rose from Palestinian- and other Arab-Americans and Muslims, as well as students and other young people, African-Americans, progressive Jews and a host of others.

There's no evidence to suggest that likely Harris voters who instead voted "Gaza" or third parties or left the top line of the ballot blank were numerous enough to account for her loss. Anger at the economy and numerous other factors played key roles. But certainly those voters were part of the equation. In Dearborn, the largest Arab-majority city in the country and historically a Democratic stronghold, Harris lost badly, with 36 percent to Trump's 42 percent. The national exit poll by the Council on American-Islamic Relations showed that among Muslim voters, a traditionally reliably Democratic constituency, Harris won only 20 percent of the vote. That was a precipitous drop from the 2020 election, when 69 percent of Muslims voted for Biden, and 2016, when a CAIR study showed 72 percent of Muslims supported Hillary Clinton.

Politico made clear that the "protest vote was not limited solely to Arab Americans, who make up a fraction of the U.S. population. Their furor toward the Biden administration over Gaza spilled out onto college campuses across the nation and among progressives of all ages, amounting to the most significant anti-war protest in a generation." There was no question that the loss of that whole range of other key progressive constituencies weakened her campaign. Students came to the campaign fresh from their ceasefire-based encampments on campuses across the country, facing potentially harsh consequences for their nonviolent protests. So they were far less likely to volunteer for long stints knocking on doors, staffing phone banks, or mobilizing voter registration drives for a candidate/vice-president who had refused to break with her administration's complicity in Israel's genocide in Gaza through the provision of weapons.

As Peter Beinart, a noted Jewish intellectual and strong critic of Israel, wrote in the *New York Times*, "Despite overwhelming evidence that the Democratic Party's most devoted constituents wanted to end sales of weapons to Israel, the Biden administration kept sending them, even after Prime Minister Benjamin Netanyahu of Israel expanded the war into Lebanon. And not only did Ms. Harris not break with Mr. Biden's policy, she went out of her way to make voters who care about Palestinian rights feel unwelcome. ... For decades, the party's politicians and operatives have treated the struggle for Palestinian freedom as a taboo. They've grown so accustomed to sequestering it from their stated commitment to human rights that, even amid what prominent scholars call a genocide, Ms. Harris thought it wiser to campaign with Ms. [Liz] Cheney than, say, Representative Rashida Tlaib. Despite overwhelming evidence, her campaign could not see that among progressive voters, the Palestine exception no longer applies."

Harris's embrace of Dick Cheney, the infamous architect of the Iraq war and its lies about Iraq's nonexistent weapons of mass destruction, as a favored supporter, while campaigning arm in arm with his arch-Republican daughter (and strong backer of her father's war), former congresswoman Liz Cheney, hit many progressives, certainly including the Uncommitted voters, very hard. Welcoming the Cheneys into the "big tent" of the Democratic Party, while denying access to elected Palestinian Democrats who remained unswerving if critical supporters of their own party, showed all too clearly the priorities of the Democratic leadership. And those priorities did not match the urgencies of the activists trying to make real the Biden-Harris claimed commitment to ending Israel's war in Gaza.

Even beyond longstanding US strategic interests, Joe Biden's personal "I am a Zionist" commitment to Israel was the basis for his continued provision of weapons that enabled Israel's war. In doing so, he stood against large majorities of the American people and still larger majorities of his own party, who were demanding a permanent ceasefire including an end to US arms transfers. He refused to change policy, even when faced with the likelihood that, after a fifty-plus-year career in US politics, he would go down in history as "Genocide Joe." Kamala Harris did not seem to share all of Biden's personal and/or ideological commitment to Israel, but she maintained a kind of reflexive transactional support for Tel Aviv that had been the position of mainstream US political figures for decades. Her refusal to break with Biden lay at the core of many Democrats' anger and sense of betrayal by party leaders.

Though many voters withheld their support to Democrats because of their outrage at the complicity of Biden and Harris in Israel's war, their votes alone would not have changed the overall election results. But it is clear that for many voters in key components of the Democratic base—Arabs and Muslims certainly, but also numerous young, Black, and overall progressive communities—the available choice, between what many saw as fascism and what many saw as the enabling of a genocide, was simply not an acceptable choice.

In Trump's second term, Washington's virtually unlimited level of military support for Israel will almost certainly remain in place, regardless of civilian deaths or violations of US or international law. From the beginning of his term in 2021, even before the 2023 war began, Biden had left standing key aspects of Trump's 2018 policy shifts that enabled some of the most extreme goals of the Israeli right wing. Those included recognizing the annexation of Jerusalem as Israel's capital and moving the US embassy there, accepting Israeli sovereignty over the Syrian Golan Heights, legitimizing settlements and future annexations in the West Bank, closing the US consulate in East Jerusalem that had served Palestinians, and shuttering the Palestinian diplomatic office in Washington.

Biden had also accepted, and to some degree tried to build on Trump's embrace of Arab dictators, most significantly the crown prince of Saudi Arabia Mohammad bin Salman, and the Abraham Accords that normalized relations between Israel and various Arab governments. During the second Trump term, efforts to expand that process will likely continue, and will likely continue to ignore or directly undermine Palestinian rights and Palestinian lives, as his policies always have.

The United Nations, and especially its agencies that help support Palestinians, are likely to come under greater attack. One indication was evident in Trump's announcement that he would appoint Elise Stefanik, the far-right congresswoman known for harsh anti-Palestinian rhetoric and positions, as the US ambassador to the UN. The Israeli newspaper *Ha'aretz* responded to the announcement saying, "the New York Representative, who has a history of propagating antisemitic conspiracy theories, is widely expected to prioritize attacking the United Nations' criticism of Israel during her tenure as ambassador." Any effort to reverse the congressional halting of funds to UNRWA (legislated to remain in place through March 2025) will likely fail under the Trump administration.

What else Trump might do differently than his predecessor remains unclear. He has said he wants Israel's war in Gaza to end soon, but also made clear he would give Netanyahu everything he wants. And, as *Foreign Policy* described it, "If the Trump administration allows the Israeli government to pursue the end of the conflict in ways it sees fit, it is likely that more Palestinians will be killed along the way. Then, of course, there are Netanyahu's partners who want to resettle the Gaza Strip, the logical conclusion of which is the further dispossession of a population that was already predominantly refugees and their descendants."

That means ethnic cleansing—and a continuation of genocide. It is not surprising that polls of Israeli public opinion across the political spectrum indicated strong support for Trump over Harris. Netanyahu chose Trump as well. He was one of the first world leaders, by some reports *the* first, to turn to social media to congratulate Trump the moment the election results were called.

Changing those realities means we have a great deal of work to do.

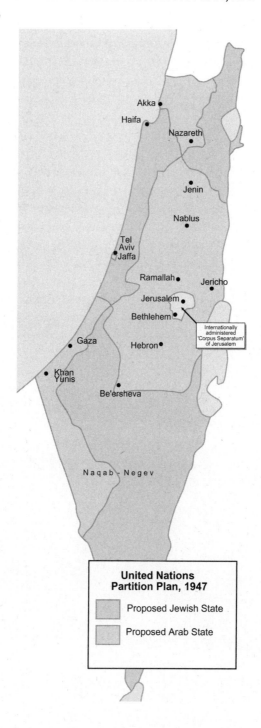

Akka
Haifa
Nazareth
Jenin
Nablus
Tel
Aviv
Jaffa
Ramallah
Jericho
Jerusalem
Bethlehem
Internationally
administered
'Corpus Separatum'
of Jerusalem
Gaza
Hebron
Khan
Yunis
Be'ersheva
N a q a b – N e g e v

**United Nations
Partition Plan, 1947**

Proposed Jewish State

Proposed Arab State

PALESTINIAN REFUGEES: UNRWA REFUGEE CAMPS, 2001

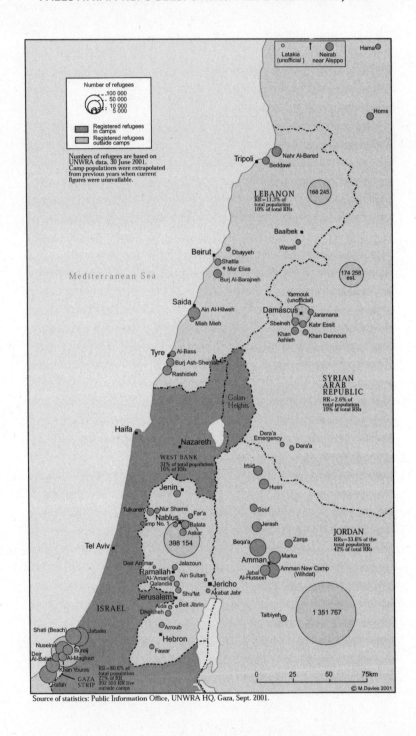

Source of statistics: Public Information Office, UNRWA HQ, Gaza, Sept. 2001.

MAP OF THE WALL

The Wall in the West Bank, December 2003

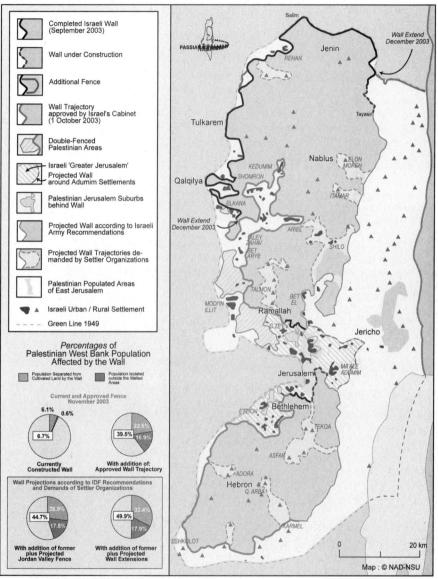

Permission to reprint graciously provided by the Palestine Liberation Organization

OSLO, 1995

0   20 km

Jenin
GANIM

Tulkarem

SHAVEI
SHOMRON

Nablus
ELON MOREH

Qalqilya

ALFEI
MENASHE

ARIEL

MA'ALE
EPHRAIM

RIMONIM

PSAGOT
Ramallah

GIV'AT
ZE'EV

Jericho

Jerusalem
MA'ALE
ADUMIM

KALYA

ISRAEL

Bethlehem

ETZION
BLOC

KIRYAT ARBA

Green Line

Dead Sea

Hebron

Area A - Palestinian cities

Area B - Palestinian villages

Area C - Israeli settlement,
military areas and state lands

▲ Main Israeli settlements

DIMINISHING LANDS OF PALESTINE

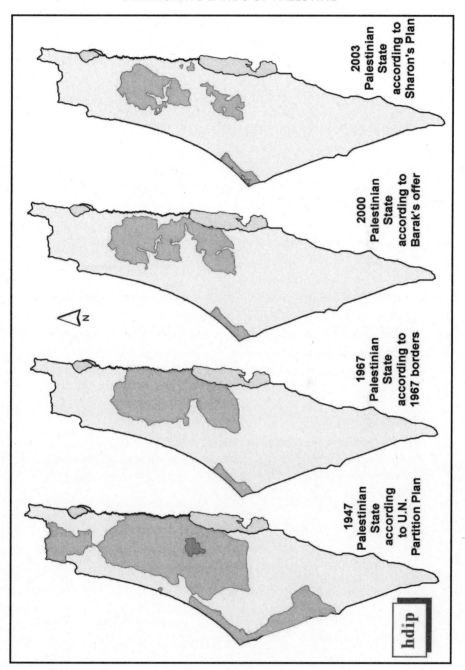

Map courtesy of The Palestinian Health, Development, Information and Policy Organization (HDIP)

RESOURCES

Organizations in the US

(This list represents a range of perspectives on Palestinian rights.)

Adalah Justice Project
Advocacy organization linking US domestic and international policies.
www.adalahjusticeproject.org

American-Arab Anti-Discrimination Committee
Supports Palestinian rights and challenges anti-Arab racism in the US.
www.adc.org

American Friends Service Committee
Quaker educational organization—its Middle East Peace division provides
resources, talking points, and educational materials.
www.afsc.org

American Muslims for Palestine
Works to educate US public and media about Palestine issues, including Israel's
occupation of Palestine, Palestinian refugees, and Israel's violations of international law and human rights.
www.ampalestine.org

Americans for Middle East Understanding
Publishes The Link newsletter to amplify analysis of scholars, activists, and
policymakers working on Middle East issues, especially Israeli occupation of
Palestine.
www.ameu.org

Black Christians for Palestine
Network of Christian scholars, educators, faith leaders, and theologians supporting Palestinian rights through organizing, education, and advocacy.
www.blackchristiansforpalestine.com

Black for Palestine
Organization of Black activists in the US doing political education to build
awareness and understanding of the Palestinian struggle in the Black
community, and mobilizing Black activists to call for an end to US support
for Israel.
www.blackforpalestine.com

Arab Center DC
Independent research organization affiliated with the Arab Center for
Research and Policy Studies in Doha, providing information on the Arab
world and US Middle East policy—including a major focus on Israel-
Palestine—through policy analysis, conferences, and academic research.
www.arabcenterdc.org

Churches for Middle East Peace
Inter-denominational faith-based organization that works to encourage US
policies that actively promote a comprehensive resolution to conflicts in the
Middle East with a focus on the Israeli–Palestinian conflict.
www.cmep.org

CodePink
A feminist grassroots organization working to end US warfare and support
peace and human rights initiatives, including support for Palestinian rights
and changing US policy in the region.
www.codepink.org

Democracy in the Arab World Now
DAWN's advocacy is centered on accountability for human rights violators in
the region, including in Israel-Palestine and on US policies that support those
violations.
www.dawnmena.org

Dissenters
A national movement of students and young people focused on opposing
militarism and on Palestinian rights.
www.wearedissenters.org

Electronic Intifada
Independent online news publication focusing on Palestine.
www.electronicintifada.net

Eyewitness Palestine
Education program that organizes delegations to Palestine for social justice,
faith-based, and other activists.
www.eyewitnesspalestine.org

Foundation for Middle East Peace
Publishes a weekly newsletter on Israeli settlements and annexation.
www.fmep.org

Friends Committee on National Legislation
Quaker lobby organization focusing on congressional and other advocacy pushing US towards diplomacy and leveraging its influence to push Israel to end the Gaza war and occupation and other policies of systematic oppression.
www.fcnl.org

Friends of Sabeel–North America
FOSNA supports the work of the Sabeel Ecumenical Liberation Theology Center through education, advocacy, and nonviolent action.
www.sabeel.org

If Not Now
Young US Jews organizing their community to end US support for Israel's apartheid system and demand equality and justice for all Palestinians and Israelis.
www.ifnotnowmovement.org

Institute for Middle East Understanding
Provides journalists with background and sources, and works to ensure Palestinian voices and analysis in mainstream and independent media.
www.imeu.org

Institute for Palestine Studies
Publishes the *Journal of Palestine Studies* and a wide variety of books and resources in English, French, and Arabic.
www.palestine-studies.org

Jewish Voice for Peace
Leading Jewish organization working inside the Jewish community and in broader coalitions in support of Palestinian rights.
www.jewishvoiceforpeace.org

J-Street
Lobby that defines itself as "pro-Israel, pro-peace."
www.jstreet.org

Middle East Children's Alliance
Supports children's projects in the occupied territories and provides educational resources in the US on human rights and peace and justice issues.
www.mecaforpeace.org

Mondoweiss
An independent news organization focusing on developments inside Israel-Palestine and related US policy. Includes debates over Israel and nationalism in US Jewish communities while committed to reflecting diverse and international views.
www.mondoweiss.net

Middle East Research and Information Project (MERIP)
Publishes the online quarterly *Middle East Report* and frequent articles and educational primers on critical analysis of current issues in the Middle East.
www.merip.org

Palestine Center
The educational arm of the Washington-based Jerusalem Fund organizes policy briefings, lectures, conferences, publications, and an extensive research library.
www.thejerusalemfund.org

Palestine Children's Relief Fund
Humanitarian relief organization, primarily focused on essential medical, food, water, and other supplies for families, especially in Gaza. It also supports rebuilding health care facilities and providing long-term support to children and the health sector.
www.pcrf.net

Palestine Legal
Legal support organization that challenges efforts to threaten Palestinian rights activists by providing legal advice, training, advocacy and litigation support.
www.palestinelegal.org

Palestine Youth Movement
Independent grassroots movement of young Palestinians and Palestinian-Americans organizing for liberation.
www.palestinianyouthmovement.com

Rabbis for Ceasefire
Created at the beginning of Israel's 2023 war against Gaza, this group of activist rabbis has mobilized for "a complete ceasefire now" and organized protests in Washington, DC, at the UN in New York, and in Israel trying to bring humanitarian aid to Gaza.
https://rabbis4ceasefire.com

Rachel Corrie Foundation for Peace and Justice
Named for the young American peace activist killed by Israeli military in 2003 while providing nonviolent support to prevent demolition of homes in Gaza, the RCF supports grassroots efforts for human rights and economic and social justice, especially in the Gaza Strip.
www.rachelcorriefoundation.org

Students for Justice in Palestine
A national organization of campus-based student groups supporting Palestinian rights, working to empower, unify, and support the student movement.
www.nationalsjp.org

Uncommitted National Movement
After mobilizing "uncommitted" votes in 2024 Democratic primaries, it now works for a just foreign policy prioritizing justice, peace, human rights, and freedom for Palestinians.
www.uncommittedmovement.com

UNRWA–USA
Independent information and fundraising arm that partners with UNRWA at the United Nations to build US public support for Palestinian refugees.
www.unrwausa.org

US Campaign for Palestinian Rights
Formerly the US Campaign to End the Israeli Occupation, a network working to end occupation and apartheid using a rights-based, accountability- and justice-oriented framework.
www.uscpr.org

Organizations in the Region

972
Online magazine run by Palestinian and Israeli journalists to provide in-depth reporting from the ground. Spotlights people and communities working to oppose occupation and apartheid.
www.972mag.com

Adalah
The legal center for Arab minority rights in Israel works to promote human rights for Palestinian citizens of Israel as well as residents of the occupied territory, including in the Israeli courts.
www.adalah.org

al Haq
The oldest human rights organization in Palestine, al Haq documents violations of individual and collective rights in the occupied territories and works to end those violations through national and international advocacy and efforts towards accountability.
www.alhaq.org

Alternative Information Center–Palestine
Palestinian NGO working to end the occupation and enabling Palestinians to attain freedom, independence, national and social rights through local and global analyses, advocacy, grassroots activism.
www.aicpalestine.org

Badil Resource Center for Palestinian Refugee & Residency Rights
Independent human rights organization working to defend rights of Palestinian refugees and internally displaced people.
www.badil.org

Boycott, Divestment, and Sanctions Movement
Based on a 2005 call from Palestinian civil society, now a Palestinian-led global movement using nonviolent economic and cultural strategies to end international support for Israel's oppression of Palestinians and pressure Israel to comply with international law.
www.bdsmovement.net

B'Tselem
The Israeli Information Center for Human Rights in the Occupied Territories was established by a group of academics, attorneys, journalists, and Knesset members endeavoring to document human rights violations in the occupied territories and educate the Israeli public.
www.btselem.org

GISHA
An Israeli organization working to protect the freedom of movement of Palestinians, especially residents of Gaza.
www.gisha.org

International Solidarity Movement
Organizes international nonviolent activist volunteers to work with Palestinians defending human rights in the occupied territories.
www.palsolidarity.org

Israeli Committee Against House Demolitions
An Israeli and international organization working to end Israel's apartheid policies and the settler colonial goals that Israel maintains over the Palestinian people, emphasizing opposition to house demolitions in the West Bank.
www.icahd.org

Israeli Physicians for Human Rights
Human rights organization based in Jaffa. Works to promote equal access "to all people under Israel's responsibility."
www.phr.org.il

Jerusalem Media and Communications Center
Started during the first intifada, it produces polls, reports, media services for journalists across the occupied territories.
www.jmcc.org

Machsom Watch: Women Against the Occupation & for Human Rights
Israeli women activists monitoring checkpoints and other aspects of occupation to defend Palestinian freedom of movement and an end to occupation through education inside Israel.
www.machsomwatch.org/en

MIFTAH–Palestinian Initiative for the Promotion of Global Dialogue and Democracy
Hanan Ashrawi founded MIFTAH in 1998 to promote democracy and good governance within Palestinian society, and to engage local and international public opinion and officials on Palestinian rights.
www.miftah.org

Palestinian Center for Human Rights
One of the most internationally recognized Gaza-based Palestinian human rights groups, it works to protect civil and political rights in Palestine and in using the law internationally to fight for Palestinian rights.
www.pchrgaza.org

The Palestinian Center for Rapprochement Between People
A Palestinian NGO based in Beit Sahour that works to inform the global public about the reality in Palestine and empower the community through nonviolent direct action.
www.pcr.ps

Rabbis for Human Rights
An Israeli organization founded in 1988 in response to serious human rights abuses by the Israeli military in the occupied territories. Publicizes causes, helps victims, engages in civil disobedience, and promotes Jewish ecumenical dialogue and education in human rights.
www.rhr.israel.net/overview.shtml

Stop the Wall
A grassroots Palestinian organization that works to bring civil society together to build campaigns against the apartheid wall, supports BDS, and raising global awareness and joint action against the increasing dominance of walls dividing people around the world.
www.stopthewall.org

Taayush
A joint Palestinian–Israeli organization that works against occupation, focusing on protecting Palestinians in Area C (fully Israeli controlled) of the West Bank from forcible dispossession of homes and agricultural land.
www.taayush.org

Who Profits
An Israeli research center dedicated to exposing the commercial involvement of Israeli and international companies in the continued Israeli control over Palestinian and Syrian land; includes access to comprehensive lists of relevant companies.
www.whoprofits.org

Books

Nonfiction

Abunimah, Ali. *One Country: A Bold Proposal to End the Israeli–Palestinian Impasse*. New York: Metropolitan Books, 2007.

Aranguren, Teresa & Barrilaro, Sandra. *Against Erasure: A Photographic Memory of Palestine Before the Nakba*. Chicago: Haymarket, 2024.

Aruri, Naseer. *Dishonest Broker: The US Role in Israel and Palestine*. Cambridge: South End Press, 2003.

———. *Palestinian Refugees: The Right of Return*. London: Pluto Press, 2001.

Asali, K.J. *Jerusalem in History*. Northampton: Olive Branch Press/Interlink Publishing, 1999.

Barghouti, Omar. *Boycott, Divestment, Sanctions: The Global Struggle for Palestinian Rights*. Chicago: Haymarket Books, 2011.

Baroud, Ramzy & Pappe, Ilan. *Our Vision for Liberation: Engaged Palestinian Leaders & Intellectuals Speak Out*. Atlanta: Clarity Press, 2024.

Batarsa, Aline. *Visualizing Palestine: A Chronicle of Colonialism and the Struggle for Liberation*. Chicago: Haymarket Books, 2024.

Beit-Hallahmi, Benjamin. *Original Sins: Reflections on the History of Zionism and Israel*. Northampton: Olive Branch Press/Interlink Publishing, 1998.

Bennis, Phyllis. *Before and After: US Foreign Policy and the War on Terrorism*. 2nd ed. Northampton: Olive Branch Press/Interlink Publishing, 2003.

———. *Calling the Shots: How Washington Dominates Today's UN*. Northampton: Olive Branch Press/Interlink Publishing, 2000.

Carter, Jimmy. *Palestine: Peace Not Apartheid*. New York: Simon and Schuster, 2007.

Chomsky, Noam. *The Fateful Triangle: The United States, Israel and the Palestinians*. Cambridge: South End Press, 1999.

Coates, Ta-Nehisi. *The Message*. New York: One World/Penguin Random House, 2024.

Cobban, Helena & Khouri, Rami G. *Understanding Hamas: And Why That Matters*. New York: O/R Books. 2024.

Corrie, Rachel. *Let Me Stand Alone: The Journals of Rachel Corrie*. New York: W.W. Norton & Co, 2008

Davis, Angela. *Freedom Is a Constant Struggle: Ferguson, Palestine, and the Foundations of a Movement*. Chicago: Haymarket 2016.

Dittmar, Linda. *Tracing Homelands: Israel, Palestine, and the Claims of Belonging*. Northampton: Olive Branch Press/Interlink Publishing, 2023.

Erakat, Noura. *Justice for Some: Law and the Question of Palestine*. Stanford: Stanford University Press, 2019.

Falk, Richard, Dugard, John, Lynk, Michael. *Protecting Human Rights in Occupied Palestine: Working through the United Nations*. Atlanta: Clarity Press, 2023

Falk, Richard. *Palestine: The Legitimacy of Hope*. Charlottesville: Just World Books, 2014

Farsoun, Samih, and Aruri, Naseer. *Palestine and the Palestinians: A Social and Political History*. 2nd ed. Boulder: Westview Press, 2006.

Finkelstein, Norman. *Beyond Chutzpah: On the Misuse of Anti-Semitism and the Abuse of History*. Berkeley: University of California Press, 2005.

Hadawi, Sami. *Bitter Harvest: A Modern History of Palestine*. 4th ed. Northampton: Olive Branch Press/Interlink Publishing, 1998.

Halper, Jeff. *An Israeli in Palestine: Resisting Dispossession, Redeeming Israel*. London: Pluto Press, 2008.

Hass, Amira. *Drinking the Sea at Gaza: Days and Nights in a Land under Siege*. New York: Henry Holt, 2000.

Jawhariyyeh, Wasif. *The Storyteller of Jerusalem: The Life and Times of Wasif Jawhariyyeh, 1904-1948*. Northampton: Olive Branch Press/Interlink Publishing, 2013.

Jayyusi, Lena. *Jerusalem Interrupted: Modernity and Colonial Transformation 1917-Present*. Northampton: Olive Branch Press/Interlink Publishing, 2024.

Jeffries, J.M.N. *Palestine: The Reality: The Inside Story of the Balfour Declaration*. Northampton: Olive Branch Press/Interlink Publishing, 2016.

Johnson, Penny and Shehadeh, Raja, eds. *Seeking Palestine: New Palestinian Writing on Exile and Home*. Northampton: Olive Branch Press/Interlink Publishing, 2023.

Karcher, Carolyn, ed. *Reclaiming Judaism from Zionism: Stories of Personal Transformation*. Northampton: Olive Branch Press/Interlink Publishing, 2019.

Khalidi, Rashid. *Palestinian Identity: The Construction of Modern National Consciousness*. New York: Columbia University Press, 1998.

———. *The Iron Cage: The Story of the Palestinian Struggle for Statehood*. Boston: Beacon Press, 2006.

———. *The Hundred Years' War on Palestine*. New York: Metropolitan Books, 2020.

Khalidi, Walid. *Before Their Diaspora: A Photographic History of the Palestinians 1876–1948*. Washington, DC: Institute for Palestine Studies, 2004.

———. *All That Remains: The Palestinian Villages Occupied and Depopulated by Israel in 1948*. Washington, DC: Institute for Palestine Studies, 1992.

———. *From Haven to Conquest: Readings in Zionism and the Palestine Problem until 1948*. Washington, DC: Institute for Palestine Studies, 1987.

Levit, Daphna. *Wrestling with Zionism: Jewish Voices of Dissent*. Northampton: Olive Branch Press/Interlink Books, 2020.

Lim, Audrea, ed. *The Case for Sanctions against Israel*. London: Verso Books, 2012.

Masalha, Nur. *Imperial Israel and the Palestinians: The Politics of Expansion*. London: Pluto Press, 2000.

McGowan, Dan, and Ellis, Marc. *Remembering Deir Yassin: The Future of Israel and Palestine*. Northampton: Olive Branch Press, 1998.

Mearsheimer, John, and Walt, Stephen. *The Israel Lobby and US Foreign Policy*. New York: Farrar, Straus and Giroux, 2007.

Niseibeh, N.S. *Namesake: Reflections on a Woman Warrior*. Olive Branch Press/Interlink Publishing, 2024.

Pappé, Ilan. *The Ethnic Cleansing of Palestine*. London: One World Publications, 2007.

Prior, Michael, ed. *Speaking the Truth: Zionism, Israel and Occupation*. Northampton: Olive BranchPress, 2004.

———. *Lobbying for Zionism on Both Sides of the Atlantic*. London: One World Publications, 2024.

Rogan, Eugene, and Shlaim, Avi. *The War for Palestine: Rewriting the History of 1948*. 2nd ed. Cambridge: Cambridge University Press, 2007.

Roy, Sara. *The Gaza Strip: The Political Economy of De-Development*. Washington, DC: Institute for Palestine Studies, 1995.

Ruebner, Josh. *Shattered Hopes: Obama's Failure to Broker Israeli–Palestinian Peace*. London: Verso Books, 2013.

Said, Edward W. *The Question of Palestine*. New York: Vintage Books, 1992.

———. *Peace and its Discontents: Essays on Palestine in the Middle East Peace Process*. New York: Vintage Books, 1996.

———. *The End of the Peace Process: Oslo and After*. New York: Vintage Books, 2001.

———. *The Selected Works of Edward Said.* Moustafa Bayoumi & Andrew Rubin, eds. Vintage Books, 2019.

Shahin, Mariam and Azar, George. *Palestine: A Guide.* Northampton: Interlink Books, 2006.

Suárez, Thomas. *Palestine Hijacked: How Zionism Forged an Apartheid State from River to Sea.* Northampton: Olive Branch Press/Interlink Publishing, 2022.

———. *Writings on the Wall: Palestinian Oral Histories.* Olive Branch Press/Interlink Publishing, 2019.

Suleiman, Michael W. *US Policy on Palestine: From Wilson to Clinton.* Washington, DC: Association of Arab-American University Graduates, 1994.

Swisher, Clayton E. *The Truth about Camp David.* New York: Nation Books, 2004.

Tamimi, Azzam. *Hamas: A History from Within.* Northampton: Olive Branch Press/Interlink Publishing, 2007.

Usher, Graham. *Dispatches from Palestine: The Rise and Fall of the Oslo Peace Process.* London: Pluto Press, 1999.

Vilkomerson, Rebecca & Wise, Rabbi Alissa. *Solidarity is the Political Version of Love: Lessons from Jewish Anti-Zionist Organizing.* Chicago: Haymarket Books, 2024.

Wagner, Donald E. *No Place Left to Go: Why Palestine Matters.* Northampton: Olive Branch Press/Interlink Publishing, 2025.

Zertal, Idith, and Eldar, Akiva. *Lords of the Land: The War for Israel's Settlements in the Occupied Territories 1967–2007.* New York: Nation Books, 2007.

Fiction

Habib, Dr. Nejmeh Khalil. *A Spring That Did Not Blossom: Palestinian Short Stories.* Northampton: Interlink Books, 2024.

Glick, Alison. *The Other End of the Sea.* Northampton: Interlink Books, 2021.

Habiby, Emile. *The Secret Life of Saeed: The Pessoptimist.* Northampton: Interlink Books, 2024.

Kanafani, Ghassan. *All That's Left to You.* Northampton: Interlink Books, 2023.

Khalifeh, Sahar. *Wild Thorns.* Northampton: Interlink Books, 2024.

Nimr, Sonia. *Wondrous Journeys in a Strange Lands.* Northampton: Interlink Books, 2024.

Poetry

Alareer, Refaat. *If I Must Die*. New York; O/R Books, 2024.

Barghouti, Tamim. *In Jerusalem and Other Poems 1997-2018*. Northampton: Interlink Books, 2016.

Boullata, Kamal, and Engel, Kathy, eds. *We Begin Here: Poems for Palestine and Lebanon*. Northampton: Olive Branch Press/Interlink Publishing, 2007.

Darwish, Mahmoud. *Almond Blossoms and Beyond*. Northampton: Interlink Books, 2024.

——. *I Don't Want This Poem to End*. Northampton: Interlink Books, 2017.

——. *Palestine as Metaphor*. Northampton: Interlink Books, 2019.

Children's and Young Adult

Kassis, Reem. *We Are Palestinian: A Celebration of Culture and Tradition*. Northampton: Crocodile Books/Interlink Publishing, 2023.

Lester Murad, Nora. *Ida in the Middle*. Northampton: Crocodile Books/ Interlink Publishing, 2022.

Mattar, Malak. *Sitti's Bird: A Gaza Story*. Northampton: Crocodile Books/ Interlink Publishing, 2022

Robinson, Anthony and Young, Annemarie. *Young Palestinians Speak: Living Under Occupation*. Northampton: Interlink Publishing, 2024.

Sokolower, Jody. *Determined to Stay: Palestinian Youth Fight for Their Village*. Olive Branch Press/Interlink Publishing, 2021.